Financial Reform in Central and Eastern Europe

Financial Reform in Central and Eastern Europe

Edited by

Dr. Andy Mullineux
Director of Money, Banking and Finance Programmes
Department of Economics, University of Birmingham,
United Kingdom

Nova Science Publishers, Inc.
Commack

Art Director: Maria Ester Hawrys
Assistant Director: Elenor Kallberg
Graphics: Denise Dieterich, Kerri Pfister,
Erika Cassatti and Barbara Minerd
Manuscript Coordinator: Roseann Pena
Book Production: Tammy Sauter, Benjamin Fung
Circulation: Irene Kwartiroff and Annette Hellinger

Library of Congress Cataloging-in-Publication Data

Financial reform in Central and Eastern Europe/Andy Mullineaux, editor.

Includes bibliographical references and index.

ISBN 1-56072-231-2

Library of Congress Cataloging-in-Publication Data available upon request.

6080 Jericho Turnpike, Suite 207
Commack, New York 11725
Tele. 516-499-3103 Fax 516-499-3146
E Mail Novascil@aol.com

Printed in the United States of America

CONTENTS

Preface

This book contains updated versions of papers presented at a conference held in Prague, 3-4 September 1993 to mark end of the second phase of a collaborative project for which funding was gratefully received from the Commission of the European Communities under the ACE programme of the Phare initiative in 1992/2. The collaborators, who are listed separately along with the invited discussants, are associated with the Departments (Institutes) of Economics at the Universities of Birmingham (UK), Bordeaux (France), Lodz (Poland) and the Czech National Bank. The Project (No: ERB4012PL910252) was entitled "Hard Budget Constraints, Privatisation and Financial Reform in Eastern Europe with Particular Reference to Poland at Czechoslovakia". This book is a companion to a previous volume entitled: "Financial Reform in Central and Eastern Europe: Lessons from the `West', Poland and Further East". That book was also published by Nova Science Incorporated and edited by Dr Andy Mullineux and contained papers produced in connection with the first phase of the collaborative research sponsored by the ACE programme. In the second phase, the Institute of Economics at the Czech National Bank joined the project and in the current (third) phase the collaboration has been further broadened to include the Baltic States and Bulgaria. It is hoped that the work in progress will lead to a third volume following our conference in Warsaw on the 2nd and 3rd of September 1994. The continuing support of the ACE programme is gratefully acknowledged.

List of Contributors

Akira Ariyoshi
Economics Division
European Bank for Reconstruction and Development
London

Prof. King Banaian
Department of Economics
The Claremont Graduate School
USA

Jaroslaw Bauc
Institute of Economics
University of Lodz
Poland

Marek Belka
Institute of Economics
University of Lodz
Poland

Christian Bordes
Laboratoire d'Analyse et de Recherche Economiques (LARE)
Faculty of Economics
University of Bordeaux 1
France

Aleš Buliř
Institute of Economics
Czech National Bank
Czech Republic

David Dickinson
Department of Economics and International Finance Group
The University of Birmingham
UK

Maxwell Fry
Internat. Finance Group,Sch. of Bus.
University of Birmingham
UK

Eric Girardin
Laboratoire d'Analyse et de Recherche Economiques (LARE)
Faculty of Economies
University of Bordeaux 1
France

Daniel Goyeau
Groupe de Recherche en Intégration Économique et Financiere (GRIEF)
Department of Economics
University of Poitiers
France

Boguslaw Grabowski
Institute of Economics
University of Lodz
Poland

Eduard Hochreiter
Foreign Research Division
Austrian National Bank
Austria

Miroslav Hrnčíř
Institute of Economics
Czech National Bank
Czech Republic

Jan Klacek
Institute of Economics
Czech National Bank
Czech Republic

Dominique Lacoue-Labarthe
Laboratoire d'Analyse et de Recherche Economiques (LARE)
Faculty of Economies
University of Bordeaux 1
France

Roman Matoušek
Institute of Economics
Czech National Bank
Czech Republic

Andy Mullineux
Department of Economics and International Finance Group
The University of Birmingham
UK

Jerzy Pruski
Institute of Economics
University of Lodz
Poland

Andrzej Raczko
Institute of Economics
University of Lodz
Poland

Amine Tarazi
Centre de Recherche en Macroéconomie Monetaire (CRMM)
Department of Économiques
Université de Limoges
France

Josef Tošovský, Governor
Czech National Bank
Czech Republic

Clas Wihlborg
Gothenburg School of Economics and Commercial Law
Gothenburg University
Sweden

Thomas D Willett
Department of Economics
The Claremont Graduate School
USA

Frank Wykoff
Department of Economics
Pomona College
Claremont
USA

Editor's Introduction

Andy Mullineux

This volume contains papers presented at a conference held in Prague on September 3-4, 1993. The overall theme was financial reform in central and Eastern Europe. An overview of the issues, particularly relating to the experience of the ex-Czechoslovak Federal Republic (CSFR) and the future prospects of the Czech Republic, was provided by Mr. Josef Tošovský, the Governor of the Czech National Bank, whose keynote speech is Chapter 2 of this book.

Eleven papers were presented at the conference in three sessions, which form the three parts of this book. Part 1 deals with monetary and exchange rate policies in Poland and the ex-CSFR, the two countries under consideration in this book. Part 2 covers banking sector and enterprise restructuring, including privatisation and the hardening of budget constraints and the micro level. The final part considers bank regulatory and supervisory issues. Discussants' comments are reproduced at the end of each part.

As explained in the Preface, the conference concluded the second stage of an ongoing and expanded, to cover Bulgaria and the Baltic States in addition to Poland and the Czech Republic, research programme. The conference itself concluded with a panel discussion led by Max Fry and Eric Girardin which aimed to draw lessons from the first and second phases of the collaborative research programme and to consider their implications for the third phase of the programme and challenges facing policy makers in transforming economies in general. Max Fry emphasised the importance of the institutional framework, and particularly the role of auditing. In the absence of rigorous internal and external auditing, banks have little incentive to identify performing and non-performing loans and impose the necessary financial discipline. In Indonesia, for example, long term (`evergreen') lending relationships, are common and banks have little knowledge of the borrowing firm's situation. A legal system capable of ensuring that debts are honoured and executing bankruptcy proceedings efficiently is also essential to avoid the need to take physical possession of collateral.

Max Fry also observed that the Baltic States, with their small populations could only support two or three indigenous banks of minimum efficient scale and consequently foreign bank entry should be encouraged to generate an adequate level of competition. Finally, he warned against using wide spreads between borrowing and lending rates as a means of recapitalising banks since this acts as a discriminatory tax on savers and/or borrowers, impairs growth, and drives banking business abroad.

Eric Girardin drew four main lessons. Firstly, that there was a considerable gap between decreed measures and actual practice; particularly with respect to bankruptcy, which had not been rigorously pursued. Secondly, that deregulation of financial markets can be dangerous in the sense that they can give rise to asset price inflation and speculative bubbles and subsequent debt deflation. The market economy, and particularly the financial system, had to be controlled using appropriate regulatory and supervisory arrangements. He also felt that it was necessary to look again at recent French and Italian experience before advocating the lifting of foreign exchange controls in formerly centrally planned economies at an early stage in their transition. Thirdly, that it is insufficient simply to declare a commitment to fixed exchange rates. The credibility of the commitment takes time to establish and, until this has been achieved, the initial capital inflows in the `honeymoon' period following the announcement, can be quickly reversed at the first sign of faltering. Finally, Eric Girardin observed that transmission mechanisms may be different in emerging market economies (EMEs), from those in OECD countries, because of the higher level of uncertainty. There is a need to develop appropriate instruments of control and to consider how economic agents behaviour can be made responsive to such instruments. In order to stabilize EMEs it was necessary to consider, for example: how the central bank should control aggregate bank lending (monetary base multiplier versus refinancing approaches); how to deal with demand shocks; and how to integrate monetary and exchange rate policy.

The discussion then opened up with Marek Belka observing that the most valuable comparisons were between EMEs, rather than between `eastern' and `western' economies. In the second phase of the programme a lot had been learnt by comparing the Polish and the ex-CSFR cases, and the third phase provided the opportunity for further comparative study of this sort due to the inclusion of the Baltic States and Bulgaria.

Jan Klacek noted that, unlike Poland, the Czech Republic was still in recession, but that the service sector was booming. He warned that newly privatised state owned enterprises (SOEs) may well take time to significantly change their behaviour and that during the restructuring some sectors and regions would experience expansion whilst others would continue to suffer from contraction. Too much emphasis on a general macroeconomic policy should be avoided and more attention needed to be paid to supply side policy, including the role of banks, and to its relationship with monetary (interest rate) policy. Further initiatives seemed to be required because the restructuring of enterprises was taking much longer than expected.

Eduard Hochreiter observed that dialogue between economists and central bankers was extremely useful but, at the end of the day, it was the central bankers, at least in countries with independent central banks, which made the monetary policy decisions. With this in mind, as an economist advising central bankers, he noted that economists still had much work to do. In particular they needed to satisfactorily explain why the depth of the transition recession exceeded widely held expectations and to persistently argue against protectionism. He also noted that expectations are important and that as long as it is expected that living standards will converge on EU levels migration will be deterred. Price stability is another key issue, given the inverse correlation between growth and inflation, and fixing the exchange rate to a low inflation anchor currency whilst developing internal flexibility, as Austria has done, seemed to be a route that other similar sized Central and Eastern European economies could pursue. The issue of sustainability of the monetary/exchange rate regime was likely to be decisive. He judged that with wages at 10% of those in Germany and productivity at 50 to 65% of German levels, the Czech republic, with its balance of trade surplus and scope for productivity increases, should be able to sustain its currency peg.

Eduard Hochreiter also observed that the importance of financial, and particularly banking, sector reform had not been recognised initially and consequently the reform of this sector now needed to be given the highest priority. Key issues were the extent to which foreign banks should be allowed to dominate the system and the design of optimal regulations and supervisory arrangements. Finally, he observed that even though each of the EMEs had their own structural peculiarities, there was no need for a separate economic theory to cover each country.

At the end of the first session of the conference (corresponding to Part 1 of the book) Eduard Hochreiter also observed that in order to conquer inflation, it was necessary to have a social consensus in favour of price stability and to employ simple transparent policy rules which can be readily understood by workers and members of parliament. Policy makers, such as independent central bankers, must be able to rely on political support to overcome political manoeuvring, as in Germany and Austria. Britain, in contrast had no social consensus, no parliamentary consensus, and little dialogue between the government and trade unions. He further noted that a wage anchor was needed to control inflation. The aim should be to achieve the highest equilibrium wage rates that the economy can sustain over time by encouraging average wages to grow in line with average productivity growth, and thereby keeping unit labour costs under control and maintaining the link between work effort and wages. The key to success, he concluded, is to create an environment in which workers work hard and are suitably rewarded for doing so.

Tom Willett concurred that empirical evidence, from his own and other research, demonstrated a negative trade-off between inflation and growth. There was less agreement about how to control inflation, but it was increasingly being recognised that central bank independence was a necessary, though not a sufficient, condition for inflation control. The institutional form of central bank independence was also important. In many EMEs independence is from the executive government, but the central bank is accountable to Parliament. This is potentially dangerous, as the Russian case demonstrates. Independence of all parts of government is required and yet accountability to the public must be assured. Central bank independence, and a good institutional structure in general, is not sufficient either, since it has to be backed by credibility, which takes time to build. A currency peg may help to establish credibility but it is best not to announce that the peg will hold for all time, since this creates a hostage to fortune. The longer the peg is held, however, the more widely accepted is the view that the intention is to maintain the peg and the more likely are speculators to test the resolve of the government and/or the monetary authorities. There is therefore a need to look at the impact of the Polish move to a crawling peg, after the first year of its transition, on the credibility of its policy and the reputation of its policy makers. Another promising research area is the impact of changes in the exchange rate on wages under different incomes policy mechanisms. Tom Willett further observed that current and expected future trading patterns should be taken into account when choosing a currency peg,. It was sensible for Austria to peg to the Deutsche-Mark, for example. It was also important to choose a realistic initial exchange rate and to decide on the appropriate foreign exchange market intervention policy. Minor fluctuations can and should be ironed out by `leaning into the wind' but it is not clear that exchange rate movements in response to major shocks can and should be opposed.

In the opening discussion, following the Governor's Keynote speech, Max Fry expressed alarm at the use of an exchange rate peg as the backbone of monetary policy. He concurred with Tom Willett's view that it was alright as a hidden agenda, but dangerous if announced as a policy commitment; as the UK had discovered in September 1992. Policy independence and inflation control were better pursued via a policy of balancing budgets and through wage control or incomes policy, especially whilst banks are unable to impose hard micro budget constraints. Further, capital account liberalisation increases the problems associated with exchange rate targeting. When a fixed exchange rate is combined with capital mobility, then overnight interest rates need to be extremely flexible - triple digit overnight rates are common in Switzerland and Singapore at the end of reserve accounting periods - in order to inflict a high cost on potential speculators. Capital account convertibility should therefore be postponed until policy credibility has been further enhanced. Such issues are pursued further in Part 1.

Keynote Speech

Governor J. Tošovský

First of all, I would like to say that many things have been done on the political scene which are very important. We certainly have made a lot of good steps from our previous totalitarian regime to democracy. Sometimes, I have to confess, when I watch the parliament, particularly in 1990 - 1991, I feel that their democratic development is a "kindergarten" one: a real mess of ideas. But step by step and quite quickly it achieved a normal well formalized democratic approach for MPs and government: the cooperation between all institutions. The situation in this respect is much better, and I think there is now a strong democracy in the Czech Republic. Many things were done in the economic field regarding the change of the central planning system towards the market economy system. Of course in a certain sense we are still at the beginning, which I will explain later.

Our reform package, as you probably know, was quite radical. It started basically in 1991 and continued step by step up to now. Without drawing any conclusions, I would like to mention some of our achievements thus far.

First we started with really sweeping liberalisation. We started with convertibility and privatization, which I will explain. I will also explain our macroeconomic policy in brief and I will mention that the government also prepared a social safety net, which was very important to preserve the social concensus on political reform.

Let me comment on this a little bit.

The liberalization of prices was done on a really massive scale with an overnight liberalisation of price control on January 1, 1991. Now about

95% of all prices in the Czech Republic are fully liberalized. What happened is obvious and you have probably seen our results: at the beginning, after the price liberalization, a jump in prices occurred. They were stabilized after three or four months, and since that time we have been able to keep inflation under 1% on monthly basis for, I think, 20 months, which is not bad in our situation, given that we have had so many structural changes.

Another small shock had something to do with the consumer price level. It started at the beginning of this year with the introduction of a new taxation system, particularly VAT and income tax. Again a jump in prices occurred: a small one, but again a shock. And the same pattern followed. In March and April, we were able to stabilize the new high price level at an average of half per cent and it is holding. So the liberalization of prices was something we were afraid of, and it was quite difficult macroeconomically, but finally we succeeded.

Concerning the liberalization of foreign trade: foreign trade was liberalized from the central planning system immediately opening the economy for imports and at the same time for exports. The approach of our government is very liberal and our protectionist measures are very small. On the contrary, we are facing protectionist barriers from other countries, especially from the members of the EC. The opening of economy was a little bit dangerous in the context of currency convertibility. We, however, successfully overcame the collapse of COMECON and the losses of former Soviet markets. The change or re-orientation of trade was really remarkable, because we now have about 70% of all of our exports and imports with OECD countries. The ratio was in favor of COMECON some two or three years ago. It was done very quickly, and some flexibility can certainly be seen in our corporate sector.

Foreign Exchange Regime.

There were long debates preceding the switch from central planning system of foreign exchange allocation on how to go about it in the new system. There were many proposals and we finally, without explaining the reasons, opted for convertibility on current account transactions. We sometimes call it internal convertibility (only domestic legal entities may make use of it rather than individual citizens). Introduction of such convertibility was another risky step, especially with very low foreign exchange reserves, at a time when in fact nobody knew anything about the proper exchange rate level. But at that time we thought it was very compatible with our whole reform package, and especially with the liberalization of prices. The economy was still very widely monopolized. It was necessary to open trade and to keep access to foreign exchange in order to enable competition within the domestic economy. Again, one month before the start of convertibility and for one or two months afterwards we could not sleep well. It was really very difficult because we launched our convertibility with 300 mil. US dollars of foreign exchange reserves. But as you probably know, we made an agreement with IMF which brought us a standby credit of about 1 bil. US$ at the beginning and some additional amount afterwards which was sufficient to kick-start convertibility and to give confidence both at home and abroad that we would be able to survive. At the beginning of economic reform, some support from international financial institutions and governments is very important, because there is a reluctance, I would say both at home and abroad, to borrow money from the capital market and from banking sector. So at the beginning, support from international institutions (EC, G24) was crucial. Otherwise, our radical reform package could not have been started. As far as convertibility is concerned, I would add one or two things. Since the introduction of convertibility - preceded by a heavy devaluation before - we have kept the exchange rate stable, i.e. stable against a basket of currencies. We have only changed the composition of the basket. Now it is a two-currency basket with a 65% DEM share and a 35% USD share. But we have kept the nominal exchange rate stable since January 1, 1991 (which is 32 months now). This is completely different from all the other countries in a similar situation - i.e. in the process of transition. In Poland there is a crawling peg and perhaps from time to time some additional devaluation. In Hungary, there are continuous small devaluations. They more or less try to keep the exchange rate stable in real terms, while we keep it stable in nominal terms. I think this is an issue, which I would like to discuss with you a little bit more. Of course, you can ask me: "How long do you want to continue with such policy? Your inflation is higher than Germany's and some other countries, and the margin is quite high. Sooner or later, you will be forced to devalue."We think that under certain conditions this is not true. This is a very important issue for us - I dare to say it might be even the backbone of our economic policy for the future and, at the same time, it is a really difficult issue. So if you would elucidate "hard crown" policy for the future I would be very happy to hear the results of your debate. I am going to make only two or three comments in this context. First, you know that to continue our policy, we must bring inflation down. We are expecting a single digit inflation next year. We would like to succeed, and this is our target. But we think that we could tolerate points above that, say, 3 or 4% provided we have something which I call hidden reserves in productivity. Therefore, if the inflation in our country is 8% next year and in Germany or in another country 4% we should still be able to survive this. This is my first observation. Of course, it would be necessary to make an assessment of where we are now as concerns the exchange rate and to compare the real effective exchange rate, purchasing power parity, with the nominal exchange rate. And we think that we still have something which could be called a cushion. We do not want to sleep on it, but it can help us. The third issue is that this policy of a stablenominal exchange rate is very useful for us as an anchor for domestic price levels and it has helped tremendously in the first two and half years to keep inflation down. We feel that it has a good impact on microeconomy as well. Especially when certain exporting companies, to put it very bluntly, are in trouble, if they are hesitant to do something about their costs, to restructure the company and to bring their costs down. This policy is pressing the corporate sector to improve the productivity of labour and to bring down labour unit costs. The question is how far we can proceed, and how long we can continue. And in this respect, I will be very pragmatic: Let us not promise anything, let us make no irrevocable commitment and, instead let us watch carefully what is happening on the export and output side, let us consider costs and benefits. When the costs (i.e. the output losses and social problems) outweigh the benefits of this exchange rate policy we have to consider a change. Now, if you could help us throw some light on this issue in the debate we would be very happy.

Let me mention privatization very briefly. You have been informed that the privatization process goes on very fast here and nowadays the private sector's share of GDP might be higher than 30 percent, according to our assessments. According to the Statistical Bureau, as I was informed, it is even higher. Privatization was fast due to the quick, I would say, conventional, traditional techniques of privatization, and due to the nonstandard voucher privatization. We are now in the situation where we have done something, and I hope that the critical mass of ownership change was effectively accomplished, and we are now waiting to see what will happen in the real economy. So we are now wondering whether there will be some time delay or not, and how fast companies will adopt market behaviour. This is basically what we are waiting for. I have already mentioned the importance of macroeconomic stability at the beginning of the economic reform - particularly of consumer prices and inflation and exchange rate stability. I would only add, that good macroeconomic results were achieved by a combination of three policies - a restrictive monetary policy, a reasonable and quite restrictive budget policy, and control of wages. This approach functioned for two years, in 1991 and 1992. At the beginning of this year the control of wages was abolished but, after a couple of months, we had to return to the control of wages again. I do not want to say that it was a mistake but, probably, it was, given that we liberalized wages before ownership rights. So we had to go back but something happened here and it is possible that some inflationary gap was created in the economy. Now we have to try to eliminate the possible consequences of the jump in wages in the first half of the year. Finally I would like to mention the social safety net. I do not want to add anything to the existing safety net because, in my opinion, a relatively good package of social measures was created and I think that the government is watching these things very carefully. Whenever there is a debate in the government on a proposal for a price increase, e. g. public transport, apartment rents, or elsewhere, there is always a second paper concerning its possible effect on low income groups of citizens. It is always a balanced package aimed at keeping the social consensus in our society in favor of a peaceful continuation of our economic reforms. My notes include some data about a better rating of our country and you will be informed by my colleagues about a successful improvement of our international image. I mean especially our ratings in the United States where, for example, Standard and Poor's has given us the best investment rating in Central and Eastern Europe.

I have mentioned our basic package of economic reform and some results but I have not tackled the issue of real economy. Output has been going down from the beginning of 1991, and even before that. Up to now we have had a more or less permanent decline in output. This recession was much deeper than we had expected but at the same time the revival of certain segments of the economy came perhaps sooner than we had expected. Certain signs of recovery were visible in the second half of last year and then there was a break connected with the dissolution of the country. The dissolution of the country has effected not only the macroeconomic data, but also our results for this year. So our output is declining, but there are still many unresolved questions about output. When Mr. Greenspan was here in May last year, his first observation, was that the decline of GDP was not as deep as our statistics were showing. The other data, such as unemployment were simply not compatible with such a decline in output. So it is necessary to to make a deeper analysis somehow. Probably the statistics are not now able to cover all our economic activities and, probably, the so-called grey economy or black economy is growing quite fast. The service sector is growing, or even booming, and this is very difficult to record is statistics. Therefore, it is necessary to carefully interpret the decline of output. And at the same time it is very difficult to make sound economic monetary policy because output is one of the elements of our monetary program. This is the only remark I have on real economy: output is declining but we have probably reached the bottom.

Now I would like to mention shocks. We have gone through several shocks in the economy. One of my colleagues, Mr. Klacek, during the board meeting when we were considering the economic and monetary situation in the economy, mentioned that shocks in our economy have actually helped us. After each shock we immediately made faster progress, for example reorientation of trade. Of course, as we have mentioned, we do not want to initiate additional shocks. What do I mean by these shocks? The first shock for the economy was at the beginning of 1990. The government was dismantling the central planning system without replacing or, better, without quickly replacing it with something else, which was quite a big shock for certain companies. The establishment of a two-tier banking system, which I will mention later, was another shock. The collapse of COMECON was also a major shock effecting output. The next shock was the start of our radical economic reform, then a value added tax and, of course, the dissolution of the country and split of the currency with all its consequences, which I do not want to talk about now, but it could be of great interest to you to hear what this has meant for monetary policy and these kinds of issues. We have gone through many shocks, and immediately after each we tried to stabilize the economy at a new price level. And in this we were quite successful.

Let me change now to the banking sector. I mentioned that we established a two-tier banking sector at the beginning of 1990 and that we established an independent Central Bank. And of course, new commercial banks started to grow here. We had seven commercial banks at the beginning of 1990, and now we have about 50 commercial banks. The Central Bank is, in my opinion, a normal classic central bank, based on the model of the Bundesbank, with quite a great deal of independence and it is probably more powerful than some other central banks in two particular areas, which are banking supervision and the exchange rate policy, which are both controlled by the Central Bank. We could now discuss the issue of independence of the Central Bank, but I do not want to talk about it for too long. It was vested in the Law, but this does not mean anything. In fact, the important and necessary issue is to build, day by day, the credibility of the Central Bank at home and abroad. Only the credibility of the Central Bank will generate its independence. This is my observation from the past. And, of course, credibility can be lost equally so easily and quickly, within a matter of a few minutes.

We have slightly impaired our credibility now as the exchange of coins was not done as carefully as some of our previous actions. I hope it was just a minor thing, but certainly the general public was not satisfied with our actions this time.

I would now like to mention two major problems within the economy and the banking sector. The first one is the problem of old non-performing loans, and the second is inter-enterprise debts. I would even add one new problem, which is the problem of new non-performing loans. I will explain later why I am presenting this problem for your consideration.

As concerns the burden of the old non-performing loans there are two or three basic courses of action. The first possibility is to make a clear division between the debts from the past and those incurred in the transition. The second possibility is to do nothing and to wait and hope that through the privatization process the problems will somehow be solved.

The third possibility is to do something in-between, to find a compromise. We have made such a compromise - I use the term "salami approach" for the steps we have taken. We sliced a piece of salami when the situation was really hot. We established the so-called Consolidation Bank and put there the "perpetual" credits from balance sheet of the commercial banks. And the effect was good: it enabled us to reduce the balance sheets of the commercial banks, to improve the capital/asset ratio at the same time and of course to shift the bad debts somewhere else, to improve the quality of their portfolios. The second thing we did was to re-capitalize our large domestic commercial banks. Third, we gave a certain amount of money to our commercial banks to write off non-performing loans of the companies. Then we tried to make some attempt at netting out bilateral and multilateral overdue credits among companies. The current situation is that we will probably continue step by step on an individual basis to solve the problem of non-performing loans. The economic ministers are now discussing how to resolve the non-performing loans of some foreign trade companies which were hit hard by large devaluation, especially at the beginning of 1991, and the problem has not yet been solved. On a case by case basis, the government will probably deal with a few commercial banks. So we do not expect any general scheme for addressing this problem, but rather a case by case approach. Perhaps only one general scheme was prepared - buying out some of the non performing loans from companies going bankrupt. The government prepared a certain amount of money for the Consolidation Bank to buy credits. These are the more or less bankrupt companies. Everything I have mentioned is done according to a compromise scheme of sharing losses. The burden is practically split among many entities: the government, banks, citizens and the corporate sector. By the way, the privatization process was conducted according a similar scheme.

The second issue I will mention is the problem of inter-enterprise indebtedness. It means the debtors failure to fulfil an obligation to a supplier at maturity. The size of this problem is quite large and we do not see any miracle solution to it. I do not want to talk about the causes, but the main problem is that there are still some companies in our economy which are not healthy and are not yet bankrupt, even though they probably should be, and they are causing secondary payment problems for other companies which are otherwise normally or potentionally healthy. The solution will probably not be easy, and it will be connected with cleaning up the problems of bankruptcy within the economy. Of course, financial discipline must be restored in this context.

I also mentioned the problem of new non-performing loans. In all of the Central and Eastern European countries in transition, the problem is that the banking sector is practically new and the bottle-neck of this system is the quality of its employees. Currently, banks are expanding their activities while they lack experienced people. When I compare the inexperience in commercial banks, particularly in the new commercial banks, with the many new private individuals entering the private sector for the first time, I see that many mistakes are made on each side in the initial stages. New banks have an especially easy beginning position because they do not have any problems with inherited non-performing loans. They simply see the profit and immediately start granting new credits. After a year they suddenly recognize that certain clients are not repaying their loans, and that they are not even recovering their interest. Only then do they realize that something is happening. The problem arises if they do not draw any lesson from this and continue with their expansionary credit policy. Then the dynamism of non-performing loans can be faster than the new credits and problems start very soon thereafter. And then, when you combine the new inexperienced banks, many new inexperienced companies and many new private individuals, plus the inexperienced supervision of the Central Bank, problems can because really bad. We must keep this in mind and be very careful, otherwise the entire banking sector will be fragile within two or three years time.

We went through the stage which Mr.Hrnèíø called a "stabilization stage". We are now entering an adjustment and consolidation period. Basically, it means that all the market "embryos" present here must be developed very fast. We used, as I mentioned, some non standard methods of privatisation and ownership change, and we are waiting now for faster restructuring of the economy now. We hope that despite the fact that this stage will be very long, perhaps even longer than we expected, and probably more painful and costly than we expected, that it can generate some economic activity. We realize that it will be a long marathon and that we are still at the beginning, having run only the first few kilometers.

DISCUSSION

Prof. Willett: One follow-up question on the trade decline between the Czech Republic and Slovakia after the split. To what extent do you think it is temporary because of getting used to the new system?

Mr. Tošovský: We, of course, expected some decline in bilateral trade with Slovakia because we had to split the currency and because the balance of payments between our countries was not in equilibrium. We very carefully prepared the options for the trade arrangement and payment system between the two countries. I think that my colleagues helped very much in this. The three policy options under consideration were a payment system in national currencies to make them convertible despite the fact that they are not convertible outside, trade with payments in convertible currencies, or a clearing payment system. We opted for the clearing payment system because we were quite confident that it could help prevent the collapse of trade. Therefore the payment system was organized in such a manner. We expected a possible trade decline of 20% - 30% and our rough assessment is that a 10% decline in trade with Slovakia means something around a 1% loss in GDP for the Czech Republic. Our estimate was not far off. There was about a 25% decline in trade with Slovakia in the first half of this year. As far as the Czech Republic is concerned, we were able to partly offset this decline with an increase of exports to other countries, primarilly to EC countries, but not only to them. The export index for the first half of this year compared with the same period for last year was 7.8%, close to 8%, due to the fact that the 8% is of course from a bigger base - I mean our trade to convertible area is bigger than exports to Slovakia. This did not fully offset the trade decline with Slovakia but helped to partly solve the problem. There is a certain impact here: Our country is paying a certain price for dissolution - no question about it. As your question is concerned whether it is short-term or long-term matter, I would only say that this decline of trade was partly the result of our new lower GDP. We are not quite sure what will happen in future. We were really surprised at how quickly our companies redirected their exports to other locations. The impact on Slovakia was more dramatic. When we compared the results of the first half of this year in several macroeconomic categories we were quite surprised at how fast the divergence of economic performance was. For example, the GDP in the Czech Republic during the first half of this year was, according to official statistics, minus 0.9. But this is only an estimate and it will be probably closer to 0 (stagnation). In Slovakia, there was a decline of 6,4% in GDP in the first half of this year. I would like to continue with other data like exports, but we do not have any information about Slovakias trade balance. We only have information on foreign exchange reserves. The foreign exchange reserves at the beginning of this year were divided 2:1 between the Czech Republic and Slovakia, respectively. The overall reserves in the Czech banking sectors now are 5.5 bil. while in Slovakia they are only 1.4. So the ratio certainly is not 2:1. But I should say one thing: We were able to raise some money from the market economy while Slovakia was not. Our current account is in surplus by about 320 mil. US dollars in the first half of the year. Smaller divergence is visible as concerns the inflation. The difference is only 2 or 3% between the Czech Republic and Slovakia in the first half of the year. The biggest divergence is in unemployment, but this was already big at the beginning of this year, and it has continued to widen. In the Czech Republic unemployment is now 2.6%, and in Slovakia it is about 13.5%, and this is visible. I would add one more figure, concerning the performance of the budget. Our budget is officially in surplus for the first half of this year by 3 bil. Czech crowns. Officially. But unofficially there are many hidden reserves and the surplus is really very large. I must admit that the performance of the budget was a little bit surprising to us especially in the first half of this year. The fiscal policy of the budget was very restrictive in the first half of the year. We are in surplus whereas Slovakia has a deficit of about 14 bil. Czech crowns. This, I think, reflects the transfers which were made from the Czech budget through the federal budget to Slovakia. It was partly hidden but now it is visible, with a surplus on one side and deficit on the other.

Prof. Wihlborg of the University of Gothenburg, Sweden: After listening to your interesting description of your policy there is one thing. As the Central bank you said that you might be willing to give up the nominal peg if the cost is too high, otherwise the Central bank, as you say, will stick to this. But I wonder by what mechanism then are you trying to establish credibility for the long term. Do you think you have succeeded? What are interest rates for example?

Mr. Tošovský: This is a broader issue. I have few remarks on exchange rate policy. We discussed it with Mr. Hrnčíř, as he is an expert on exchange rate regime and system. And it seems to me that we will soon be at a crossroads as the exchange rate regime is concerned. We think that the policy of keeping the nominal exchange rate pegged is good and healthy but at the same time we realize it can be quite difficult from the social and, of course, from the political point of view. And certainly we would not be interested in keeping this policy if the economic ministers, I mean the Minister of Economy, the Minister of Industry and Trade, and the Minister of Finance are shooting at us with strong ammunition in the press, in Parliament or elsewhere. We would be isolated and it would be very difficult to survive it. So we have to reach some consensus to maintain a certain policy. At the same time I am a little bit skeptical, and I think that these ministers will be reluctant to come to any consensus, because they would like to have free hands. So we will continue with this policy and sooner or later we will be criticized despite the fact that we are trying to achieve a consensus. We will have to consider a little bit more the signals towards a change of our policy. Under certain circumstances, I think, even a deficit of current account should not be a signal to change policies. It depends on how the exports develop, whether there is some acceleration of exports, and how our country is re-gaining its position in the world market. The assessment will not be easy and I cannot give you any prescription for how we shall solve this problem. But certainly we will be watching many indicators. Of course if we decide to continue with this policy this means we must, for example, continue to build strong foreign exchange reserves. If, on the other hand, the given policies are not maintained, it would not be desirable to increase the reserves too much, because big reserves increase costs.

As far as the interest rate is concerned, I did not mention anything about monetary policy. But our experts here can explain what our monetary policy is. I will only mention that we are not using any administrative instrument now in our monetary policy. The key issue of this policy is to keep the nominal exchange rate unchanged. We have a certain programme of money supply growth; we especially watch M2 and we are preparing a monetary base and the problem is that we are short of reliable data. What we are doing is partly an analysis of the situation and an assessment and then we look out of the window and say, " this program, this alternative is the best one." I will tell you why we have not already done this.

After the dissolution of the country and the split of the currency we did not have any information about currency in circulation. For example, there was one currency circulated both in Slovakia and in the Czech Republic and nobody knew what amounts were circulating in the two parts of the former Czechoslovakia. Preparing the split of the currency, we had to ask our citizens, practically speaking, to put all cash into saving accounts, otherwise we would not be able to withdraw the banknotes from circulation and stamp them. It would not be technically possible in any other way, and there was no another solution. So at the beginning of this year, we had a dramatic distortion between M0, M1 and M2. Even at the beginning of the next year we will not be fully informed about it. We can only make an assessment - a reconstruction of the actual volume of M0, M1, and M2 in our economy. So, we are partly blind. It is very difficult to conduct monetary policy under such circumstances. Also, for example, the coefficient between the monetary base and M2 is permanently moving due to the currency split. We are waiting for its stabilization. Should we pump liquidity into the market, we cannot predict exactly what will happen by simple multiplication. We have some more stable data now but we are still not sure whether it is valid for increments - and increments are very important to us. We are doing the normal things that all central banks do. All the instruments have been developed, and for successful monetary policy the banking system must be, of course, sensitive and ready.

The interest rate level is a different issue and the interest rate spread is another special one. Spreads are higher than normal - around 6 - 7% spreads between what the banks pay for deposits and what they charge their clients for credits. Again, there are many reasons for it, e. g. lack of competition, the things I mentioned before, that the excess liquidity is somewhere else, the problem of non-performing loans the banks being left alone to solve these problems. It means that somebody has to pay for it and they are simply drawing money from the private sector to build reserves with this mechanism, through wide spreads. The market is now in better shape, the interbank market is now the overnight market, its level of interest rate is about 9% and the discount rate is currently 8% and the prime rate for large domestic banks is somewhere between 11 - 13%. I would say that for foreign investors, a very good investment during last two years was to go from German marks or even US dollars to Czech crowns. Because we peg our currency, we keep the exchange rate unchanged in nominal terms and difference between interest rate in our country and in Germany and especially in the USA was at least 10 percent. This was the best investment, and some foreign capital investors came to make some profit on it.

Prof. Maxwell Fry: I am very alarmed by the idea of using the currency, or the exchange rate as the major platform or backbone of monetary policy basically in any country. I think one might have that as a hidden agenda but to put it out is an incredible mistake. Because as you have very rightly said it is very easy to destroy credibility, and if your exchange rate is the backbone of your annouced policy then, of course, any sensible change in exchange rate would assumably destroy credibility. And independence, of course, is very dependent on, it seems to me, budget balance and currently on wage control. So I just would like to suggest that it would be a very sensible aim that should certainly perhaps be kept as un-publicized aim. Secondly, that if you are thinking of liberalizing the capital account, that can make problems infinitely greater. And again, if you are thinking in next five years of capital account liberalization, I would not want to, in any way, say that the exchange rate was the linchpin or backbone of monetary policy because, goodness, what will happen with any capital account liberalization. The situation is extraordinary difficult and it seems to me that one of the things that happens in the monetary sphere when you have a fixed exchange rate with capital account liberalization is the ability to allow overnight rates to be very volatile. It is, I think, extremely interesting to know that both Switzerland and Singapore, countries with the two hardest currencies in the world have experienced overnight rates in triple digits, over 100%, and this has happened several times. And unless you impose costs on speculators, incredible costs, you cannot defend a fixed exchange rate. So it seems to me that if there is any agenda, I would keep the fixed exchange rate target very much in the background.

Mr. Tošovský: I think this was not a question, but rather it was comment to our discussion. I would mention that we do not promise anything. This is very important. And we will certainly act in such a was as not to lose our credibility. We will concentrate on this but still there are several good possibilities that we will be able to continue with our policies. Certainly, as I mentioned, there are some hidden reserves in the economy which we could use. In the short term we basically have to be careful about wages and in the long term it is a question of investment. As concerns the further liberalization of the exchange rate regime, I would say that we do not need capital account convertibility at the present time. It would be too dangerous. I would say, basically, the capital account convertibility is a question of confidence and credibility. And as we have gone through so many shocks and there is the possibility of some further shocks - I do not see any immediate shock on the horizon - but always in shock situations people start to change their behaviour: citizens and companies start to change and they are always thinking about their money, their savings, and about convertible currencies. So it would probably be very dangerous to do this now and it is perhaps not so good that now our foreign exchange law is overly flexible and quite free, and that the extent of liberalization is surprisingly bigger than would be expected. So basically the inflow of capital is possible only with the authorization of the central bank but are very flexible about this, and we go through the process of registration just to know what will happen in the future, and what we can expect. All foreign investors can buy treasury bills and they can then back out of this transaction the following day. Without authorization. It is the same with shares - it is possible to buy shares without any authorization. So portfolio investments are practically open. And as concerns the outflow of capital, again the authorization of the Central bank is needed and here we are, of course, conservative and very careful. So we are considering further small steps to partially liberalize the capital account but we do not plan anything dramatic or quick because it could be dangerous for us.

Part I:

Monetary and Exchange Rate Policies

THE EFFECTS OF SHOCKS TO BANK CREDIT DURING THE TRANSITION:

LESSONS OF SIMULATIONS OF A MACROECONOMETRIC MODEL OF CZECHOSLOVAKIA*

Eric Girardin and Velayoudom Marimoutou
LARE - University Bordeaux IV, France

It is widely recognized that macroeconomic stabilization programs, including restrictions in real money supply and/or bank credit, in transitional economies will have simultaneous effects on real activity (output, employment) and nominal variables (wages and prices)[1]. While a number of theoretical or descriptive studies have attempted to give an account of such effects in qualitative term, little has been done to try and quantify the relationships among major macroeconomic variables in the context of formerly planned economies. This absence of a quantified framework is particularly damaging when one wants to evaluate the contribution that specific monetary policy initiatives can make to real and nominal developments, or their responsibility in past movements of such variables.

The actual operation of the transmission mechanism in transitional economies, and the relative size and timing of the effects of a change in

* The present version of this chapter benefited from comments by Keith Cuthbertson. However, we remain responible for all remaining ends.

[1] On alternative hypotheses recently put forward to try and explain nominal and real macroeconomic developments in formerly planned economies, see Bruno, 1992.

policy are a matter of considerable doubt. This is similarly the case in many developing countries. However, the experience gathered in the latter countries (especially by the IMF, see Kahn, Monthiel and Haque, 1991) can be built upon in modelling transitional economies. Typically, such modelling emplasizes the role played by the demand for money and monetary disequilibrium in the behaviour of major macroeconomic variables such as output and prices. The main stress being put on monetary factors and short run dynamics, this type of model focuses essentially on the demand-side. A simplified theoretical version of this model, also located in the tradition of the monetary view, has been developed by Berg and Sachs (1992) in order to interpret the Polish stabilization program of the early 1990's. However these authors do not attempt any estimation.

The defect of such a monetary view, well emphasized for instance by Bernanke (1983), is that it does not seem to represent a complete explanation of the link between the financial sector and output. Indeed the latter can involve not only the money supply, as emphasized by the monetary view, but also bank credit, as stressed by the credit view.

The main approach which portrays the way in which restrictions in bank credit can potentially affect output in transitional economies emphasizes supply-side effects[2]. This supply-side view has been modelled by Calvo and Coricelli (1992a and c). The key assumption of their model is that firms face the constraint of needing liquidity in advance to finance intermediate inputs. In such a context, the supply side shock that economics like the CSFR faced in 1991 can be seen as stemming from the combined effects of a steep rise in input prices (i.e. energy) together with an expansion of credit that failed to keep pace with input prices. As a result, firms curtailed their demand for other firms' products and, eventualy, their demand for labor. Firms tried to offset the liquidity crunch by drastically lowering real wages, i.e. by borrowing from workers.

By setting credit ceilings for the entire banking system, the stabilization program limited the amount of credit that banks could offer to enterprises. However, the initial price jump of about 40% was much higher than envisaged (table 1). This implied that the programmed monetary targets became more restrictive than anticipated. In addition, cautious behaviour on the part of banks slowed credit to enterprises even more than targeted, particularly in the first quarter of 1991.

[2] In developed economies, analysts like Bermanke (1983) prefer to stress demand-side channels for credit-market effects on output.

Table 1: Rate of variation of bank credit to firms
and of inflation in the CSFR. (in%)

	Real credit to enterprises		inflation	
1991	actual	target	actual	target
First quarter	- 28.3	- 11.4	- 39.5	25.0
Whole year	- 18.4	- 8.1	58.7	30.0

Source: Calvo-Coricelli (1992b).

Credit tightness, measured in terms of bank credit seems to have eased later in 1991, (see figure 2 below). However, output responded much less to this credit expansion than to the credit contraction which occured earlier. One explanation, put forward by Calvo and Coricelli, is that the objective of firms is to maximize current wages[3]. Thus, the easing of credit conditions would lead firms to offer higher wages instead of using the proceeds to relieve the liquidity squeeze and increase production. This would explain the sharp increase in real wages.

In the present paper we use a macroeconomic approach[4] in the spirit of Bermanke's (1983) in that we argument the purely monetary approach by bank credit effects in order to improve the explanation of the financial sector-output correlation in the short run. We estimate and simulate a small-scale macroeconomic model of Czechoslavakia, trying to isolate more precisely the ways in which bank credit to firms empirically plays a role in the formation of nominal as well as real magnitudes. Using monthly data, we study the February 1991-September 1992 period. This leads us to focus on the industrial sector of the Czechoslovak economy which is still mostly made up of state firms, and represents roughly 50% of overall GDP. We leave aside January 1991 since the opening and liber-

---

[3] Another explanation is that a credit crunch signifies a fundamental shake-up of interfirm relationships, leading firms to fall into arrears with one another and to break all sorts of explicit and implicit contracts. In such an environment, a later expansion of credit may not be able to mend the damage caused by the initial credit crunch, thus leading to a slower recovery. Furthermore, some of the arrears with other firms will be repaid. Therefore easing up bank credit would lead to a repayment of debts to both workers and suppliers (rather than an expansion of output) leaving total credit for enterprises roughly unchanged.

[4] Borsenzstein *et alii* (1992), implementing an econometric procedure that separates the effects of national and industry specific shocks on output changes, show that the bulk of output variance in Czecoslovakia is accounted for by aggregate or national factors, with industry specific components playing only an insignificant role. Therefore they conclude that the data support the adoption of a macroeconomic approach.

alization of the economy involved specific developments and must have generated instabilities which we do not intend to examine.

The paper is divided into two sections. The first will specify a small-scale macroeconomic model made up of a real sector, a wage-price one and a monetary sector. We will also present the results of the estimation of such a model. The second section will examine the overall performance of the model. Using dynamic ex-post simulations, we will also study what would have happened to real and nominal magnitudes if, after the initial credit crunch of january 1991, bank credit to firms had been increased immediately.

I. Specification and Estimation of the Model

A. Specification

The model comprises six equations and a set of six identities. Before mentioning these identities, we will examine behavioural equations in turn by considering the real side, the wage-price sector, and the monetary sector.

1. The Real Sector

Industrial output (Q) is modelled to depend both on monetary disequilibrium, proxied by the excess supply of real balances ($MQMP_{t-1}$ - $MQMP^d_t$), using consumer prices as a deflator. External factors are proxied by exports to market economies (XMP) deflated by producer prices. The ration of the producer price index to the price of energy (RPEN) and the wage bill deflated by the CPI, (WLP) also appear a possible explanatory variables. All variables are in log.

$$Q_t = \alpha_0 + \alpha_1(MQMP_{t-1} - MQMP^d_t) + \alpha_2\, RPEN_{t-i} + \alpha_3\, WLP_t + \alpha_4\, XMP_t \qquad (1)$$

An excess real supply of money inherited from the previous period relative to what agents desire should generate an increase in industrial output. Agents would adjust their money holdings to their desired level by increasing their spending[5]. Exports to market economies and the real

[5] This specification has been shown by Clements and Jonson (1979) to be equivalent, under some specific conditions, to the use of unancipated changes in the money stock.

wage bill are supposed to influence positively industrial production. The relative price of energy should also exert a positive influence on the latter.

Employment in the industrial sector (L) is to be explained by the real product wage (real wages deflated by producer prices, WP), plus the levels of industrial production and of real bank credit to firms, the relative price of energy, and the minimum wage[6]
(DUM_{wMIN}).

$$L_t = \beta_0 + \beta_1 WP_{t-m} + \beta_2 Q_{t-u} + \beta_3 RPEN_{t-j} + \beta_4 CEP_{t-j} + \beta_5 DUM_{wMIN} \quad (2)$$

We expect real wages as well as the minimum wage and the relative price of energy to exert a negative impact on the level of employment, while industrial production should have a positive effect.

2. *The Wage-Price Sector*

Nominal wages in the industrial sector depend on labor productivity (r), on the change in real bank credit to enterprises ($\triangle CEP$), and on the level of consumer prices (P).

$$W_t = \omega_0 + \omega_1 r_{t-i} + \omega_2 \triangle CEP_{t-k} + \omega_3 P_{t-f} \quad (3)$$

Wages should be linked positively to labour productivity and to the consumer price level. Enterprise credit should influence them positively in as much as firms use extra credit to finance wage increases

Nominal incomes of the population (YR) are equal to the sum of industrial wage income plus transfers from the government. The latter are considered to be a function of government expenditure (G).

$$YR_t = \nu_0 + W_t + \nu_2 G_{t-k} \quad (4)$$

The coefficient of wages is thus constrained to be unity, while government expenditure should determine positively the income of individuals.

---

[6] Details about the minimum wage policy in Czechoslovakia are to be found in Ham, Svejnar and Terrell (1993)

Consumer price inflation is modelled to depend on the level of real bank credit to firms, on excess real cash balances, on the change in the level of employment, on the rate of variation of the exchange rate of the koruna vis a vis the dollar, and on rate of change of labour productivity (ΔP).

$$\Delta P_t = \lambda_0 + \lambda_1 \Delta CEP_t + \lambda_2 (MQMP_{t-1} - MQMP^d_t) + \lambda_3 L_t + l_4 \Delta S_{t-i} + \lambda_5 \Delta P_{t-l_2} \quad (5)$$

Consumer price inflation is assumed to be positively related to the excess supply of real cash balances. In other words, an expansion of the money stock that generates in the next period an excess supply of real money balances will create inflationary pressures wich should eliminate the disequilibrium in the money market. We also expect consumer price inflation to be related positively to the change in the level of employment for standard reasons and to the rate of change of the exchange rate. The sign of the coefficient of real bank credit is a priori ambiguous. Indeed all depends on the way this extra credit is used by firms. Besides, the growth in labour productivity should have a negative effect on inflation.

3. The Monetary Sector

The demand for broad money (M1 plus quasi-money) is here a standard one, with real balances function of an activity variable (incomes of the population deflated by the consumer price index, noted YRP), and of the short-term rate of interest (i). We also include an influence of inflation:

$$MQMP^d_t = q0 + q1\, YRP_t + q2\, i_t + q3\, \Delta P_{t-n} + q4\, MQMP_{t-1} \quad (5)$$

The influence of the exchange rate on the demand for real balances should be positive. The same should be the case for the level of real incomes of the population. The interest rate should by contrast have a negative influence.

4. Identities

Two identities define the rate of change of a variable as a function of its level or vice versa: this is the case for employment (6) prices (7), productivity (8) and real cash balances (9). One identity (10) establishes the rate of change of labour productivity as a function of the rate of change of two endogenous variables: industrial production and employment.

$$\Delta l_t = l_t - l_{t-1} \quad (6)$$

$$P_t = P_{t-1} + \Delta P_t \quad (7)$$

$$p_t = p_{t-1} + \Delta p_t \quad (8)$$

$$\Delta p_t = Q_t - Q_{t-1} - (L_t - L_{t-1}) \quad (9)$$

Another group of two identities define respectively real incomes of the population (10) and real wages (11), using respectively the consumer price index and the producer price index as a deflator. The twelveth identity gives the real wage bill.

$$YRP_t = YR_t - P_t \quad (10)$$

$$WP_t = W_t - Pp_t \quad (11)$$

$$WLP_t = W_t + L_t - P_t \quad (12)$$

The last identity sets nominal money demand equal to money supply, where the latter is equal to the sum of bank credit to enterprises, credit to households and to the State and foreign assets (aggregated into CHS) which are exogenous in the model·

$$CE_t + CHS_t = MQMP^d_t + P_t \quad (13)$$

B. Estimation

The model was estimated as a system with monthly data over the February 1991-September 1992 period, with lags using data over the second half of 1990, (on the data used see the note at the end of this paper). We used the instrumental variables method, taking as instruments current and lagged values of the exchange rate, of enterprise credit, of the rate of unemployment, of government expenditures, of imports from market economies, and lagged real wages. The estimated stochastic equations are summarized in table 1.

Most of the coefficients have the expected sign. The excess supply of real cash balances exerts a sizable and significant effect on industrial output. Indeed it more than spills over to the goods market. This direct monetary effect on production contrasts with the absence of any direct credit effect. Indeed, we checked that when external (foreign trade) and domestic exogenous (the relative price of energy) variables are taken into account, there is no direct effect of bank credit. The direct influence of these other variables is sizeable. This is particularly true for the price of energy: each 10% increase in the latter over producer price inflation decreases industrial production by nearly 8%. The same is true for real exports to market economies: every 10% increase in these exports seems able to generate directly a 7% increase in industrial production. We tested for a specific influence of exports to (or imports from) COMECON, but this never appeared significant over the period examined here. Besides, the current level of the real wage bill exerts a sizable effect on industrial production.

In the employment equation, the absence of lag in the influence of the real product wage is striking: the direct negative influence is such that each 10% increase in the real product wage is associated with a 1.4% fall in industrial employment over the same month. Although similar direct effects of the relative price of energy and of real bank credit to firms are to be noticed, they are only weakly significant.

In the nominal industrial wage equation, two effects seem to be at work. On the one side the traditional positive influence of labor productivity operates here with a one month-lag. Moreover there is an under-indexation of wages on consumer prices with a five-month lag. On the other side, a factor specific to transitional economies seems at work. Indeed, the growth in real bank credit to firms influences strongly the nominal wage (every 1% increase in credit leads directly to a 0.6% increase in wages). Besides, incomes of the population are influenced very strongly by the level of government expenditures, showing the importance of transfers.

Consumer price inflation is linked positively to monetary disequilibrium. The depreciation of the koruna and the growth in the level of industrial employment generate inflation with similar coefficients. The negative effect of the growth in productivity on consumer price inflation is only weakly significant. Quite surprisingly the growth in bank credit to firms has a negative effect on inflation. This may be rationalized by the fact that the availability of credit enables firms to avoid using price increases as a source of internal finance.

In the demand equation for real monetary balances (broad money), the cœfficient of private real income is around 0.22. A 1% increase in the exchange rate seems to generate directly a 1.8% reduction in desired real cash balances while an increase of the interest rate of the same order of magnitude generates a 0.03% fall in money demand. Long term elasticities of the demand for money are, in absolute value, about twice as big as short term ones.

Table 1. Estimated equations

Industrial production:

$$Q_t = 2.49 + 0.72\ XMP_t + 1.29\ (MQMP_{t-1} - MQMP^D{}_t)$$
(1.61) (5.94)(4.49)
$$- 0.49\ PEN_{t-1} + 0.95\ L_t$$
(-4.67)(3.68)
$R^2 = 0.911$ $\overline{R}^2 = 0.887$ $Q(5) = 3.59$ $SEE = 0.04$

Industrial employment:

$$L_t = 4.93 - 0.13\ (WP)_t - 0.26\ (CEP)_t$$
(12.8) (-2.34) (-1.32)
$$- 0.06\ PEN_{t-1} + 0.13\ Q_t - 0.007\ DUM_w MIN$$
(- 1.31) (2.78) (-7.47)
$R^2 = 0.95$ $\overline{R}^2 = 0.94$ $Q(5) = 1.19$ $SEE = 0.01$

Industrial wages:

$$W_t = 8.29 + 0.41\ r_{t-1} + 1.23\ CEP_t - 0.801\ L_t$$
(5.59) (2.57) (2.22) (-2.46)
$R^2 = 0.748$ $\overline{R}^2 = 0.701$ $Q(5) = 12.5$ $SEE = 0.06$

Incomes of the population:

$$YR_t = -3.07 + W_t + 0.27\ G_t + 0.19\ G_{t-1} + 0.2\ G_{t-2}$$
(-2.67) (2.99) (2.19)(2.15)
$R^2 = 0.777$ $\overline{R}^2 = 0.718$ $Q(5) = 3.24$ $SEE = 0.07$

Consumer price inflation:

$$D\,P_t = 1.83 - 0.09\ CEP_t + 0.148\ L_t$$
(6.95) (-2.16) (5.08)
$$+\ 0.11\ DS_{t-3} - 0.27\ P_{OECD\ t} + 0.07\ (MQMP_{t-1} - MQMP^D{}_t)$$
(2.25)(8.51)(2.63)
$$R^2 = 0.943\ \overline{R^2} = 0.923 Q(5) = 4.66 SEE = 0.005$$

Demand for real cash balances:

$$MQMP^d{}_t = -\ 1.35 + 0.53\ MQMP_{t-1}$$
(- 2.88)(3.88)
$$+\ 0.16\ YRP_t - 0.04\ i_{t-1} + 0.42\ S_{t-4}$$
(2.62)(-3.05)(3.56)
$$R^2 = 0.986\ \overline{R^2} = 0.983 Q(5) = 4.16 SEE = 0.026$$

List of Variables*

Q =volume of industrial production
MQMP =real money supply (M1 + quasi money) (deflator: CPI)
S =exchange rate: koruny per US dollar
XMP =real exports to market economies (deflator: producer price index)
P =consumer price index
L =industrial employment
W =nominal wages in the industrial sector
CEP =real bank credit to entreprises (deflator: producer price index)
r =productivity of labor in the industrial sector
i =rate of interest on short term deposits
YR =nominal income of the population
YRP =real income of the population (deflator CPI)
WP =real wages in the industrial sector (deflator: producer price index)
RPEN =energy price index
DUM_WMIN =dummy for minimum wage = 0 up to January 1991, 1 from February to December 1991, 1.1 as of January 1992.
PP =producer price index.
P_{OECD} = Producer price index of OECD countries in koruny.

* All variables are in log except for the rate of interest.

II. Simulation Results

Two series of simulations were performed. The first one aimed at appreciating the capacity of the model to track actual developments of the endogenous variables. The second examines the impact of the removal of the credit crunch for firms on major macroeconomic variables.

A. The Overall Performance of the Model

In order to assess the overall performance of the model, we implemented dynamic ex post simulations of the system of estimated equations and of identities. The graph of the fit of the estimated equations is given in figures 1.a to 1.f. The comparison of the actual and fitted values of endogenous variables suggests that the model tracks macroeconomic developments reasonably well, over the February 1991-September 1992 period. Major turning points are generally captured. This is especially true of the

Graph 1a: The performance of the model:
Graph 1a: Industrial production (in log)

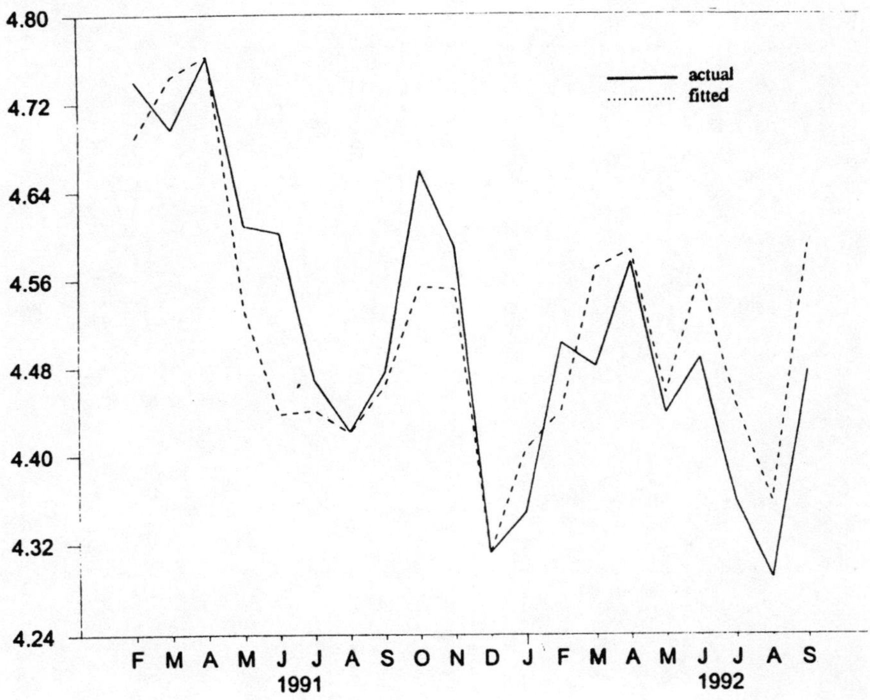

Graph 1.b: Industrial employment (in log)

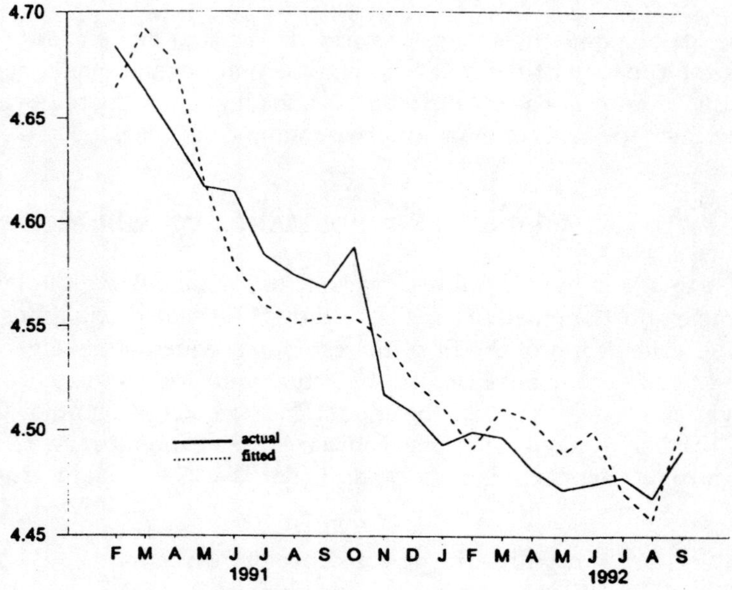

Graph 1.c: Industrial nominal wages (in log)

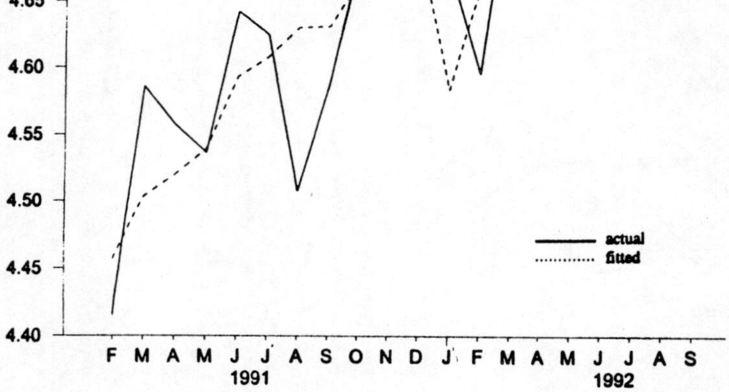

Graph 1.d: Nominal incomes of the population (in log)

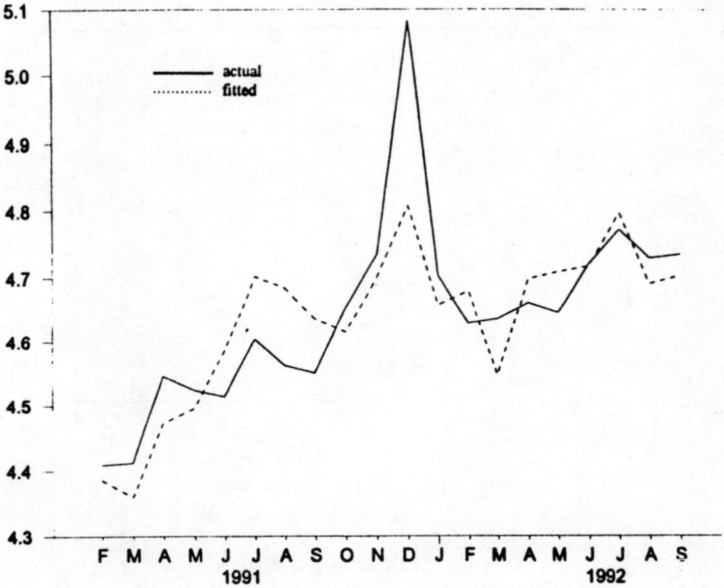

Graph 1.e: Consumer price inflation (percentage points)

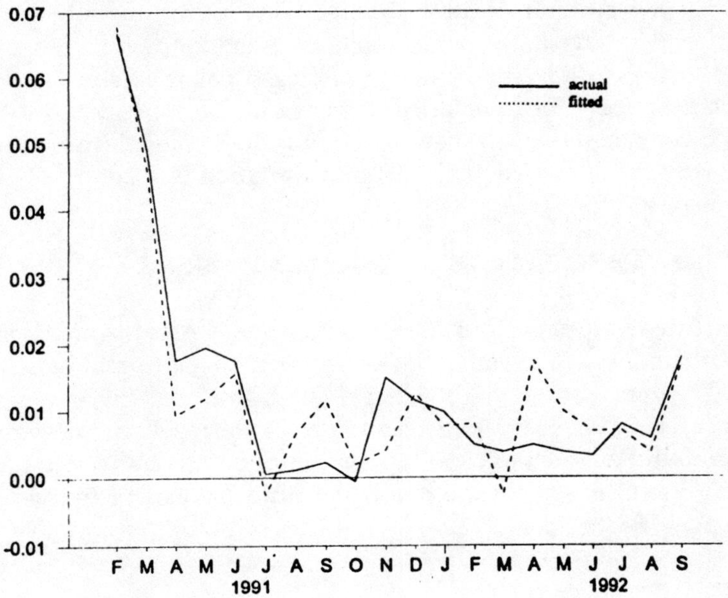

Graph 1.f: Demand for real cash balances (in log)

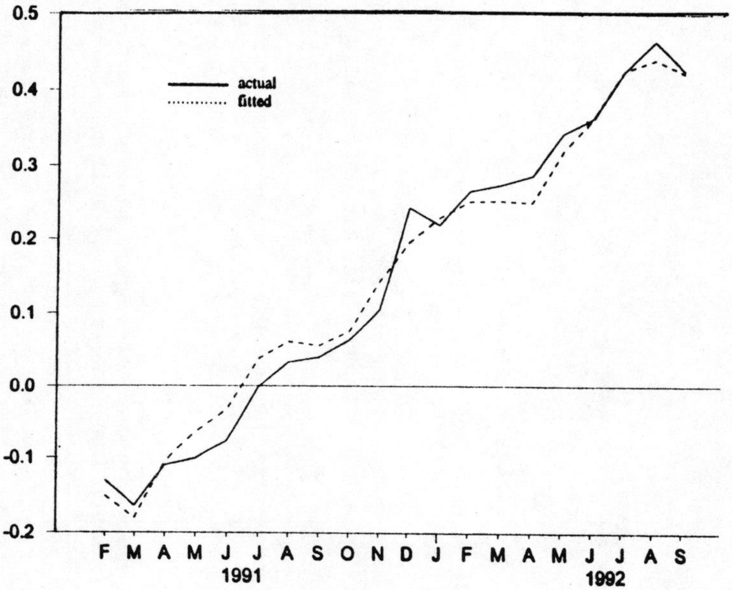

fall in industrial production in the early spring of 1991, and of its movements after the autumn of 1991. Overall movements in industrial employment and in consumer price inflation (over the disinflation period) are quite well proxied. The fit of the real cash balances equation seems quite good. Some difficulties arise however in the industrial wage and nominal income equations, especially during the first semester and occasionally with the inflation equation after disinflation is over.

B. The Effects of Shocks to Bank Credit

Using the fitted values of the model as a baseline, we now implement dynamic simulations. We examine the impact of a shock to real bank credit to firms. We thus assume that the 13.5% fall in this bank credit aggregate which occured in February 1991 (see figure 2) is cancelled. Subsequently real bank credit is assumed to follow its actual path.We study the effects of this shock on the endogenous variables until the end of the period of estimation, i.e. September 1992.

Figure 2: The rate of growth of real bank credit to firms (%).

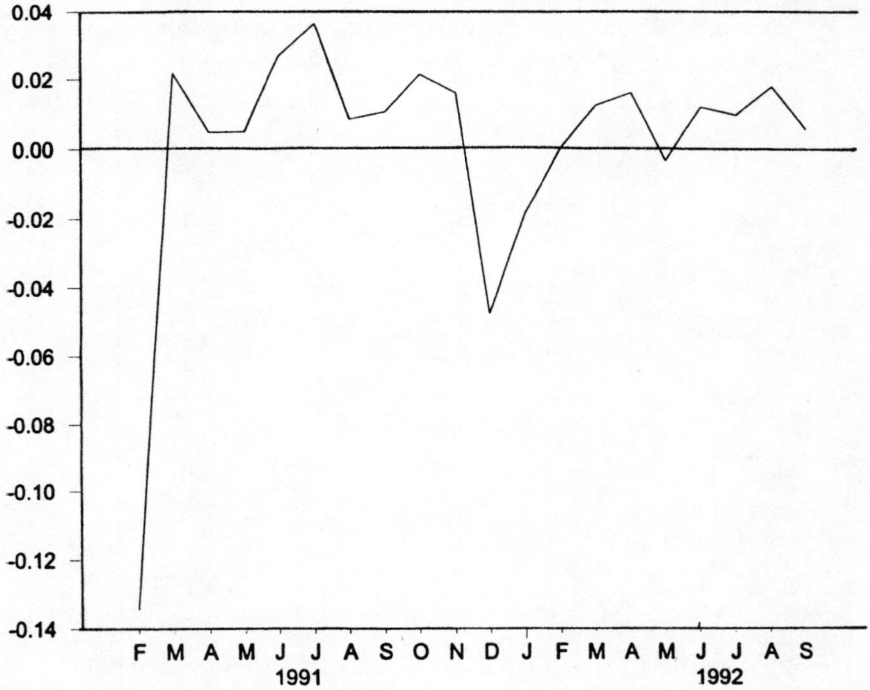

The level of industrial employment reacts to this shock (figure 3.a) with a typical J-curve effect. Indeed, on impact the fall in employment is around 5% while its increase in the medium run is close to 1.5%. The reaction of industrial production is completely different, since this variable increases with a one-month lag by around 3.5%. Thereafter its growth slows down gradually to a rate a little smaller than the rate of growth of employment.

Consumer price inflation is reduced by around 4 percentage points (monthly rate) on impact, and by 0.5 points in the subsequent month (figure 3.c). Therafter inflation is unaffected. Thus the direct reaction of inflation and employment to the increase in bank credit goes in the same direction.

The fall in inflation has a positive impact on the level of industrial production through the improvement in the purchasing power of the wage bill. Indeed the fall in inflation, plus the positive reaction of nominal wages more than compensate the fall in the level of employment.

Graph 3: Effects of a shock to the growth of real bank credit to firms: (cancelation of its 13.5% fall in February 1991)

Graph 3a: Effects on industrial production and employment (% deviation from fitted value)

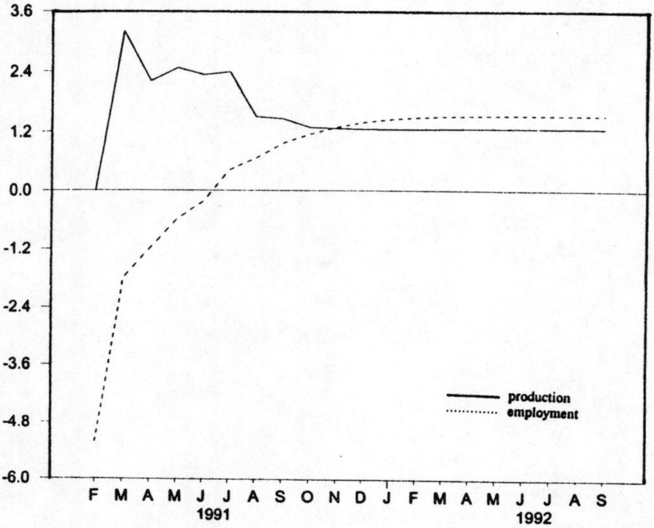

Graph 3.b: Effects on industrial nominal wages (percentage points)

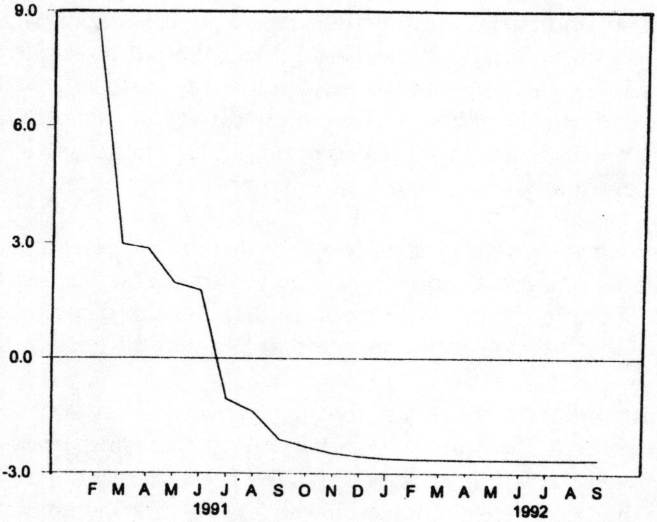

Apart from this direct negative effect of increased bank credit on inflation, the source of the negative impact effects of the increase in real bank credit on economic activity and inflation seems to lie in the reaction of industrial wages and desired real cash balances.

Indeed nominal wages (and thus nominal income of the population) increase substantially on impact (19%) and during the subsequent four months (figure 3.b). This effect is however short-lived since afterwards wage growth is negative, and this goes on for a year with a decrease of up to 2.5% per month. This may explain why employment is able to recover at about this time. The combined movement in nominal wages and consumer prices imply that the shock to bank credit seems to generate initially an increase in real wages, followed by a fall.

Graph 3.c: Effects on consumer price inflation (percentage points)

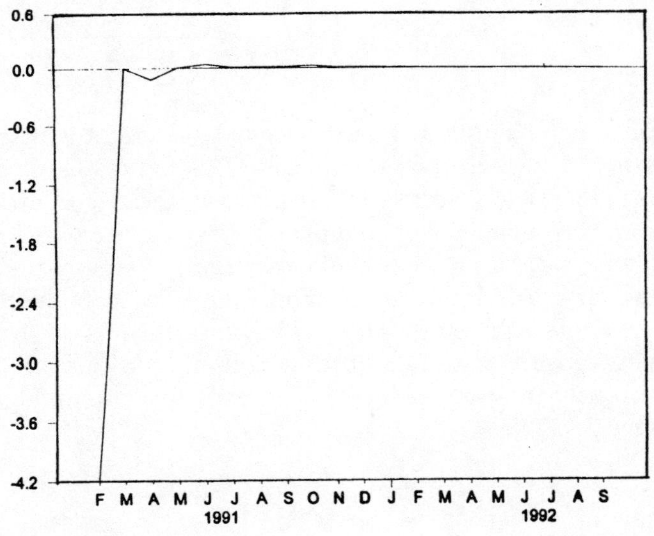

The increase in nominal (and real) income of the population induced by the rise in wages (and accentuated by the fall in inflation) implies that the demand for real cash balances (graph 3.d) increases immediately after the shock to bank credit. This rise is substantial (reaching 3.5%) but gradually falters over the semester following the shock. Desired cash balances are thus higher than their actual level over this period. This disequilibrium initially reinforces the downward pressure on production and inflation and subsequently it moderates their recovery.

Graph 3.d: Effects on the demand for real cash balances

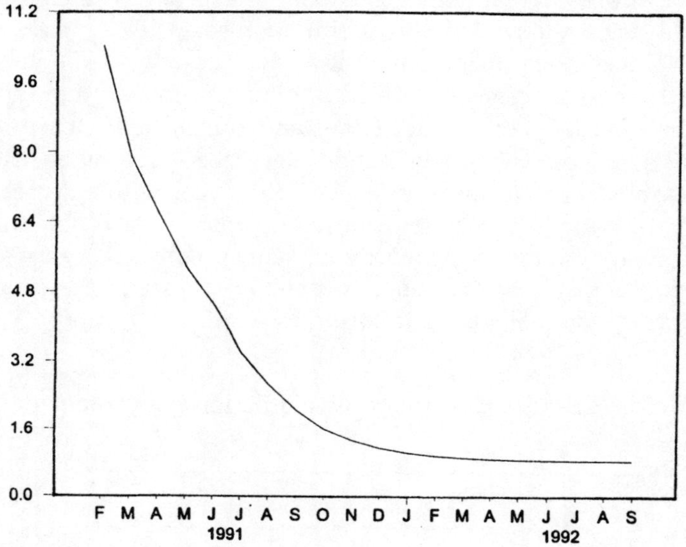

These movements imply that an increse in bank credit is first used by industrial firms to increase nominal wages. This depresses directly employment in the industrial sector. Simultaneously the rise in credit has a negative impact on consumer price inflation. Besides, the positive impact of increased wages on desired cash balances reinforces these direct effects by generating an excess demand for money and this combines with an increased real wage to generate an increase in production. When wages stop increasing, positive effects on production and on inflation materialize. Simultaneously the rise in employment leads to a negative growth in nominal wages.

CONCLUSION

In the macroeconometric model estimated for Czechoslovakia over the February 1991-September 1992 period shows that money and bank credit variables play a major role in the determination of real as well as nominal magnitudes in this economy. Indeed monetary disequilibrium affects directly production and consumer price inflation, while bank credit to firms influences also directly industrial employment and wages as well as inflation.

The simulation of positive shocks to the growth of real bank credit to firms which have been carried out indicate that such shocks are followed in the very short term by a J-curve type reaction of employment and inflation. Thus, rather unexpectedly, the impact effect on these variables is negative. This can be explained since firms seem initially to use extra bank credit to grant wage increases, which depresses both economic activity and employment. This exerts direct and indirect negative effects on inflation. Moreover, the positive impact of increased wages on desired cash balances reinforces these direct effects by generating an excess demand for money.

This pattern of reaction of nominal wages to the shock in bank credit seems to fit well with the idea that coming after the initial credit crunch (January 1991)- that firms tried to side-step by borrowing from each other and by reducing nominal wages (borrowing from workers)- a pause in credit restrictions (in February 1991) would have led firms, among other things, to repay workers by increasing nominal wages. This would have affected employment negatively in the very short run, and may have thus eased inflationary pressures.

Source of the Data

Trade flows, incomes of the population and the rate of unemployment are from the *Monthly Statistical Bulletin* of the Czech Statistical Office.

The consumer price index, the producer price index, government expenditures, industrial production, nominal industrial wages and industrial employment are from the *Quarterly Statistical Bulletin* of the Czech and Slovak Federal Statistical Office.

Money supply, bank credit to firms and the short term interest rate are from *Financial Statistical Information of the CSFR*, State Bank of Czechoslovakia.

The exchange rate is taken from IMF *International Financial Statistics*, while the producer price index of OECD countries is from OECD *Main Economic Indicators.*

References

Aghevli, B.B., Borensztein, E. and **T. van der Willingen** (1992) "Stabilization and structural reform in the CSFR: first stage". *IMF Occasional Paper.* N° 92. March.

Asselain, J.C. (1993) "Transformation et ouverture des économies européennes: les enjeux de la fixation du taux de change". (resarch contract of the LARE with the French planning Commission). Mimeo. LARE-University Bordeaux I. January.

Begg, D. (1991) "Economic Reform in Czechoslovakia: should we believe in Santa Klaus ?". *Economic Policy.* Vol. 13. October. pp. 243-285.

Berg, A. and **Sachs, J.** (1992) "Structural adjustment and international trade in Eastern Europe: the case of Poland". *Economic Policy.* Vol 14. October. pp. 175-225.

Bernanke, B. (1983) "Non-monetary effects of the financial crisis in the propagation of the Great Depression". *American Economic Review.* Vol. 73. June. pp. 257-276.

Borensztein, E. R., Demekas, D. G. and **Ostry, J.S.** (1992) "The output decline in the aftermath of reform: the cases of Bulgaria, Czechoslovakia and Romania". *IMF working paper* n° 59. July.

Bruno, M. (1992) "Stabilization and Reform in Eastern Europe: a preliminary evaluation". *IMF Staff Papers.* December.

Calvo, G.A. and **Coricelli, F.** (1992a) "Stagflationary effects of stabilization programs in reforming socialist countries: enterprise-side and household-side factors". *The World Bank Economic Review.* Vol. 6. N° 1. January.

------------ (1992b) "Output Collapse in Eastern Europe: the role of credit". *IMF Working Paper.* August.

------------ (1992c) "Stabilizing a previously centrally planned economy: Poland 1990". *Economic Policy.* Vol. 14. October. pp. 175-225.

Clements, K. W. and **Jonson, P.D.** (1979) "Unanticipated money, 'disequilibrium' modelling, and rational expectations. *Economic Letters.* March, p. 303-308.

Dyba, K. and **Svejnar, J.** (1991) "Czechoslovakia: Recent economic developments and prospects". *American Economic Review. Papers and Proceedings.* May.

Ham, J., Svejnar, J. and **Terrell, K.** (1993) "The Czech and Slovak labour markets during the transition" . University of Pittsburg and CERGE, Prague. April

Hrncir, M. and **Klacek, J.** (1991) "The stabilization policies and currency convertibility in Czechoslovakia". *Eurropean Economy.*

Kahn, M.S. and **Knight, M.D.** (1981) "Stabilization programs in developing countries: a formal framework". *Staff papers.* Vol. 28 - March pp. 1-53, reprinted in KAHN, MONTHIEL, HAQUE (1991).

Khan, M.S., Monthiel, P.J. and **Haque, N.U.** (1991). *Macroeconomic models for adjustment in developing countries.* IMF - Washington - 323 p.

Exchange Rate and Stabilization in Process of the Polish Type Transition

Jaroslaw Bauc and Boguslaw Grabowski

Introduction

The role of an exchange rate convertibility, its timing, scope and extent in the transition programs of ex centrally planned economies is the subject of extensive literature[1]. Although the detailed content of "Minimum Bang" reform package is disputable there is a fairly broad consensus that "internal" or current account convertibility should be an element of it. The following macro and micro conditions for successful currency convertibility are suggested:

1. e.g. Claassen, E.M., "Exchange Rate Policies in Developing and Post-Socialist Countries", International Center for Economic Growth, San Francisco 1991; Fry, M.J. and Nuti, D.M, "Monetary and Exchange Rate Policies during Eastern Europe's Transition: Some Lessons from Further East", Oxford Review of Economic Policy, 8(1), Spring 1992; Williamson, J., "Currency Convertibility in Eastern Europe", Institute for International Economics, Washington DC, 1991; Green, J.E., Isard, P., "Currency Convertibility and the Transformation of Centrally Planned Economies", Washington DC, IMF Occasional Paper 81, June 1991.

1. an appropriate exchange rate scheme,
2. a sufficient level of foreign exchange reserves (in case of fixed exchange rate regime),
3. sound and credible macroeconomic policy,
4. an economic and institutional environment in which economic agents have incentives and ability to respond to market prices.[2]

Full, current and capital account, currency convertibility is still rare among market oriented economies. It is confined to the major OECD countries. "Internal" or current account convertibility is a common phenomenon amongst IMF members. Though some authors differentiate between these two terms we use them as synonymous terms to mean " current account convertibility with some sectoral trade (e.g. tourism) excluded and repatriation of capital and profit by foreign investors permitted"[3] .

When the key prerequisite conditions are satisfied the policy makers who opt for convertibility also have to:

- select an exchange rate regime,
- decide on the extent of convertibility.

The former broadly entails the choice between a fixed and a flexible exchange rate regime. The latter is equivalent to the question: should the full capital account convertibility be introduced at the outset of convertibility or not?

The choice of an exchange rate regime is not simply between pure fixed and purely flexible schemes. In fact crawling peg (passive or active) regime and managed floating are much more common. The most important difference between fixed and floating exchange rate systems is the role of Central Bank in the exchange rate level determination. Therefore, for the sake of simplicity, we will not differentiate between fixed and crawling peg schemes and therefore between floating and managed floating systems.

2.See: Green, J.E., Isard, P., (1991), Ibid, p.9

3.See: Dickinson, D., Mullineux, A.W., "Currency Convertibility, Policy Credibility and Capital Flight in Poland and the CSFR", unpublished manuscript, p.3.

1. Fixed Versus Flexible Exchange Rate

There is considerable debate about which regime is the most advantageous for economies in transition. The choice must take into account specific features of economic and political situation and the institutional environment in each country.

From 1 January 1990 Poland and a year later Czechoslovakia introduced convertibility based on fixed exchange rates while Romania and Russia decided to rely upon floating rates.

A fixed exchange rate system may be better than a flexible one when the domestic money market is underdeveloped. The proper functioning of flexible rate schemes requires an adequate level of money market development and an institutional environment providing for forward foreign exchange or exchange rate risk insurance. The absence of such an institution and separation from the world financial markets would expose the exchange rate level to volatility. This would raise the level of uncertainty for exporters and importers. In addition, speculation on such a foreign exchange market would make a floating rate very unstable even in very short term. The Russian experience seems to be very didactic in this respect.

On the one hand a volatile and difficult to predict foreign exchange rate level would be a serious obstacle for the development of an export sector. On the other hand, through the price level of tradable goods it would entail high variability of the inflation rate and the price structure[4] . In general proponents of flexible rate regimes think that it is the best and quickest way for the economies in transition to attain the appropriate exchange rate level. The problem is however that in the absence of the afore mentioned institutional arrangements there is more room for market imperfections and distortions.

Under fixed exchange rate system money supply can be recognized as endogenous. In case of formerly centrally planned economies with an underdeveloped money market and the lack of open market operations, sterilization is hardly possible. The endogeneity of money supply may be very advantageous in the transition when the money demand function is not stable and monetary authority lacks experience in monetary management. It could guarantee that the central bank mistakes will not be so

4.It should also be noted that high variability of inflation rate makes monetary policy ineffective. Thus exogenouity of money supply seems useless. See: Lucas, R., "some International Evidence of Output Inflation Trade-offs", American Economic Review, vol. 63, No 3, June 1973.

costly and reinforces resistance to the automatic monetization of budget deficit. Too fast an increase in domestic credit due to excess domestic credit supply to the government would result in the declining foreign exchange reserves. This seems to be a stronger and more visible argument against monetary expansion, especially when the governments is committed to a fixed exchange rate. In general fixed exchange rate systems are more suitable in situations when domestic nominal shocks are more likely to happen.

The next advantage of a fixed exchange rate scheme is its ability to serve as a nominal anchor. Under flexible exchange rate the contribution of instruments other than exchange rate to stabilization policy must be stronger and greater attention should be paid to fiscal and monetary restriction and income policy. On the other hand however "the exchange rate can hardly be relied upon to anchor an economy in which competition is limited, marketing nonexistent and communications appalling"[5] .

In this case other nominal anchors should be used to achieve price stabilization while the exchange rate policy ought to be used to promote exports.

Fixed exchange rate systems also serve as an instrument for suppressing inflationary expectations. This is especially important in countries like Poland with experience of high but only partially open inflation and serious dollarization of the economy. In such circumstances the parallel market exchange rate is the main factor of inflationary expectation formation. A fixed exchange rate with only small revaluation may be the most useful instrument for reducing inflationary expectations. In this case however gross exchange rate misalignment must be avoided.

A key requirement for a fixed exchange rate system is an adequate level of foreign exchange reserves at the outset of convertibility. A weak foreign exchange position and/or huge and no-restructured foreign indebtedness make a fixed exchange rate regime impossible to constitute. Foreign financial help seems to be the only remedy for this. In Poland the introduction of "internal" convertibility based on fixed exchange rate was supported by the Stabilization Fund of $1 bln.

Maintaining of the fixed exchange rate strengthens the stabilization program. But the recessionary effects of such a stabilization program are expected to be more significant than with the floating exchange rate sys-

5.Fry, M.J., "Monetary and Exchange Rate Policies in Poland and others Eastern European Countries: Some Lessons from Further East", International Finance Group, University of Birmingham, Manuscript 1992, p.19.

tem. The price increase despite anti inflationary policy will lead to overvaluation of the domestic currency. Thus the undervaluation of the exchange rate at the outset of convertibility, like in Poland, seems to be necessary. A failure in the maintaining of the exchange rate level declared as fixed undermines the credibility of the government. This may threaten not only convertibility but the successful accomplishment of the stabilization program. On the other hand credibility of the government and the public support for its economic transition program is an important factor for the successful and less costly maintaining of the fixed exchange rate.

2. Exchange Rate Policy in Transition - A Model Approach

After describing pros and cons of an exchange rate targeting we shall try to model the possible consequences of different kinds of the exchange rate policy on the stabilization process during transition. Our model analysis will rely on the features of the Polish-type stabilization program.

The analysis consists of two parts. First, the fixed exchange rate will be examined from the viewpoint of open and closed capital account. The second part embraces the floating exchange rate system. This option will also be described in accordance with both approaches to the capital flight control.

The main criterion for our conclusions will be the impact of exchange rate policy on the deepness of recession during stabilization. In addition, advantages and disadvantages of a given policy choice for other economic variables like the level of foreign reserves and domestic price index will be evaluated. In addition to that, the analysis will include plausible effects of expected inflation and devaluation.

The formerly centrally planned economy which is to implement the stabilization program usually faces a macroeconomic disequilibrium. It is assumed, what occurred in the polish case, that the economy experiences a hyperinflation both in a repressed form but also in the form of actual price increases. Wages and other forms of income are assumed to be highly index-linked and far above a market clearing level. The country has no capital market. This implies that the public sector deficit can almost exclusively be financed by printing money rather then saling of bonds. It is assumed that the economy has to deal with a large stock of external debt which makes the access to external credit on commercial terms severely restricted.

These unfavorable circumstances imply some peculiarities both with respect to the goods and the money markets. Therefore to make the economy controllable it is necessary to set some nominal and real anchors. The choice is always disputable and is one of the main focuses of this paper. In the case of Poland, at least at the first stage of the stabilization program, anchoring the nominal wage and the real interest rate seemed to be the proper and justified measures. The freeing of prices and the removal of subsidies along with the liberalization of the foreign trade and "internal" convertibility of the domestic currency in the "Big Bang" of January 1990 also had implications for the labour, goods and money markets.

(A) Labour Market

Since the nominal wages are set exogenously employment is determined by the demand side of the labour market. Unemployment rate is therefore set by the price level. We have then:

$$L = L^d\left(\frac{W}{P}\right) \tag{1}$$

where L represents employment, L^d - demand for labour, W - nominal wage and P is the price level.

(B) Goods Market

The direct implication of the situation in the labour market boils down to the fact that the GDP level (Y) appears to be endogenous variable. The equilibrium on the goods market occurs when:

$$C(Y-T)+I(R-\pi^e)+G+X\left(Y,\frac{P}{EP^f}\right)-Y=0 \tag{2}$$

The signs in parentheses reflect whether the function with respect to given argument is increasing (positive sign) or decreasing (negative sign). Consumption (C) is then positively related to disposable income Y-T (where T indicates tax revenue). Investment demand depends negatively on the real interest rate (where R stands for the nominal interest rate while

π^e represents the expected inflation[1]). Net export function (X) decreases with respect to both GDP and the real exchange rate, where P^f indicates the foreign price level and E is the nominal exchange rate (number of units of domestic currency for one unit of foreign currency).

(C) Money Market

The supply of money in real terms consists of the domestic credit DC and the foreign reserves Res:

$$\mu^s = \frac{DC}{P} + \frac{Res}{P} \tag{3}$$

However in order to specify the demand for money function, one has to identify the most important substitutes for money.

Because of the absence of a capital market people do not invest in bonds or equities. Thus saving deposits are used as a substitute for buying the government debt. The expected rate of depreciation (devaluation) has usually played an important role in countries with unstable economies. Dollarization appears everywhere whenever there is a lack of trust in the domestic currency. Another common response to hyperinflation is that people invest in goods whether they need them or not. For all these substitutes there are some opportunity costs of holding money:

- the opportunity cost of holding money against saving deposits i.e.: R,
- the opportunity cost of holding money vs foreign exchange i.e.: $dE/E=\varepsilon^e$,
- the opportunity cost of holding money against holding goods i.e.: π^e

---

[1] Our econometric estimations for Poland show that the inflationary expectation formation during the first stage of the transition program can be best described by the first order adaptive expectation model (PISTAR model). The best results were obtained when l=0.75 in the following equation:

pte=(1-l)(pt-1-pt-1e)+lpt-1

It means that the expected inflation was mostly dependent upon the past inflation (see fig.1) where dE is the expected depreciation or devaluation (and depends on the exchange rate regime) of the exchange rate, ε^e shows the expected rate of depreciation or devaluation of the exchange rate[2].

In general the demand for real money balances can be written as:

$$\mu^d = \mu^d(Y; R, E^e, \pi^e) \tag{4}$$

where the semicolon separates the transaction from non-transaction motives of holding money. The equilibrium on the money market occurs if:

$$\frac{DC}{P} + \frac{Res}{P} = \mu^d(Y; R, E^e, \pi^e) \tag{5}$$

One of the most significant categories for the economy during the stabilization program is the stock of foreign reserves (Res). Its changes are determined by the following relation:

$$\frac{d\,Res}{P} = X(Y, \frac{P}{EP^f}) + F(R - \varepsilon^e - R^f) \tag{6}$$

where F indicates the capital inflow which positively depends upon the difference between the domestic R and the foreign R^f interest rate covered by the expected devaluation (depreciation) of the domestic currency.

(D) Budget Identity

Confining budget revenues and expenditures to taxes, government spending and debt service, the simple version of a budget identity can be defined as:

$$G + \frac{B}{P}R - T = \frac{dDC}{P} + \frac{d\,Res}{P} + \frac{dB}{P} \tag{7}$$

where B is a stock of the government debt.

---

[2] The expected devaluation is defined as the difference between the zloty deposit interest rate and the dollar deposit interest rate.

2.1 Fixed Exchange Rate Case

2.1.1 Closed Capital Account

The economy in question is implementing a stabilization program. Very restrictive monetary policy is therefore assumed in the sense that there is no increase in the domestic credit (dDC=0). For the simplicity we assume that the fiscal policy can be described by the following equation:

$$dT = (1+\alpha)dG \tag{8}$$

where a is the degree of fiscal policy restriction. One can expect that the stabilization program should entail restrictive fiscal policy, i.e. $\alpha>0$. We also assume that the foreign general price level does not change (i.e. dP^f =0).

The first relation used in the model is exactly the equilibrium condition on the goods market i.e. eg.(1).

The equation (6) represents an identity and in that sense does not show any behavioural relation. For the fixed exchange rate model changes in the foreign reserve stock are crucial. It seems reasonable to combine this category with the role it plays in the budget identity.

Before starting stabilization program the stock of internal debt in Poland did not exist (B=0). In the model we also reject the possibility of financing the budget deficit by means of open market operations. Since at the first stage of transition the budget deficit is typically low (in 1990 in Poland there was a surplus of 0.7% of GDP) and as it is impossible to create a capital market within a short period and we assume that dB=0. Therefore combining equations (6) and (7) and reminding our assumptions that dDC=0, B=0, dB=0 we get:[3]

$$G-T = X(Y, \frac{P}{EP^f}) \tag{9}$$

Under these conditions internal deficit (surplus) is equivalent to a current account deficit (surplus) since the net capital inflow component disappears in the case of closed capital account.

---

[3] Because of the way the inflationary expectations are formed (see fn 1) both nominal and real interest rates can be recognized as exogenous.

The equations (2), (5) and (9) constitute the model of an economy with initial conditions similar to those in Poland while implementing a stabilization program with fixed exchange rate under closed capital account.

Solving this system by means of a Cramer's rule with respect to dY, dRes and dP we obtain the following changes of GDP:

$$dY = \frac{1}{1-C_y} [I_r(dR - d\pi^e) + (1 - \alpha - c_y(1+\alpha)dG] \tag{10}$$

Since the denominator is positive, an increase in the real interest rate has the negative impact on GDP. This negative effect may partly be offset by a loose fiscal policy which in this situation means:

$$\alpha < \frac{1-C_y}{1+Cy} \tag{11}$$

Otherwise even though dG>0 restrictive fiscal policy (in terms of the value of α) deepens the recessionary effect of the first stage of transition.

As one can see, devaluation of the exchange rate appears to be entirely passive with respect to a drop in GDP.

Its also worth stressing that neither expected inflation nor the expected devaluation exert any influence on the deepness of the recession caused by a stabilization program. In other words, under fixed exchange rate and closed capital account the recession of the very first stage of transition can be described only in terms of a fiscal squeeze and a monetary restraint.

It is not possible to determine what may occur to the foreign reserve stock. We can however depict the difference in foreign reserve changes between the situation of devaluation or revaluation and the case of constant exchange rate:

$$dRes_{dE\neq 0} - dRes_{dE=0} = \frac{H}{eX_e} dE \tag{12}$$

where H represents the monetary base and e is the real exchange rate. An increase in the foreign reserves in case of devaluation of the domestic currency turns out to be higher than under the constant exchange rate policy. If however the economy is loosing the international reserves their outflow in the case of devaluation is smaller. The revaluation acts in the opposite direction. In other words, from the viewpoint of the foreign reserves it is more favourable to keep devaluing the domestic currency rather than setting it once and for all. Thus the crawling peg system seems to be more appropriate than a fixed exchange rate.

2.1.2 Open Capital Account

In case of an open capital account one has to include an impact of the inflow and outflow of capital on changes in the stock of foreign reserves. In other words equation (8) takes now the following form:

$$G - T = X(Y, \frac{P}{EP^f}) + F(R - \varepsilon^e - R^f) \tag{13}$$

This relation together with the remaining two equations i.e. (2) and (5) constitutes the model of the economy in question under the fixed exchange rate regime and open capital account.

Solving the system by applying the same procedure we come to the following conclusions.

Openness of the capital account weakens the recessionary effect by:

$$dY_{open} - dY_{closed} = \frac{F'(dR - d\varepsilon^e - dR^f)}{1 - C_y} \tag{14}$$

Assuming that changes in the foreign interest rate are insignificant and that the expected devaluation follows the expected inflation i.e. $d\varepsilon^e = d\pi^e$ (fig.2, tab.1 and fn 2), we obtain:

$$dY_{open} - dY_{closed} = \frac{F'(dR - d\pi^e)}{1 - C_y} \tag{15}$$

Openness however is less advantages if the foreign reserves are regarded. The difference between systems of restricted and free capital flow in this respect is determined by the following relation:

$$d\,Res_{open} - d\,Res_{closed} = F'(dR - d\pi^e)\ \left(\frac{\mu_y}{\frac{1}{p}(1 - C_y)} - \frac{H}{eX_e}(1 + \frac{X_y}{1 - C_y})\right) \tag{16}$$

If the marginal propensity to save exceeds the reaction of the net export on income i.e.

$$if\ |X_y| \leq 1 - c_y\ then\ dRes_{open} - dRes_{closed} \geq 0 \qquad (17)$$

it would pay to open the capital account in the fixed exchange rate framework of the examined economy.

It is however very unlikely for the transition economy to fulfill the requirement. At the outset of the stabilization program (as the Polish experience shows) the marginal propensity to save shrinks to a considerable extent. That requires for the net export be inelastic with respect to income. In other words, from the viewpoint of reserves the transition economy of fixed exchange rate should rather rely on the closed capital account.

2.2 Flexible Exchange Rate Case

2.2.1 *Closed Capital Account*

Under a floating exchange rate system the monetary authorities do not intervene on the foreign exchange market. This implies that the stock of foreign reserves remains unchanged (i.e dRes=0).

No change in foreign reserve stock and a closed capital account means that the equation (6) can be reduced to the following form:

$$X(Y, \frac{P}{EP^f}) = 0 \qquad (18)$$

A freely floating exchange rate must ensure the equilibrium between exports and imports.

Goods market equilibrium occurs now if:

$$C(Y-T) + I(R-\pi^e) + G - Y = 0 \qquad (19)$$

The only difference between the former and current model results from the fact that now the trade balance equals zero.

A credible announcement that the government is determined to lower inflation substantially will be taken seriously if a restrictive monetary policy is adopted. Therefore the assumption of no domestic credit expansion is still valid. Under this condition we consider the money market equilibrium in the previous form.

In this case the system depicts changes in the level of exchange rate instead of changes in foreign exchange stock. As before the foreign price index changes are assumed to be insignificant.

The most important variable is the GDP path:

$$dY = \frac{I_R (dR - d\pi^e)}{1 - C_y} + dG \tag{20}$$

For no fiscal expansion (dG=0) and if $dR > d\pi^e$ $dY < 0$. If then all crucial features of the stabilization package are in work its implementation inevitably leads to a recession. It is again worth underlying that under floating exchange rates, the expected depreciation of the domestic currency has no influence on the change in real GDP.

As far as the direction of the exchange rate movement is concerned, one can examine the influence of the expected depreciation or the appreciation exerted on the actual exchange rate.

$$dE_{dE^e \neq 0} - dE_{dE^e = 0} = \frac{\mu_E}{\frac{DC + Res}{P^2}} - dE^e > 0 \tag{21}$$

As we can see expected depreciation of the domestic currency results in actual depreciation. The same applies to the expected appreciation.

There can be noticed that if initially, i.e. at the moment of introducing stabilization program the domestic price index were equal to the nominal exchange rate (P=E) both variables would behave exactly in the same way with respect to expected depreciation or appreciation:

$$dP_{dE^e\_0} - dP_{dE^e = 0} = --dE^e > 0 \tag{22}$$

In other words expected depreciation (appreciation) makes the actual price level and the actual exchange rate grow at the same rate.

It also turns out that the expected inflation exerts an impact on the actual inflation according to the following rule:

$$dP_{d\pi^e\_0} - dE_{d\pi^e=0} = -\frac{\mu_E}{\frac{DC+Res}{P^2}} dE^e > 0 \qquad (23)$$

The stronger the impact of the demand for money on expected inflation, the higher the actual price index increase.

2.2.2 *Open Capital Account*

Under the flexible exchange rate where the international reserves do not change net exports is equal to net capital outflow. Therefore the third equation from the previous model takes the following form:

$$X(Y, \frac{P}{Ep^f}) + F(R - \pi^e) = 0 \qquad (24)$$

The condition for the money market equilibrium remains the same while the goods market equilibrium again includes the net export part.

Taking into account all these changes, and differentiating the whole system, the model can be solved with respect to dY, dE and dP. It turns out that openness of the capital account, given the flexible exchange rate regime, might deepen the possible recession of this type of a transition economy i.e:

$$dY = \frac{I_R(dR - d\pi^e) - F(dR - d\pi^e)}{1 - c_y} + dG \qquad (25)$$

Comparing this result to the solution obtained for the previous model of no capital flow, we can see that the difference boils down to the net capital inflow effect i.e.:

$$dY_{open} - dY_{closed} = -\frac{F'(dR - d\pi^e)}{1 - c_y} \qquad (26)$$

For $dR > d\pi^e$, which is the prerequisite for the anti-inflationary stabilization program, the increment of net capital inflow is positive. Under the flexible exchange rate net capital outflow has to equilibrate net export. Keeping the assumptions of no domestic credit expansion and of the absence of open market operations also the budget must be balanced. In other words the whole net capital inflow brings about an import leakage which reduces the total demand by the amount of net capital inflow. This is the additional recessionary effect which might occur if the economy had adopted this kind of stabilization framework.

Unfortunately it is not possible to determine the impact of freeing the capital flow on the exchange rate.

CONCLUSIONS

(i) "Internal" convertibility of the domestic currency is an indispensable element of the stabilization program for the previously centrally planned economies.

(ii) Although the choice of the exchange rate regime eventually depends on individual economic and institutional conditions prevailing in particular country there are more arguments for adopting the fixed exchange rate system at the outset of convertibility.

(iii) From the model which is analyzed in this paper based on the assumptions stemming from the shape of the Polish stabilization program (i.e.: restrictive fiscal and monetary policy, wages as a nominal anchor, interest rate as a real anchor), the following conclusions can be derived:

- both systems of pure fixed exchange rate and crawling peg one result in a recession;
- under fixed exchange rate regime the openness of the capital account may exert a negative impact on the foreign exchange reserves;
- given the flexible exchange rate regime, openness of the capital account may alleviate the recessionary pressure.

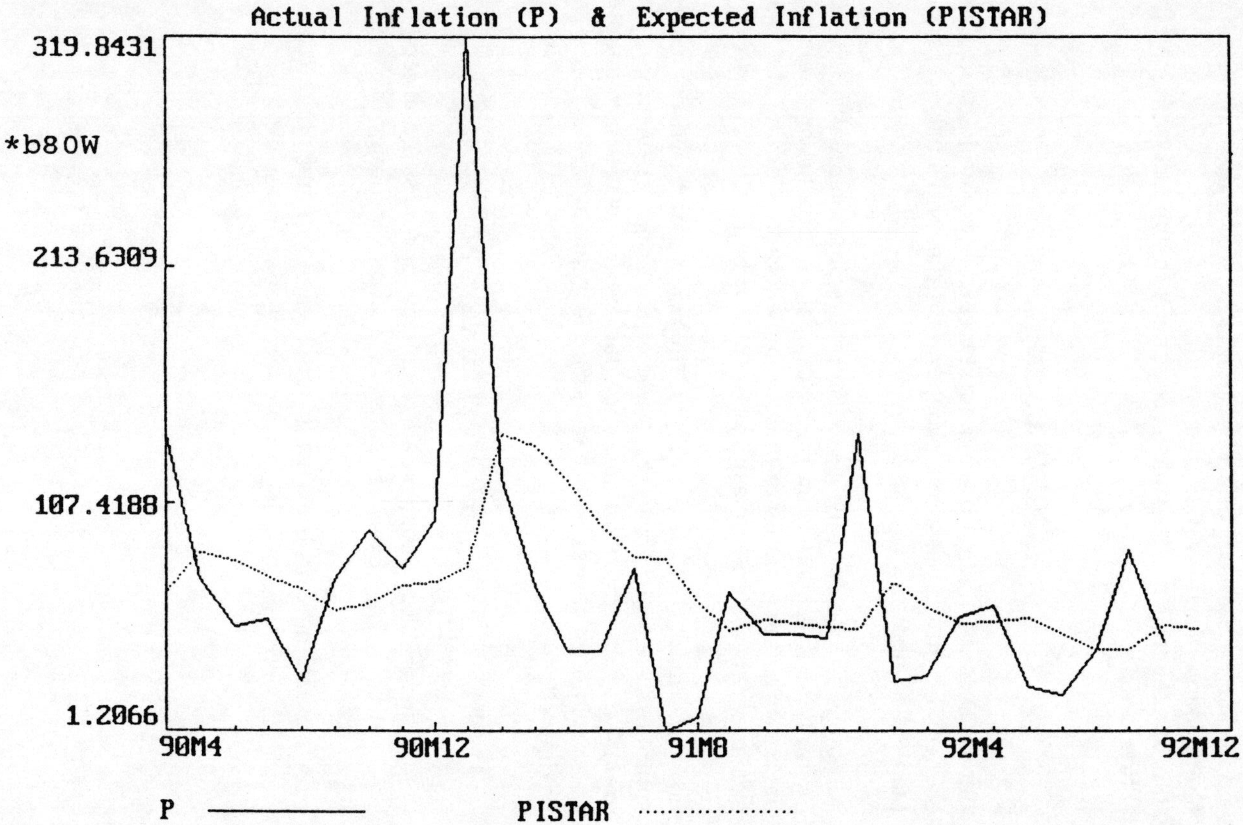
Actual Inflation (P) & Expected Inflation (PISTAR)
319.8431
*b80W
213.6309
107.4188
1.2066
90M4
90M12
91M8
92M4
92M12
P
PISTAR

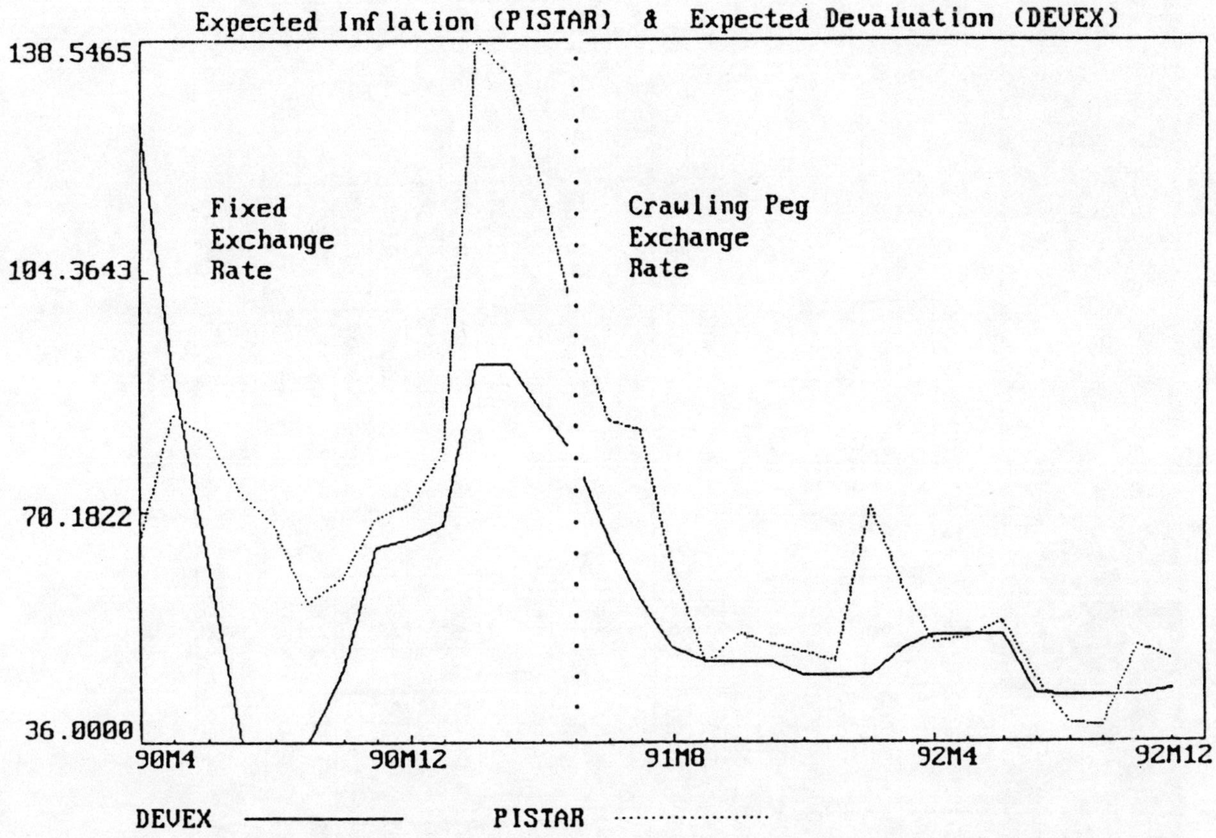
Expected Inflation (PISTAR) & Expected Devaluation (DEVEX)
138.5465
104.3643
70.1822
36.0000
90M4
90M12
91M8
92M4
92M12
Fixed
Exchange
Rate
Crawling Peg
Exchange
Rate
DEVEX
PISTAR

Expected Rate of Devaluation (Depreciation)

m.y	Foreign currency population deposits in bn zł.	Exchange rate	Foreign currency population deposits in mln US$	Interest rate on short term zloty deposits	Interest rate on short term foreign cur. deposits	Expected rate of devaluation (depreciation)
12.89	45,926					
3.90	47,232	9,500	4,972	117.00%	6.50%	110.50%
4.90	48,058	9,500	5,059	108.00%	6.50%	101.50%
5.90	49,000	9,500	5,158	75.00%	6.50%	68.50%
6.90	49,445	9,500	5,205	55.50%	6.50%	49.00%
7.90	50,976	9,500	5,366	33.50%	6.50%	27.00%
8.90	52,389	9,500	5,515	37.50%	6.50%	31.00%
9.90	53,193	9,500	5,599	33.50%	6.50%	27.00%
10.90	54,044	9,500	5,689	43.50%	6.50%	37.00%
11.90	54,600	9,500	5,747	57.50%	6.50%	51.00%
12.90	55,505	9,500	5,843	64.00%	6.50%	57.50%
1.91	55,623	9,500	5,855	65.00%	6.50%	58.50%
2.91	52,294	9,500	5,505	85.00%	6.50%	78.50%
3.91	49,885	9,500	5,251	85.00%	6.50%	78.50%
4.91	47,141	9,500	4,962	81.50%	6.50%	75.00%
5.91	55,161	10,290	5,361	72.00%	6.50%	65.50%
6.91	57,560	11,392	5,053	66.00%	6.50%	59.50%
7.91	57,908	11,457	5,054	56.00%	6.50%	49.50%
8.91	58,639	11,286	5,196	49.00%	6.50%	42.50%
9.91	59,436	11,154	5,329	48.00%	6.50%	41.50%
10.91	62,447	11,151	5,600	46.00%	6.50%	39.50%
11.91	63,967	11,111	5,757	46.00%	6.50%	39.50%
12.91	62,747	11,072	5,667	45.00%	6.50%	38.50%

Discussion of Exchange Rate and Stabilization Policy

Thomas D. Willett
Horton Professor of Economics
Claremont Graduate School
and
Claremont McKenna College

This stimulating paper by Bauc and Grabowski (B and G) nicely illustrates that it is not easy to determine the optimal exchange rate regime for an economy which needs to achieve macro economy stabilization at the same time as it begins to move toward a market oriented system. The authors rightly stress that policies which may work satisfactorily for countries with well developed financial markets may perform quite differently where effective financial markets are only just beginning to be created. They likewise make clear that there are advantages and disadvantages to both pegged and flexible exchange rates. I found their analysis, however, to somewhat overstate the potential advantages of pegged rates relative to what I perceive to be their costs and, in several instances, I felt that their characterization of the issues failed to adequately treat what I consider to be important considerations.

Let me begin with their statement that "The most important difference between fixed and floating exchange rate systems is the role of the Central Bank in exchange rate level determination. Therefore, for the sake of simplicity, we will not differentiate between fixed and crawling peg schemes and therefore between floating and managed floating systems."

Whether such a simplification is relatively harmless or creates considerable problems depends critically on the issue being considered. For many purposes I believe that the key distinctions are between "permanently" fixed, adjustably pegged, and flexible rates. While it is an important issue for central banks to consider to what extent and with what strategy flexible rates should be managed, this typically can be considered largely independently of stabilization policy strategies. Because of the infancy of financial markets in the former communist countries a good case can be made for smoothing intervention by central banks in the foreign exchange market to reduce the problems of excessive short term volatility that could be caused by thin markets. (Note that this is a different rationale for Central Bank intervention than the case of destabilizing private speculation.) In this regard I believe that there is no need for us to consider B and G's case of flexible exchange rates and no capital mobility. In such a case because of J curve effects the initial worsening of the trade balance following a depreciation would make a freely floating exchange rate dynamically unstable. For a freely floating rate to be stable, one needs not only the absence of destabilizing speculation but also the presence of stabilizing speculation. From this perspective a crawling peg might be viewed as a special form of managed flexibility. Certainly from the standpoint of the analysis of the credibility effects of pegged exchange rates on macroeconomic stabilization policy, a crawling peg would come closer to a managed float than to genuinely fixed exchange rates.

B and G argue that "A fixed exchange rate with only small revaluation may be the most useful instrument for reducing inflationary expectations." They go on to correctly stress that "In this case, however, gross exchange rate misalignment must be avoided." I do not believe that they emphasize enough the problems that this creates for the use of exchange rate policy as a movement anchor for stabilization policy in the case of initial high inflation. As B and G note, a substantial initial devaluation to temporarily undervalue the currency in the short run is necessary if the new peg is to be sustainable in the long run. It is a virtually impossible technical task to choose what this new level of the exchange rate should be. It requires knowing not only the level of the equilibrium real exchange rate but also how much the transitional inflation will be while the domestic inflation rate is brought down to world levels. One should not believe any economist who tells you that they can forecast this with any reasonable degree of accuracy. Furthermore, the initial substantial devaluation will have direct feedback effects on prices in the home country. To the extent that inflationary expectations are formed adaptively, and B and G suggest that this is largely the case in Poland, then the initial devaluation will complicate the task of reducing inflationary expectations.

In this regard I believe that B and G need to refine their theoretical analysis. They indicate in section 2 that the main criterion for the conclusions of their analysis "will be the impact of exchange rate policy on the deepness of the recession during stabilization." I think that this is quite reasonable. However, in their formal analysis they address primarily the effects of alternative policy regimes on aggregate demand through Keynesian current account effects. At least equally, and I'm inclined to think a good deal more, important for the amount of employment and output lost during the stabilization process is the speed with which inflationary expectations are dampened. Recent work by Burdekin, Westbrook , and myself (1994) on this issue for the members of the European Monetary System suggests that the rate of exchange rate pegging in reducing inflationary expectations has often been greatly overstated. We found that pegging was no substitute for tight monetary and fiscal policies. It appears that in some cases pegging may have been a useful complement to domestic macroeconomic tightening, but at present I believe that the case for pegged versus flexible exchange rates for stabilizing economies must be viewed as an open question, with the answer likely varying from one country to another as would be suggested by the theory of optimum currency areas.

Let me turn to a final point. B and G emphasize the argument that during the process of development of money and financial markets the demand for money function is likely to be unstable. In such circumstances fixed exchange rate can have attractions. Indeed where demand for money shifts are the only disturbance, fixed exchange rates can be shown to be optimal. In my view, however, the economies in transition typically face not only instability in the demand for money but also considerable uncertainty about, and likely shifts in, equilibrium real exchange rates. The latter type of disturbance of course calls for flexible exchange rates, or at least exchange rate adjustments. Furthermore where the pegged nominal rate strays substantially from equilibrium, rational speculative capital flows may destabilize domestic monetary conditions. Once again I believe that it is difficult to generalize across most countries about the comparative costs and benefits of alternative exchange rate systems. We have developed a rich set of theories which point to important considerations. The task of the applied policy economists is to attempt to understand the situations of particular countries and provide help in judging the relative importance of this variety of theoretical considerations in concrete cases.

Reference

Burdekin, Richard C.K., and Westbrook, Jilleen R., "Exchange Rate Pegging As A Disinflation Strategy: Evidence From The European Monetary System." In Pierre L. Siklos (ed) *Varieties of Monetary Reform: Lessons and Experiences on the Road to Monetary Union*, Kluwer Academic Publishers, 1994.

Credit Crunches in the CSFR: A Comment on Girardin and Marimoutou

King Banaian
Pitzer College*

The monetary portion of the policy prescription for historically planned economies ("HPEs") has typically included a curtailment of credit emissions while allowing prices to rise from suppressed levels under economic planning. If done properly, the level of real credit in the economy will be sufficiently constrained so that a continuing inflation does not develop. Part of the recent history of the HPEs, however, has been the stubbornly high inflation rates and the depth of economic contraction each country has faced. Girardin and Marimoutou (hereinafter GM) argue in the present paper that the monetary prescription has been a culprit of the recessions the HPEs now endure. Each of these has created a "credit crunch" that has sharply curtailed demand growth, in particular for investment.

My comments on GM turn on two issues. First, I address whether the credit "crunch" GM describe was somehow different from the typical restriction on credit that forms the base of most disinflation strategies. The data show that the real money stock of the CSFR was in decline before prices were liberalized. Real currency grew in 1991, though most of this growth occurred after the middle part of the year. I argue that this very

---

*Visiting Associate Professor, Pitzer College, Claremont, California, USA. I thank Tom Willett and Frank Wykoff for helpful discussions. Any errors are my responsibility alone.

temporary disruption may have caused an adverse change in firms' balance sheets different from the type of shock GM theorize.

Second, GM analyze the Czechoslovak economy after the period of price liberalization using a model appropriate for developing economies. They then apply the model, which has 27 parameters for estimation to a data set that has 20 observations. This gives the appearance of a *very* overfitted equation. As every equation has an adjusted R-squared greater than 0.7, there is the appearance that the model is too successful. GM recognize this problem, but note that it is not possible to obtain more data. But this defense begs the question: Is it too soon to try to fit macroeconometric models to post-communist Eastern European data? Have the data ripened enough to harvest? Also, what is the appropriate model? This is the latest in a series of papers[1] that employ developing economy models to analyze Eastern European economies. I will argue below as well that the metaphor is wrong. There is a sharp difference between unwinding huge misallocations of capital as have occurred in Eastern Europe and building new capital in previously agrarian economies like most developing ones.

How Credit Crunches Occur in Historically Planned Economies

GM argue that a credit crunch afflicted the CSFR in 1991-92, due to insufficient monetary expansion after the price liberalizations of January 1991.

CHART 1. (Source: PlanEcon.)

[1]See, for instance, Edwards [1992] or Calvo and Kumar [1993].

As with most historically planned economies, the real money supply fell immediately after price liberalization. Chart 1 shows that a decline of both narrow and broad money supply measures after the 25.8% increase in prices in January 1991. But these measures were already in decline before that month. Money issue seems to have recovered to at least the trend that existed before price liberalization.

If this is a credit crunch, however, one expects that the velocity of circulation should rise. In the CSFR, it fell between 1990 and 1992: M2 velocity was 2.47 in 1990, 2.38 in 1991, and 2.09 in 1992.[2] Demand for currency should rise in a credit crunch as the demand for base money increases from banks seeking to make new loans at high real rates. The National Bank did provide additional currency in real terms, ending 1991 with 6.7% additional real currency in an economy that had experienced inflation near 60%. The IMF estimates that domestic credit as a share of GDP in Czechoslovakia fell from 74.7% in 1990 to 72.1% in 1991. There was also no tendency towards directing credit towards the state sector in that year. This experience contrasts with the situations in Poland in 1990 or Bulgaria and Romania in 1991, where domestic credit fell dramatically.

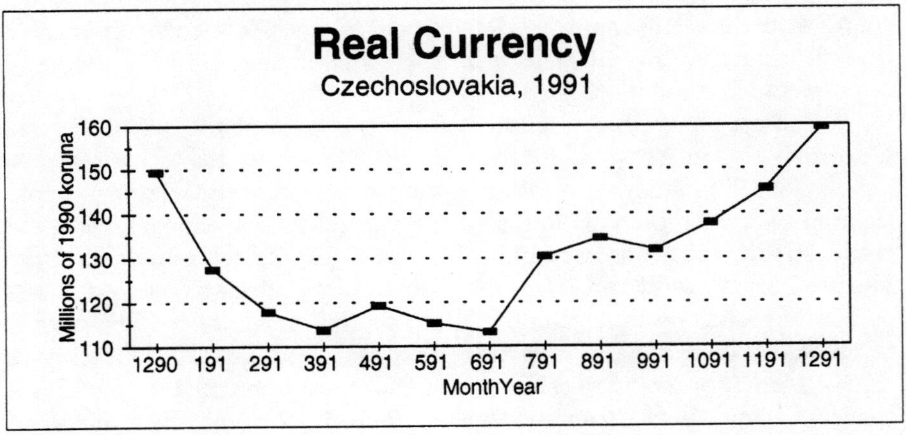

CHART 2. (Source: PlanEcon.)

[2]Drabek, Janacek and Tuma [1993] provide a study of velocity movement in Czechoslovakia in 1991. One could question the data on the basis that official price indices did not reflect repressed inflation or "shortageflation", but Feltenstein and Ha [1993] conclude that there was little repressed inflation in Czechoslovakia in the latter half of the 1980s.

GM argue that firms in a credit crunch can bargain for loans from their wage bills to workers, and that an easing of the credit crunch leads first to repayment of the loan to the workers. GM do not explain the mechanism that induces workers to strike that bargain. In developed economies with many small unions, the bargain would be quite difficult for firms to obtain. If some unions do not accept the bargain, those that do accept will experience a decline in their relative wages, and likely a decline in their real wages. Union membership in the conciliatory unions will attack their leadership. Leaders, knowing this, will thus be wary to accept a temporary wage cut without assurances that all will share in the sacrifice. Certainly, corporatist structures may be helpful in reducing the transactions costs of making this bargain. But GM are not clear that they are assuming this or any other labor market structure.

Another issue GM do not address is the relative effects of privatization and price liberalization among the various industries of the former CSFR. In employing a macroeconomic model of this degree of aggregation, the authors are assuming that the effects of the reforms are symmetric across all industries. Yet I take it as trivial that the liberalization process lead to large changes in the structure of relative prices, with different changes in different countries. With such changes it seems implausible that all industries are effected *in the same way*. At a minimum, the issue requires much more discussion.

The most compelling argument for the impact of the credit crunch, unfortunately relegated to footnote 3 in GM, is that the price jump in January of 1991 caused a set of interenterprise arrears that damaged contractual relationships. This implies therefore that a one-time shock to the credit stream causes a disequilibrium that does not self-correct rapidly. The temporary credit shock leads to uncertainty both in terms of defaults on accounts receivables and in the term and risk structure of the accounts receivable ledger. Increased variability in cash flow is very damaging to capital formation by increasing the risk premia open financial markets charge Czechoslovak firms. Moreover, failures of some firms have increased impact on other firms, by causing a markdown of the receivables on their balance sheets. All of the transitioning economies experienced some interruption in credit flow (though the CSFR had less than many others), and the explanation here would explain many other macroeconomic observations of the transitioning economies: high real interest rates, declining output, a rise in the currency to money ratios, declines in the money multiplier. Regrettably, GM did not pursue the idea further.

WHAT MODELS? WHICH DATA?

GM employ a model used by Khan, Monthiel and Haque [1988] for developing economies. The implication is thus that the CSFR was like a developing economy. But the starting points for economies like the Czech Republic and Slovakia are far different from those of developing economies. HPEs have much more capital than the traditional developing economy. Capital in HPEs is badly misallocated after decades of the state stifling relative price adjustments. Still, as long as that capital has some positive marginal product, new investment will have to overcome a higher hurdle in HPEs than the hurdle to be cleared for new investment in developing economies. It may be better for a country's growth prospects to have no capital at all than misallocated capital on this scale. With such different starting points it seems better to build models on the assumption of misallocated capital and large relative price changes.

GM undertake this study with the idea that there is a need for empirical models for policy evaluation. This may be a desirable goal, but one must appreciate the fragility and unreliability of the data upon which these models are built. The period of transition is short: GM are extracting 27 parameters from a data set containing 20 observations. There is little more one can do, as that is all the data they had. Yet two questions must be addressed in empirical studies of historically planned economies. First, one should pause to interpret what data mean in a period of such rapid relative price adjustment. What do international trade data tell you when you have simultaneously domestic price liberalization and reductions in energy subsidies and import tariffs? How much of the current inflation in HPEs is relative price adjustment towards world levels, and how much is the result of excess money creation? I am pessimistic that one will be able to apply the *ceteris paribus* conditions of multiple regression analysis in a world where everything changes at once. Second, there is at the same time changes in the structure of data collection. One hears stories from before the transition of the statistical agencies being told in advance of what the data are expected to show, and lo and behold, it comes to pass. Now we have not only new data, not only new data collectors, but one suspects a whole new paradigm for data collection itself. As the paradigm is developed, the number and quality of data collectors and data itself will change. We know from econometrics that a systematic change over time of measurement errors can create unpredictable biases in estimation of macroeconometric models. We should also consider perhaps an inquiry of *meta-econometrics*, in which we address the process of data generation before we employ the data in econometric analysis.

Are Credit Restrictions Necessary in HPEs?

The policy question remains: Was the CSFR too tight in its monetary policy? In developing economies such as Mexico or Israel, successful stabilizations have often had designs that included the restriction of credit demands.[3] In the United States 12 years ago we had a substantial inflation halted by a very deep, relatively long recession. At the time many U.S. economists had argued that better policies were available that would have imposed a smaller cost on the economy. Such criticism visits every policymaker that attacks inflation, yet they do not adopt these "better" policies. This may be because there is no better policy. While there may be several reasons for inflations to begin, inflations are not sustained without accommodating monetary policy. Thus an antidote to inflation -- and I would argue the only one we currently know -- is to curtail monetary expansion.[4] Every disinflation thus generated comes with a significant rise in business failures and unemployment. This is true of developing and industrialized economies, and there is no reason why that cure would be any less painful in HPEs. Painless antidotes remain only in the heads of the theorists. Educating the public that inflation is harmful and the pain of disinflation is worth sustaining is a duty we should all undertake in earnest, and quickly. To do otherwise erodes the political willpower necessary to ensure price stability.

Bibliography

Bruno, Michael and **Leora Meridor**, "The Costly Transition from Stabilization to Sustainable Growth: Israel's Case," in Bruno et al., eds., *Lessons of Economic Stabilization and Its Aftermath.* Cambridge: MIT Press, 1991.

Drabek, Zdenek, Kamil Janacek and **Zdenek Tuma**, "Inflation in Czechoslovakia, 1985-91," International Economics Department, The World Bank, WPS 1135, May 1993.

---

[3] See Bruno and Meridor [1991] for Israel and Oritz [1991] for Mexico.

[4] The point is most forcefully and eloquently made in Sargent [1982].

Feltenstein, Andrew and **Jiming Ha**, "An Analysis of Repressed Inflation in Three Transitional Economies," International Economics Department, The World Bank, WPS 1132, April 1993.

Girardin, Eric and **Velayoudom Marimoutou**, "The Effects of Shocks to Bank Credit During the Transition: Lessons of simulations of a macroeconometric model of Czechoslovakia," this volume.

Kahn, Moshin S., **Peter J. Monthiel** and **N. U. Haque**, *Macroeconomic models for adjustment in developing countries.* Washington: International Monetary Fund; 1991.

Ortiz, Guillermo, "Mexico beyond the debt crisis: Towards Sustainable Growth with Price Stability," in Bruno et al., eds., *Lessons of Economic Stabilization and Its Aftermath.* Cambridge: MIT Press, 1991.

Sargent, Thomas. "The Ends of Four Big Inflations." In Robert Hall, ed., *Inflation: Its Causes and Cures.* Washington D.C.: National Bureau of Economic Research; 1982.

PART II:

BANKING SECTOR AND ENTERPRISE RESTRUCTURING

Hardening Micro Budget Constraints:

Bank Behaviour and Corporate Governance in Poland*

Andy Mullineux
Department of Economics and International Finance Group,
University of Birmingham, Birmingham B15 2TT,
Britain

and

Marek Belka
Institute of Economics, University of Lodz,
41 Rewolucji 1905r., 90--214 Lodz,
Poland

Summary

This paper investigates progress made towards the hardening of budget constraints faced by state-owned and private sector enterprises in Poland since the Big Bang in January 1990 through to the end of 1992. It finds that following the 'commercialisation' of banks and the launch of the bank privatisation in 1991/2 there is evidence of more discriminating bank lending behaviour. This may however be due to 'learning by doing'

*Prepared for the Conference on Hard Budget Constraints Privatisation and Financial Reform in Eastern Europe with Particular Reference to Poland and Czechoslovakia. Prague, 3--4 September 1993 rather than commercialisation per se. The bolstering of the external governance structure: through an active involvement of a state privatisation agency, the national investment funds to be created as part of the mass privatisation programme (and possibly a development or investment bank); and a strict bank regulatory and supervisory regime, is also recommended. Additionally, attention should be given to establishing a suitable incentive structure for management and workers. Before the banks can play an active role in the restructuring process their bad debt problem must be resolved and they should be recapitalised. This will make way for rapid privatisation of banks and speed the privatisation programme as a whole. Countries such as Russia and the Ukraine, which are at an earlier stage in their transition, are advised to tackle the bad debt problems of their banks, and to recapitalise them and other state enterprises, at a much earlier stage. This will pave the way for a more rapid restructuring, via privatisation, of state-owned enterprises than proved possible in Poland; where perverse incentives persisted as a result of failure to tackle the debt problem and to launch of the mass privatisation programme at an early stage. The delay in the launch of the latter was itself due, in part, to failure to resolve the debt problem at the outset.

1. Introduction

Macroeconomic stabilisation involves the government imposing 'hard budget' constraints by adopting a 'tight' monetary policy and a conservative budgetary policy. Typically, at the beginning of the transition from central-planning toward a more market oriented economy, the state was heavily reliant for its revenue on 'taxes' on state-owned enterprises and credits were granted by the state bank in accordance with the state plan. These credits were primarily for working capital and enterprises were also allocated investment capital in accordance with the plan. If state expenditure exceeded revenue, then the state bank also granted credits to the government to fund the deficit. In more 'market oriented' economies this would be expected to generate inflation, but in planned economies, which typically had price controls and widespread subsidies, inflation was repressed.

Price liberalisation can be expected to lead to a high level inflation unless the budget deficit is brought rapidly under control. This may not be easy if, as seems to be the case, the transition reforms generate a recession and there is political opposition to the reforms. The main source of government revenue begins to dry up as state enterprises 'profits' decline.

Macro stabilisation, therefore, requires an urgent overhaul of the tax system, leading to a significant widening of the tax net and a crackdown on tax evasion and avoidance.

The reduction, and finally elimination, of price subsidies (except where they necessarily form part of a coherent regional and/or industrial or environmental policy) can be expected to help reduce government expenditure. Against this, the cost of establishing a social safety net to help the newly unemployed, who were also previously 'hidden', and fixed income groups must be provided for.

Micro-stabilisation involves imposing 'hard budget constraints' on the state-owned enterprises, and newly emerging private sector enterprises. This is related to macroeconomic stabilisation in that enterprises must not expect to receive credit on demand from the reformed[1] banking system, and the newly created (state-owned) 'commercial' banks must not count on automatic credits from the newly created central bank. The latter, as part of the macro-stabilisation programme, will instead try to restrict the supply of central bank money and credits to the banking sector. In this paper the experience of Poland during the 'transition', which started on 1 January 1990 with the 'Big Bang' reform programme, will be examined through to the end of 1992. The main focus of the paper will be an investigation of whether there is evidence of a hardening of the micro budget constraints faced by enterprises.

It should be noted that the behaviour of enterprises is also influenced by trade liberalisation and currency convertibility, which exposes them to competition from foreign firms and helps to counteract monopoly power. The impact of this competition will depend on the 'level' of the exchange rate and the degree of convertibility (Dickinson and Mullineux, 1993). Over-valued exchange rates impose discipline on the traded goods sector in the absence of protection in the form of tariffs or quotas. In contrast, a policy of undervaluation will exert little discipline, but may be desirable whilst the transforming economy is diverting traditionally eastward looking trading relations westward. On balance, an 'equilibrium' exchange rate would seem desirable (Fry and Nuti, 1992), but establishing an equilibrium exchange rate when convertibility is declared is no easy matter (Dickinson and Mullineux, 1993). Poland introduced 'current account' convertibility as part of its 'Big Bang' reform programme.

The aim of imposing hard-budget constraints on enterprises and exposing them to external competition is to bring about a change in their

---

[1] A 'two-tier' banking system (Corbett \& Mayer, 1991; Mullineux 1993) was introduced at the end of 1988.

behaviour so that productivity can be increased. Price liberalisation and convertibility support the process by importing world relative prices and thereby revealing comparative advantages and disadvantages. Inefficient firms will clearly need to be closed and the capital released for reallocation. In the transition, the new markets are unlikely to function as effectively as the market system does in 'Western' economies. It is increasingly being acknowledged that 'Western' market economies function within the context of an institutional infrastructure (O'Brien, 1992). This includes a legal system, which establishes and enforces property rights and bankruptcy laws. It also includes a system of 'corporate governance', which becomes necessary when ownership is divorced for control and it is impossible to draw up satisfactory contracts.[2].} Systems of corporate governance, as well as other elements of the institutional infrastructure (e.g., degree of central bank independence), differ considerably between 'Western' countries, but a particular distinction is often drawn between the 'German' (or 'Continental European') model and the 'Anglo--Saxon' (or 'Anglo--American' model).[3]

'Anglo--American' countries are typically more capital market oriented and control over corporate behaviour is exerted from the outside via the threat of takeover (Rybczynski, 1986). These systems are dubbed 'outsider system' by Franks and Mayer (1992). In contrast, Germanic 'insider' systems are more bank-oriented (Rybczynski, 1986) and rely on committee-style supervision of management by 'supervisory boards'. The banks, as both lenders and holders of equity participations, are the major financiers and commonly occupy prominent positions on the supervisory boards. There was a considerable literature in the 1980s examining the extent to which Anglo--American systems engender 'short termism' (see Carlin and Mayer, 1992). The issue remains contentious, but the problem is deemed to arise because of the increasing concentration of shareholding in the hands of institutional investors, rather than private investors. To date institutional investors have not become heavily involved in corporate governance in the way that German banks have. Instead, they exert pressure by demanding a satisfactory flow of dividends and are willing to sell the shares of 'underperforming' firms, exposing them to the risk of a hostile takeover. The pressure to maintain the dividend flow, it is argued, focuses firms' attention on short term profits and discourages the devel-

[2]See Carlin and Mayer (1992) and Phelps et al (1993) for reviews of the literature on the 'principle agent' and related problems.

[3]Japan is sometimes classified with Germany as an 'insider' system (Franks and Mayer, 1992) and sometimes regarded as an alternative type of system (Jackson, 1992).

opment of long term investment strategies. There is evidence, however, that some institutional investors have been more actively exercising their shareholder voting rights in the US and UK in the last few years.

The choice of a system of corporate governance clearly compliments the imposition of financial discipline, or micro-budget constraints, in bringing about the efficient restructuring of economies in Central and Eastern Europe (CEE). The role of financial institutions in this process is clearly crucial. Capital markets have not played a major role in the early stages of transformation and are unlikely to do so in the medium term (Lampe, 1992). Institutional investors, such as pension and insurance funds, are at a relatively early stage of development and, in the continental European tradition, are likely to hold a much larger proportion of government bonds than their 'Anglo--American' counterparts, which typically hold a larger proportion of shares than bonds. In Poland, state-owned banks have been the most important financial institutions in the early phase of the transition (Raczko, 1993), and are likely to continue to be so in the medium term. A Germanic model of corporate governance, in which existing state banks play a major role, thus seems most appropriate for these CEE countries,[4] especially given their historical and geographical 'closeness' to Germany. The banks will, therefore, not only have to replace the central planners as the main allocators of working and investment capital, but will also have to develop a prominent role in corporate governance. In this paper, the performance of Polish banks during the first phases of the transition will be examined and means of improving their incentives and providing them with institutional support in their 'monitoring' and governance roles during the next phase of the transition will be assessed.

2. Banks and the Hardening of the Micro-Budget Constraint

In imposing financial discipline on firms, it is important that banks have an incentive to lend to the most efficient firms and to force inefficient firms into liquidation. Through this process banks themselves will earn a return on their capital; productivity will be increased; the economy will be restructured; and exports will flow from sectors with an international comparative advantage. Additionally, capital will be released from 'old'

[4]See Phelps et al (1993) for a dissenting view and Wijnbergan (1993a,b) for arguments supporting active (former) state bank involvement in corporate governance.

state owned enterprises for investment in newly formed or privatised enterprises and the small and medium sized enterprises (SME) sector will be promoted. The SME sector is increasingly recognised as the engine of growth and the main creator of employment in western economies. Its promotion in the CEE countries is therefore crucial if the unemployment problem created in the transition restructuring is to be contained.

The 'two-tier' banking system in Poland, which was created by divesting the commercial banking functions of the state bank, which became the central bank, and concentrating them in 9 newly created, regionally oriented and state-owned, commercial banks and previously existing specialised banks (Mullineux, 1993), was ill-equipped to perform the tasks required of it at the outset of the transition. During the transition, many private sector banks were established and a 'third-tier' of banks was created, but the state-owned banks still dominate (Raczko, 1993). Not only do the state-owned and private sector 'commercial' banks lack credit appraisal skills, but they operate in a highly uncertain environment and are likely to be subject (explicitly or implicitly) to constraints as a result of government regional, industrial and environment policies, which may or may not be clearly articulated. Attempts to transfer banking skills are underway via a World Bank sponsored programme of 'twinning' the major Polish banks with western commercial banks.

Perhaps the most important impediment to banks fulfilling their recredit re-allocation function is the inherited debt structure. Under the planning system, banks lent to firms under the guidance of the state-planning authority. The liberalisation of prices, reduction of trade barriers, and establishment of convertibility meant that firms were unable to service their inherited debts, which had been substantially eroded in real terms by the pre 'Big Bang' hyperinflation but not entirely eliminated due to 'dollarisation', and banks too faced an inherited bad debt problem. The severity of the bad debt problem rapidly increased in the first phases of the transition as the inexperienced banks made further bad loans and capitalised interest rate arrears. According to most estimates, 20 to 30 per cent of total credit extended to the enterprise sector in Poland should be classified as irretrievable and a similar proportion can be regarded as of 'doubtful' quality. This dramatically undermines the asset structure of the 9 state-owned commercial banks which took over all past loans. Particularly burdensome, both for the banks and the enterprises, are credits extended in connection with the infamous central investments, which provide a good illustration of how the shortage economy functioned.

The question arises: should the heavily indebted firms be declared insolvent and forced into liquidation, or would they be viable if relieved from the inherited debts? In such an uncertain environment, it becomes even more difficult than usual for banks to decide whether enterprises are genuinely insolvent or merely illiquid. This is especially true because it takes time to establish reliable accounts, as the case of the former GDR demonstrates (Carlin and Mayer, 1992). The problem is, however, compounded by the possibility that banks will face 'perverse incentives' (Begg and Portes, 1992; Phelps et al, 1993) that lead them to continue to lend to state-owned enterprises with bad debts,seemingly compounding their own problems and blatantly misallocating credit. The problem for the banks is that, the more they force enterprises into liquidation, the more they reveal the true extent of their own bad debt problem and the more likely theyare themselves to become bankrupt. Governments should not encourage banks down this road because it will damage confidence in the banking system, with potentially serious consequences.[5]

It seems clear therefore that banks should be recapitalised and that the government should take over inherited bad debts from banks and relieve the enterprise sector of inherited bad debts at an early stage in the transition. This would allow banks to participate actively in the restructuring process and pave the way for a mass privatisation programme. To guard against any moral hazard created by 'bailing out' the banks, it is necessary to combine the financial restructuring of banks with the introduction of an effective bank regulatory and supervisory system.[6] The details of the debt workout would need to be carefully considered. Somewhat belatedly, Poland has introduced a programme to extricate banks from their inherited debt problems. This is discussed next.

3. Hardening the Micro-Budget Constraint in Poland: Policy Initiatives

The issue of enterprise debts and banks' financial restructuring has been covered by the 'Pact on SOEs' or 'enterprise pact', negotiated by the government and trade unions and signed in February 1993. The Pact's main objectives are: (1) to eliminate uncertainty facing enterprises; and (2) to involve management, workers and banks in enterprise transformation and reform. It consists of draft laws, amendments to existing laws and statements of issues and problems to be addressed. The Pact concerns:

[5]Including capital flight (Dickinson and Mullineux, 1993) and the need for lender of last resort intervention, which may possibly undermine the macro stabilisation programme.

[6]Another example of the institutional infrastructure supporting 'market' economies.

- financial restructuring of enterprises and banks;
- privatisation;
- change of the government incomes policy (the famous, or infamous, PPWW tax on excessive wage growth).

We shall concentrate exclusively on the first item here, and tackle the second later. The Act on the Restructuring of Enterprises was passed by the Parliament in 1992 and, as a result, insolvent enterprises can apply to banks holding at least 10 per cent of their total obligations to initiate a reconciliation procedure, through which an agreement with the creditors concerning debt rescheduling and/or its partial cancellation can be reached. The bank can require the enterprise to formulate a programme of restructuring. When the reconciliation procedure is unsuccessful, the enterprise should be declared bankrupt. If the procedure brings an agreement, the enterprise is transformed into a joint stock partnership with the sole participation of the State Treasury ('commercialised'), with all the concomitant legal and organizational changes. Banks holding bad assets are entitled to sell them without the consent of the debtor. Banks holding at least 30 per cent of enterprise's total obligations can acquire shares in the enterprise in question. To replace the bad assets, the Ministry of Finance, in the name of the Treasury, will transfer to the state-owned banks or to banks in which the Treasury has a majority stake, zero-interest bearing bonds which are specially issued for this purpose; thus allowing banks at least to recover the principal invested. The government has been allowed to use a part of the $1 billion 'stabilization fund', which was created but never used at the outset of the Polish transition by the IMF to support the convertibility of the zloty, to finance part of the programme. Additionally, a World Bank loan is being negotiated. According to most estimates, the operation should cost approximately $2 billion. So far, some $500 million has been found.

By taking over responsibility for the bad debts and recapitalising the banks, the government takes 'off-budget' liabilities onto the budget. As Begg and Portes (1992) note, this is not necessarily disadvantageous since it reduces uncertainty by making the government's fiscal position transparent and may enhance the reputation of the government. If recapitalisation is combined with 'commercialisation', which involves giving the state-owned firms a clear legal status as corporations and establishing supervisory boards, then the banks' incentives may be decisively changed.

As noted above, banks and other financial institutions in the west are rarely left to be governed by private sector mechanisms and oversight is increased by imposing regulations on the banking system and establishing a supervisory system to monitor compliance with the regulations. The case for privatisation has been made on the grounds that state-owned enterprises can never be truly commercialised and that efficiency will thus be enhanced by privatisation. This may well be true for banks and other enterprises, but rapid privatisation in CEE countries, prior to restructuring, which can take a considerable amount of time,[7] is probably inadvisable (Rybczynski, 1991). The launch of mass privatisation processes in Poland and the CSFR has, for bureaucratic, political and legal reasons, proved to be a lengthy process anyway (Mullineux 1982b, c). The resolution of the bank bad debt problem will facilitate the privatisation process when it comes to be launched, and 'commercialisation' seems to be a useful interim step. Evidence is presented in section 6 which suggests that bank behaviour has changed markedly since their commercialisation in Poland.

Commercialised, or genuinely commercial, banks can only operate truly commercially if freed from government guidance. If the government wishes to influence lending decisions, it should do so via incentives such as loan guarantees. To the extent that the government wishes to influence bank lending in order to support industrial, regional or environmental policy, it should establish institutions, such as a development and/or an investment bank, and a privatisation and restructuring agency, with well defined objectives, to takeover some of the responsibilities of the privatisation ministry. It is notable that the 'Treuhand', the German agency charged with privatising and restructuring industry in the former GDR, plays a major role in corporate governance in Eastern Germany. This will be discussed further in the next section, but first one further issue should be considered.

The banks may not be able to impose financial discipline, and the government's policy of monetary restraint may be undermined, if firms react to a shortage of bank credit by extending inter-enterprise credit (IEC) to each other. IEC also reinforces the tendency for credit to be misallocated towards unsound enterprises. Evidence from Poland is presented in section 6 which shows that the tight monetary policy in 1990 did seem to lead to an expansion of IEC. Begg and Portes (1992) hypothesise that, once banks are seen to be lending according to commercial criteria, IEC will contract as credit worthy enterprises will not want to be exposed to

---

[7]As the experience of the Treuhandanstalt in Eastern Germany has demonstrated (Carlin and Mayer, 1992; Mullineux, 1992d).

potential bankruptcy cases. In section 6 it is shown that there has indeed been a contraction of IEC since the commercialisation of banks in Poland.

Financial discipline has also been significantly undermined by the accumulation of tax arrears in Poland (Pinto et al 1993). To support the banks in their role as financial disciplinarians, action by the government on this front is clearly necessary.

4. Banks and Corporate Governance in Poland

Banks in Germany commonly have significant equity participations in companies to which they lend and are consequently represented on supervisory boards. Although not considered in detail here (see Mullineux and Pruski (1993) for further discussion), the swapping of debt for equity, by banks with their enterprise clients, may be a sensible way of helping to resolve the inherited debt problem given that governments in the CEE countries (including Poland) have so far chosen not to take more than a small proportion of the inherited bad debts onto their books.

Due to the aforementioned shortage of skilled and experienced personnel, it would, however, be unwise to expect banks to perform a major role in corporate governance at an early stage in the transition. The high quality staff that they do have would seem better employed in developing profitable lending strategies. Until the banks have acquired skilled personnel in sufficient abundance, it might be sensible to concentrate expertise in a semi-autonomous government agency with clearly defined policy objectives. As noted above, the Treuhand is playing a significant role in restructuring, governing and privatising enterprises in the former GDR. It has been helped considerably by banks and other 'West German' companies, which have staffed the newly established supervisory boards. It has also induced banks to help by providing substantial (up to 100 per cent) loan guarantees. Investment funds and loan guarantees have also been provided by the German development bank (KfW) and other state-backed funds and institutions (Mullineux, 1992d). The guarantees are necessary to induce banks to lend; especially to the small and medium sized enterprises (SMEs). These are typically privatised first in the transforming CEE economies, as was the case in Poland, and there number is being swelled by newly created enterprises. This is because the banks' risk threshold may be quite low in the highly uncertain transition environment and they may respond by rationing the supply of credit to SMEs (Stiglitz and Weiss, 1981).

Given that the indigenous banks in Poland were less able to assist with corporate governance than were the (West) German banks in the former GDR, and that privatisation of large enterprises is a medium to long term project, the 'privatisation agency' would appear to have a pivotal role to play in corporate governance in the early stages of transition. It should oversee the restructuring of enterprises, prior to their privatisation and in accordance with government environmental, industrial and regional policy objectives. This process will involve closing some enterprises and breaking up conglomerates. It will also involve 'commercialisation', including the establishment of supervisory boards and putting in place managements with suitable incentive (compensation) structures (Mayhew and Seabright, 1992; Pinto et al, 1993). Finally, it will need resources to induce banks to participate in restructuring on a commercial basis. To the extent that the 'privatisation' agency has to subsidize employment and investment in pursuit of regional and industrial policy, and that it meets some of the costs of dealing with inherited environmental and bad debt problems, it is unlikely to run at a profit, even after revenue from privatisation is taken into account.[8]

In Poland, a major impediment to enterprise restructuring has been the role of 'Workers Councils' in state-owned enterprises and the strength of the Trades Unions. Restructuring in Poland, considered in the next sub section, aims inter alia to clarify the power structure within the enterprises.

5. Restructuring and Corporate Governance in Poland

The position of management in the traditional Polish SOEs is extremely weak and consequently they are effectively labour-managed. Workers Councils can hire and fire the managers, set their wages and block crucial decisions concerning ownership transformation. Not infrequently they also try to influence the daily running of business. The system of managerial compensation remains basically unchanged, at least on paper. Managers still receive a multiple (between 5 and 7) of the national average wage or the average wage in the firm, which is, of course, determined by the Workers Council. There is also a bonus payment, but the link of managerial compensation to profits is weak and has been diminishing over time.

[8]Again the Treuhand demonstrates that restructuring is a costly process (Mullineux 1992c, Carlin and Mayer 1992).

Ironically, this link was the strongest (in terms of specified percentages of profits before tax minus PPWW) in 1990, when financial measurement was strongly biased by all sorts of temporary factors. To illustrate this, let us consider the following example. In 1990, if a firm registered $50 million of profits (before tax - PPWW), the manager would get about $3800 for the year. In 1991, this drops to about $2800 for the year. In a case where the manager's basic wage is 7 times the average wage in the firm, equivalent compensation can be obtained by a one-time rise in monthly wages of about $45 a month in 1990 and only $33 in 1991. This creates an automatic pre-disposition towards wage increases and emphasise upon the short-run.

In short, deeper restructuring efforts requiring painful decisions are very difficult for the managers to carry out in the SOEs, indeed they are against their interest. As a result, the necessary actions are not taken, or are taken belatedly, when the very existence of the enterprise is at stake. In the light of this, privatisation and 'commercialization' are frequently perceived in Poland as necessary to achieve an improvement in the internal incentive structure in the firms. The delay in privatisation, the need for restructuring prior to privatisation, and the need to capitalize on the big investment in managerial capital that has occurred through 'learning-by-doing' during the transformation process, highlights the importance of designing a package to strengthen the position of management. The package should include inter alia:[9]

- widespread commercialization, entailing the dissolution of Workers Councils;
- strengthening significantly the link between managerial compensation in SOEs and profits;
- clarification of the managers' position following privatisa-tionas well as their reward, e.g., through share ownership;
- inclusion of managers in the process of privatisation through the management buyouts and management contracts aimed at privatisation.

In addition attention should be paid to changing workers' incentives in order to strengthen managements' position. Commercialisation in Poland involves replacing Workers Councils with Supervisory Boards on

[9]This is taken from a report summarizing a World Bank sponsored empirical study by B.Pinto, M.Belka and S.Krajewski (1993).

which workers are represented and the privatisation programme, passed by Parliament in May 1993, will encourage employee share ownership to compliment management share ownership.

Despite repeated declarations about its highest priority and genuine efforts of the government to speed up the privatisation process (reflected in opening up numerous privatisation 'paths' meant for different types of SOEs in different economic situations), the pace of ownership transformation has been unsatisfactory. By 30 September 1992 only 43 of the large enterprises had been privatised through capital privatisation (public tender or direct offer to a potential investor) and some two hundred and fifty were being processed. 349 firms had been taken over by the employees or management (leasing of property), with some 300 being processed. Another 100 firms have been liquidated and sold, due to their poor economic condition, 700 additional ones were being processed. Including commercialization, approximately 25 per cent of 8,000 to 10,000 SOEs (the number is growing due to deconcentration process) have undergone some type of ownership or legal transformation. Nevertheless, the rapid implementation of 'small privatisations' and the establishment of new enterprises led the private sector to account for over half of GDP, exports, and employment in Poland by the beginning of 1993.

The mass privatisation programme (MPP) was conceived and prepared in 1991 by the Ministry of Ownership Transformation. The scheme was finally approved by Parliament in May 1993 and will involve selling shares in 20 National Investment Funds (NIFs) to the adult citizens of Poland. The funds will be managed by experts who will bid for the business of managing portfolios of privatised SOE shares. The shares in the NIFs will be tradable. The MPP should stimulate the development of the capital market institutions and transform a broad class of citizens into capital owners.

The firms chosen for privatisation will first be commercialized, or transformed into one-person partnerships of the State. Their shares will then be divided according to the following formula: 60 per cent for all participating citizens (but held by NIFs initially); 10 per cent for free distribution among the workers (including the management) in the firms in question; 30 per cent to be kept by the Treasury. The shares held by the Treasury will later be distributed amongst retired persons and employees to compensate for the inadequate wage and benefit increases in 1991, when the Government attempted to avoid an explosion of the budget deficit.

Much less spectacular, but more profound for the future pace of privatisation, was one of the main provisions of the aforementioned 'enterprise pact'. According to the Pact, enterprises not covered by the MPP, excluding some ('strategic') firms, will have to decide within 6 months on their preferred privatisation path. Solvent enterprise can choose one of the following options: (1) sale to a big investor; (2) public sale of shares; (3) buy-out by management or employees; and (4) transfer of controlling stake to a bank or a pension fund. Insolvent firms can also choose a method of privatisation, but must produce a draft of an arrangement with creditors (after a successful reconciliation procedure) and a plan for enterprise rehabilitation. If an arrangement with creditors is not sought or reached, bankruptcy is to be declared.

If treated seriously, this provision in the Pact may result in massive changes affecting 3,000 to 4,000 enterprises, rather than 600 or so covered by the MPP. More probably, it will result in initial chaos and a rapid deceleration of the process. However, it necessary to introduce such shocks to break the sense of temporariness prevailing in many SOEs.

There are a number of new proposals which appear to combine the needs to both restructure the internal incentives and to privatise productive assets. Let us mention just two of them:

- Privatization through Restructuring (PtR). This is meant for medium size firms with decent longer-run prospects but whose current situation is precarious. Managerial groups, both foreign and domestic, present plans to rehabilitate the firm. When the plans are acceptable, the groups take part in an auction; the highest bidder takes over the enterprise. The group pays approximately 5 per cent of the determined initial value and takes control of the firm in order to prepare it for sale within a few years. If the firm's market value grows, the group gains 70 per cent of the increase.
- Bigger firms in a similar condition need not only an arrangement with the creditors, but also an injection of capital. An EBRD-sponsored plan was recently put forward by two of its advisers (Neil Balfour and Andrzej Olechowski) to cover around 180 enterprises. It has been dubbed: Stabilization. Restructuring. Privatization (SRP). Firms which meet certain well-defined criteria, obtaining positive profit on current sales being the most important, can qualify. Commercialized state-owned banks and newly privatised commercial banks are expected to play an active role in the process as they have a stake in retrieving their bad or doubtful loans. They are ex-

> pected to submit a list of potential customers. Every participating Polish bank will form a joint-venture with the EBRD (which would hold a majority stake in it). The joint venture would take over the control of the enterprises in question and assume responsibility for their rehabilitation and ultimate sale. $480 million is said to be ready for the purpose from the EBRD, PHARE and the participating Polish banks. They hope to retrieve the money in 5 years. The programme combines some of the features of the MPP and the aforementioned PtR. A new and interesting element is the presumed active role of the existing state-owned and newly privatised large commercial Polish banks; which may become owners of the restructured and rehabilitated firms as a consequence.

The multitude of privatisation methods and gradual progress with privatisation that can be observed in 1991--1993 cannot conceal the fact that many state enterprises, maybe even the majority of them, still await significant internal changes. They face the formidable task of surviving in extremely unfavourable market conditions. In the next section evidence is presented to illustrate the change in bank lending behaviour in Poland and to show that there has been a polarisation in the performance of firms. The best performing firms are not confined to particular industrial sectors and there is considerable variation in performance within sectors. What is surprising is that this has been achieved without major changes in management incentives and without the active involvement of the privatisation ministry. Moreover, there is little evidence so far that commercialised (non-bank) enterprises fare better than other SOEs. It may be too early to draw any conclusions about this as the commercialization process in the past two years may have been heavily distorted by political influences and some adverse selection of firms may have resulted.

This contrasts with the state-owned banking sector where 'commercialisation' seems to have coincided with a marked change in bank lending behaviour. This has led to a hardening of micro budget constraints and to better performing firms getting a larger share of loans; supporting the aforementioned polarisation, and restructuring in general. The change in bank behaviour is probably not attributable to 'commercialisation' alone, however. It is also likely that 'learning by doing', learning through contact with staff from their Western bank 'twins' and growing caution as credit risks have increased in the 'transition recession' have been important. In 1990, banks simply 'rolled over' credit as most firms appeared to be profitable. This was largely an illusion due to the inappropriate inclusion of inventory 'value' appreciation under inflation (Schaffer, 1992), and matters clearly deteriorated as the transition recession gathered force in 1991.

6. Evidence of a Hardening of Micro-Budget Constraints in Poland

The lack of fundamental changes in the intra-firm incentive structure coupled with a relatively slow pace of change of ownership status does not, it seems, preclude gradual adjustment in the behaviour state-owned enterprises. The macroeconomic data and results from microeconomic research indicate that behavioral changes are taking place in bank and non-bank enterprises in reaction to the stringency of macroeconomic policy of stabilization.

In 1992, particularly in the second half of the year, the volume of bank credit to the enterprise sector started to contract in relative, and in some months even in absolute (nominal), terms. The same pattern was recorded for inter-enterprise credit. The volume of tax arrears kept growing, albeit at slower rate, suggesting that enterprise-state relations provided the most serious leakage in the hard(er) budget constraints facing firms. The aforementioned tendency, and the increasingly pronounced polarization of individual firms' performance, find some confirmation in the Pinto et al (1993) empirical study analyzing the behaviour dynamics of 62 big SOEs from 5 sectors of the Polish manufacturing industry.

The second stage of the Pinto et al (1993) study, which covers the two and a half years of transition up to mid-1992, concentrates on distinguishing between the AAA (consistently profitable) enterprises, the AA (gross profit, but net loss making) enterprises and the A (gross loss making) enterprises, rather than on sectoral differences. Most of the comparisons are between AAA and A firms, as the number of AA firms was too small to infer any well-founded conclusions. A general perception during 1990 and early 1991 was that the discipline of macro stringency was being diluted by bank loans, inter-enterprise credit and the accumulation of tax arrears. In short, the firm-level budget constraint was not hard. We shall next review the main findings of the study in this respect.

6.1 Bank Credit

Figure 1 plots the path of working capital credit loans from banks in relation to sales from the previous quarter, reflecting the firm's dependence on this source of external financing. It shows that, after an initial moderation (early 1990), bank credits rose both for AAA and A enterprises, but much more for the latter group. Looking at it in nominal terms, in the 21 months from March 1990 to December 1991, loans to A firms rose by 214 per cent compared to 92 per cent for AAA firms. This coincided with a rapid accumulation of finished goods inventories by A firms, indicating that working capital credit was indeed a factor softening their budget constraints. The period December 1991 to June 1992 is also notable. Working capital loans rose only slightly for AAA firms, but fell for A firms, suggesting that the commercialization in late 1991 of the 9 banks spun off from the National Bank of Poland and the appointment of supervisory boards, combined with closer monitoring by the Ministry of Finance of the bad loans portfolio, were having the desired effects. Some of the 9 banks had also begun to prepare for privatisation. This meant that there was more involvement of outside (usually foreign) advisers and auditors, and more caution about incurring assets that could result in a slowing down of the privatisation process or in an adverse evaluation of the incumbent management.

In sum, the data confirm the initial laxity of bank credit. The big relative increase of loans to A firms did not support a higher level of activity, but was a result of banks rolling over interest payments as they fell due, and financing growing inventory shocks.

The opinions expressed by the managers in a 'qualitative' questionnaire accompanying the statistical analysis reinforce some of the above findings. Managers unanimously reported radically changed bank behaviour. As they described it, in 1990 banks acted like 'cashiers' eager to dole out money. By 1992 banks were behaving more like 'partners' with an equity stake in the company and had become extremely cautious. Based on a 0--5 point scale ranking, the AAA managers said their firms experienced the same ease in getting loans over the period (3.0, 2.8 and 3.2) in the three years under analysis, while there was a sharp change for A firms in 1992 (3.2, 2.0, 1.2). Impressively, all firms reported increased bank involvement.

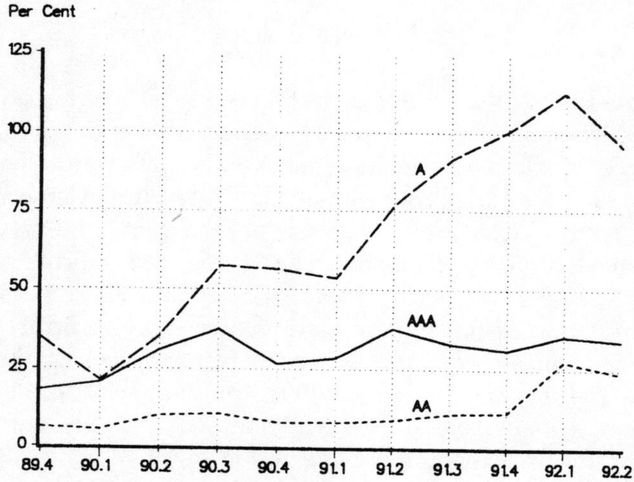

Figure 1: Working Capital Credit/Quarterly Sales Revenue.

An improvement in the credit assessment of banks can also be inferred from the fact that 25 enterprises were denied credit in the last two years, 21 were A and 4 were AAA. But the reason typically given was a general condition of the firm rather than the non-viability of the project for which the funds were sought. This points to a continuing weakness in project evaluation.

6.2 Inter-Enterprise Credit

The dynamics of net lending (inter-enterprise credit measured as receivables minus payables in relation to quarterly sales) presented in Table 1 confirms the view that such credit served as a substitute for bank loans. This shows up especially dramatically in the more recent period, when curtailment of bank loans led to a sharp increase in inter-enterprise borrowing by A firms.

Table 1: Net Inter-Enterprise Lending to Sales (per cent, selected months).

	Mar 90	Sept 90	Mar 90	Sept 91	Mar 92	June 92
AAA	27.81	28.15	23.74	24.37	20.66	17.77
A	28.71	33.79	15.39	7.6	--3.73	--10.75

Note: Manufacturing firms are net lenders to distributors and other manufacturers.

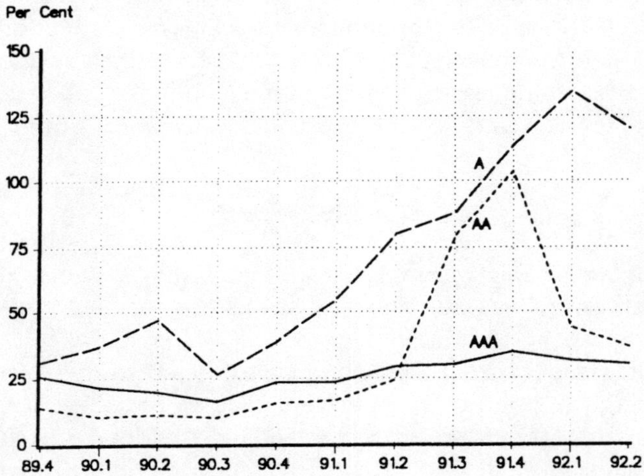

Figure 2: Inter–Firm Receivables/Quarterly Sales Revenue.

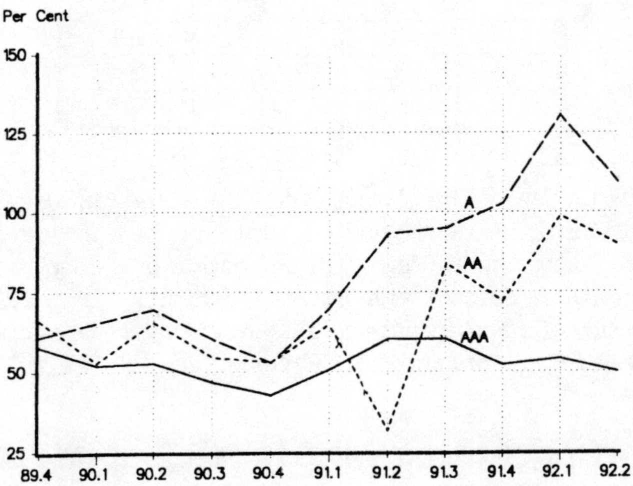

Figure 3: Inter–Firm Payables/Quarterly Sales Revenue.

Credit granted by better off AAA firms stabilized and later diminished slightly, as shown in Figures 2 and 3. Furthermore, the scale of the inter-enterprise credit, after an upward tendency for the first stage of transition, clearly levelled off and even fell. This is reinforced by the 'qualitative' information which indicates that firms created their own lists of buyers, specifying which would be dealt only on cash terms, which would receive two weeks' credit, and which will not be supplied at all.

6.3 Tax Arrears

The last leakage at micro level is tax arrears. Table 2, which gives arrears as a percentage of taxes due, shows that this has been substantial for both AA and A firms.

Further, since A firms would not be expected to owe 'profits' tax in 1992 (although this is not 100 per cent true in practice), it can be concluded that the arrears are in respect of the dividend and PPWW payments. In contrast, AAA firms are virtually current on tax payments.

Table 2: Ratio of Tax Arrears to Taxes Due (per cent).

	1990	1991	1992
AAA	1.8	3.3	3.7
AA	0.2	17.4	26.8
A	5.0	42.7	50.8

It seems that, with the glaring exception of the tax arrears accumulated by weaker firms, the budget constraint at the micro level has been hardened to some extent. Clearly, in a situation of a deep recession, the government cannot enforce widespread bankruptcy. The need to supplement the policy of macroeconomic stringency with active restructuring is, therefore, becoming more and more obvious.

7. Conclusions and Implications for Russia and the Ukraine

The imposition of financial discipline on enterprises and the establishment of an effective system of corporate governance are essential components of the successful transition of the centrally planned economies to 'market' economies.

The improvement of management incentives and internal financial discipline are key features of this process and have been discussed briefly here[10] along with the need to eliminate Workers Councils through 'commercialisation' and to provide workers with incentives through 'esops' and worker representation on supervisory boards. The role of banks and the potential role of the 'privatisation' agency, national investment funds and an investment and/or a development bank in providing external governance are, however, highlighted in this paper.

If, as seems likely, privatisation of large enterprises is to precede restructuring in the countries of the former USSR, such as the Ukraine and Russia, then heavy reliance will have to be placed on banks to impose financial discipline and to allocate resources efficiently. The experience of Poland suggests that, given their inherited debt structure, banks will be unable to perform such a role unless they are recapitalised and the bad debt problem is resolved at an early stage. Otherwise, as in Poland, banks will tend to capitalise interest arrears and there will be continued misallocation of credit. Even if the debt problem is dealt with, however, the banks will lack expertise and the degree of uncertainty is so great that disastrous consequences can be anticipated.

The most rapid restructuring and privatisation has occurred in the former German Democratic Republic (GDR) under the supervision of the 'Treuhand' and with the help of the major (former West) German banks. The Treuhand had clear constitutional goals relating to industrial, regional and environmental policies and was effectively state funded and empowered to use privatisation revenues in pursuit of its goals. It could usefully serve as a model for privatisation agencies in the Ukraine and Russia. Funding from the 'West' would seem to be appropriate in the absence of assistance from a 'rich uncle' such as the Federal Republic of Germany.

Poland trod a path somewhere between that of the former GDR and Russia and the Ukraine. Convertibility was introduced at an early stage and so too was price and trade liberalisation. Privatisation of large firms has taken longer than expected, although small privatisations, largely by auction, were executed quickly. Small privatisations by auction are scheduled to take place in Russia in the spring of 1993 and similar small

[10]See Mayhew and Seabright (1992) and Pinto et al (1993) for further discussion.

privatisation programme was approved in the Ukraine in January 1993.[11] Banks in Poland were not recapitalised at the outset. The bad debt problem was left to fester and was compounded by the growth of inter-enterprise credit leading to a misallocation of credit and a continuation of soft budget constraints in the early phases of the transition. It should be noted that a crucial difference in the former GDR was that the state could absorb the debts of the former state bank of the GDR relatively easily and the West German banks quickly took over parts of its branch network.

Banks have, however, now been 'commercialised' in Poland and the bank privatisation programme has been launched. This seems to have contributed to a significant change for the better in banks lending behaviour. The more cautious commercialised banks may now have acquired the skills[12] to impose financial discipline on state-owned enterprises and privatised firms. As their reputation for prudent lending grows, they are likely to adopt increasingly a 'monitoring' role (Phelps et al, 1993) akin to that of banks in Anglo--American-type economies. This role arises out of the information advantage enjoyed by banks, which can demand access to non-published information prior to lending to an enterprise. If enterprises can secure funding from banks of good repute, this can have a catalytic effect by giving the enterprise access to alternative, including equity and bond market, sources of finance. The banks effectively monitor the financial performance of the enterprises on behalf of the other creditors and the shareholders. The desire to gain access to these alternative sources of finance will condition the behaviour of firms.

As banks' reputations continue to grow and they acquire an ample compliment of skilled personnel, the privatisation agency could increasingly delegate restructuring and governance responsibilities to banks. As in Germany, bank representatives could serve on supervisory boards and banks could be contracted to restructure and privatise firms. In so doing, they may swap debt for equity and thereby acquire equity participation in enterprises, which in turn would increase their interest in becoming involved in corporate governance in the manner of German 'universal' banks.

There appears to be a good case for a privatisation agency in Poland to take a lead in the restructuring process prior to mass privatisation; and for countries such as the Ukraine and Russia to introduce such corporate restructuring oriented privatisation agencies as soon as possible, prefera-

[11]Russia is also planning to launch a large scale voucher based mass privatisation programme later in 1993.

[12]Through 'learning by doing' and 'twinning' and 'Western' banks, for example, in Poland.

bly with Western funding support and advisors. Following the planned mass privatisation of large enterprise in Poland and the CSFR, investment funds will control the bulk of the shares in the privatised enterprises. In the case of the CSFR, these will be in the private sector and many will be owned by banks. The viability of these funds has been questioned, but, even if the fears are unfounded, it is not clear that an adequate system of corporate governance will result because ownership may be too dispersed. The involvement of banks as both lenders and fund managers may be a redeeming feature, however. In Poland the privatised firms' shares will be held by twenty specially created, state-backed, national investment funds and investors will use their vouchers to buy shares in these funds.[13] Investors will therefore benefit from portfolio diversification in the way that unit or investment trust investors in OECD countries do. The resulting system will not be unlike the Anglo--American and one, with most shares held by institutional investors, and banks providing debt finance. The holdings of shares in Poland will, however, be much more concentrated. These funds, therefore, have a potentially important corporate governance function. Their management is to be contracted out to 'expert' western fund managers. These managers should be encouraged to play a key role in corporate governance. It is to be hoped that they develop a strategic outlook and don't come to be accused of engendering 'short termism' by demanding inappropriately high dividends from the enterprises whose shares they hold.

REFERENCES

Begg, D. and **Portes, R.** (1992), ``Enterprise Debt and Economic Transformation: Financial Restructuring of the State Sector in Central and Eastern Europe,'' CEPR Discussion Paper No 695, London: Centre for Economic Policy Research.

Carlin, W. and **Mayer, C.** (1992), ``Restructuring Enterprises in Eastern Europe,'' CEPR Discussion Paper No 700, London: Centre for Economic Policy Research.

Corbett, J. and **Mayer, C.** (1991), ``Financial Reform in Eastern Europe: Progress with the Wrong Model,'' *Oxford Review of Economic Policy,* 7(4), pp 57--75.

[13]Russia appears to be planning a half-way house system involving a small number (eight) of licensed investment trusts with western advisors/managers.

Dickinson, D. G. and **Mullineux, A. W.** (1993), ``Currency Convertibility, Policy Credibility and Capital Flight in Poland and the CSFR," Department of Economics Discussion Paper No 93--04, University of Birmingham.

Franks, J. and **Mayer, C.** (1992), ``Corporate Control: A Synthesis of International Evidence," London Business School and City University Business School, November.

Fry, M. J. and **Nuti, D. M.** (1992), ``Monetary and Exchange Rate Policies During Eastern Europe's Transition: Lessons from Further East,'' *Oxford Review of Economic Policy*, 8(1), pp 27--43.

Jackson, M. R. (1992), ``Company Management and Capital Market Development in the Transition," Chapter 5 (pp 57--74), in Lampe (1992).

Lampe, J. R. (Ed) (1992), *Creating Capital Markets in Eastern Europe* Baltimore, Maryland: The John Hopkins University Press.

Mayhew, K. and **Seabright, P.** (1992), ``Incentives and the Management of Enterprises in Economic Transition," *Oxford Review of Economic Policy*, 8(1), pp 105--129.

Mullineux, A. W. (1987), *International Banking and Financial Systems: A Comparison* London: Graham and Trotman.

Mullineux A. W. (1992a), ``Hard Budget Constraints, Credit Crunches, and Central Bank Independence," *University of Wales Business and Economic Review*, No 8 (Jan/Feb), pp 35--38.

Mullineux A. W. (1992b), ``Banking Privatisation and Restructuring in Poland," *University of Wales Business and Economic Review*, No 9/10.

Mullineux A. W. (1992c), ``Privatisation and Financial Structure in Eastern and Central European Countries," *National Westminster Bank Quarterly Review*, May, pp 12--25.

Mullineux, A. W. (1992d), ``Privatisation and Small Business Financing in the UK and Germany: Lessons for Central and Eastern Europe," Anglo--German Foundational Report, August, London: Anglo--German Foundation.

Mullineux, A. W. (1993), ``Privatisation and Banking Sector Reform: Lessons from Poland," Department of Economics Discussion Paper No 93--XX, University of Birmingham.

Mullineux, A. W. and **Pruski, J.** (1993) ``Privatisation and Banking Reform in Poland," International Finance Group Working Paper, 93--XX, University of Birmingham.

O'Brien, R. (Ed) (1992), *Finance and the International Economy 6: The AMEX Bank Review Prize Essays Oxford*: Oxford University Press.

Phelps, E. S., Frydman, R., Rapaczynski, A. and **Schleifer, A.** (1993), ``Needed Mechanisms of Corporate Governance and Finance in Eastern Europe," Working Paper No. 1, European Bank for Reconstruction and Development, London.

Pinto, B., Belka, M., and **Krajwski, S.** (1993), ``Transforming State Enterprises in Poland: Microeconomic Evidence on Adjustment," World Bank Policy Research Working Paper, WPS 1101, February, Washington.

Raczko, A (1993), ``An Analysis of Changes in the Polish Banking Sector in 1992," Working Paper, Institute of Economics, University of Lodz.

Rybczynski, T. M. (1986), ``The UK Financial System in Transition," *National Westminster Bank Quarterly Review*, November pp 26--42.

Rybczynski, T. M. (1991), ``The Sequences of Reform," *Oxford Review of Economic Policy*, 7(4) pp 26--34.

Schaffer, M. E. (1992), ``The Enterprise Sector and the Emergence of the Polish Fiscal Crisis 1990--91," Centre for Economic Performance Working Paper No 280, September, London School of Economics.

Stiglitz J. E. and **Weiss, A.** (1981), ``Credit Rationing in Markets with Imperfect Information," *American Economic Review*, 71, pp 393--410.

Wijnbergen, S. van (1993a), ``Enterprise Reform in Eastern Europe," *Economics of Transition*, 1(1), pp 21--38.

Wijnbergen, S. Van (1993b), ``Financial Aspects of Enterprise Reform," *Economics of Transition*, 1(1) pp 117--121.

Privatisation and Banking Sector Reform in Poland and the Czech Republic*

Andy Mullineux
Department of Economics, University of Birmingham

Jerzy Pruski
Institute of Economics, University of Lodz

and

Jan Klacek
Institute of Economics, Czech National Bank

1. Introduction

It is increasingly being recognised that successful transition from centrally planned to 'market' economies cannot be achieved by simply liberalising prices and trade, eliminating subsidies and establishing currency convertibility. Markets in 'Western' economies are supported by an insti-

---

* Prepared for a Conference in Prague (September 3-4, 1993) in connection with EC(ACE) Project No: ERB 4012 PL910252 entitled: "Hard Budget Constraints,Privatisation and Financial Reform in Eastern Europe with Particular Reference to Poland and Czechoslovakia".

tutional structure which include, inter alia a legal system covering property rights and bankruptcy; regulatory and supervisory (including antitrust) agencies; and a system of corporate governance. In addition, the abandonment of central planning requires the establishment of an alternative means of allocating capital and the establishment of a payments system to support the new, and more complex, commercial relationships. The payments system may be regarded as a part of the essential infrastructure of a modern economy and consequently there is often considerable public sector involvement, usually via the central bank, in Western economies. Commercial, cooperative and savings banks are, however, also normally involved in providing payments or money transmission services (MTS): either via giro transfers, or via cheque induced transfers (or through both of them).

In addition to providing MTS, banks in Western economies are involved in 'corporate governance' and in the allocation of capital by collecting deposits (often via accounts which offer MTS) and lending or granting credits. Banks, which are typically the major financial intermediaries in the transforming economies and are likely to remain so in the medium term (Lampe, 1992). They are, therefore, likely to be key players in the restructuring of the former centrally planned economies. Consequently, careful attention needs to be paid to the design of the banking system at an early stage of the transition programme and privatisation of nonbanking firms must be preceded by a fundamental reform of the banking system (Rybczynski, 1991). This is because the main source of finance for privatised firms and newly created small and medium sized enterprises (SMEs) will be the banks. Further, it is the banks which must impose financial discipline or micro hard-budget constraints (Belka and Mullineux, 1993) on private sector firms and the enterprises that remain in the state sector (SOEs) whilst they are being restructured prior to privatisation.

In the CSFR and Poland the 'monobanking' system was replaced by 'two-tier' banking system prior to price and trade liberalisation and the introduction of currency convertibility. In both cases, the 'monobank' was split into a central bank and, largely regionally based, state-owned commercial banks (SOBs).Despite the appearance of 50 or so private (nonstate owned) banks in Poland, and thus a 'three-tier' banking system (Corbett and Mayer, 1991), there has not been a substantial increase in competition in the sector.In the CSFR the SOBs were put on privatisation and are all already privatized. But the banking sector is still highly segmented. A great number of small commercial banks are specialized in only few banking operations and do not compete with large banks.

Little was done at an early stage to relieve the banks of their inherited bad debt problems. These problems arose because prior to the 'reforms', when bank lending was guided by the national plan, rather than by assessment of credit worthiness and potential profitability. Following the introduction of comprehensive reform programmes, many firms found themselves unable to service their inherited debts, leaving the banks with sizeable and accumulating through capitalisation of arrears 'bad' debts. The existence of a substantial block of bad or poorly performing assets (loans) on their balance sheets clearly inhibits the ability of banks to play a positive role in the transition process. Further, it may seem rational to the banks to lend in a 'perverse' way in order to keep the biggest debtors afloat so that the extent of their bad debt problem is not revealed, with the possible consequence that they too would be shown to be bankrupt. Another explanation of the bank behaviour is that they continued to lend because they expected the government to launch an SOE and SOB debt relief plan. To the extent that some SOEs would be solvent if relieved of inherited debts, a policy of forcing banks to cease lending to illiquid firms would lead to a misallocation of credit. There is evidence of perverse lending and a misallocation of credit in the early stages of transition in Poland, at least prior to bank 'commercialisation', and that it was compounded by a growth in inter-enterprise credit (IEC) (Belka and Mullineux, 1993; Begg and Portes, 1992).

The approach adopted in the former Czechoslovakia and the Czech Republic seems to be more coherent and promising. The bad debt issue is, however, not yet fully resolved. The constraint was not so much on the institutional side - Consolidation Bank was established in 1991 - but more on the side of financial resources allocated for the purpose of clearing operation of the commercial banks' portfolios. (The Czechoslovak approach is analyzed in section 4 of the paper.)

It is clear, therefore, that if SOBs are to play a constructive role in allocating credit to the most efficient firms in sectors with a comparative advantage, and in corporate governance, then the inherited bad debt problem should be dealt with at an early stage in the transition.

It should be noted that in resolving the SOBs' inherited bad debt problem, the debt burden of SOEs to be privatised will also be relieved and thus privatisation of non-financial SOEs will be made easier. Once relieved of their debts, SOBs themselves will, of course, be more readily privatised.

Given that governments initiating a transition must effectively create banking systems from scratch, what type of banking system should they establish? The broad choice is between the 'universal' (Germanic-continental) banking model and alternative systems in which banks play more limited roles (Mullineux, 1987). The choice of system has a profound influence and the nature of corporate governance. The Germanic universal banking system leads to 'internal control' (Corbett and Mayer, 1991, Carlin and Mayer, 1992), in which banks, as creditors and equity holders, play a key role and often supply staff to serve on the supervisory boards of their clients. In more capital market oriented financial systems (Rybczynski, 1986), which are sometimes called Anglo-Saxon (or Anglo-American) systems, 'outside control' is exerted, largely via shareholders. As shareholding has become concentrated in 'institutional shareholders (insurance companies and pension funds etc), the behaviour of institutional investors has become pivotal. In the US and the UK, it is only in the last few years that the institutional investors have shown signs of taking their corporate governance responsibilities seriously. This follows a decade when they were accused, not least by the US and UK treasurers, of causing 'short-termism' in the corporate sector.

If ever a long-term perspective is needed, it is in the restructuring of the SOEs in the transforming economies. In Anglo-American systems, banks play a 'monitoring' role by virtue of their asymmetric access to information (Diamond, 1986). In universal banking systems, the banks are more closely involved in the governance, and occasionally the restructuring, of firms and do seem to take a longer term perspective as a result of their combined debt and equity exposure. The Germanic universal banking model would, therefore, seem to be recommended for transition economies, especially as it will take time to reduce reliance on the banking system and enhance the role of the capital markets (Lampe, 1992; Rybczynski, 1991). The choice will be reinforced by the fact that the '2nd EC Banking Directive' takes a very broad view, which encompasses the range of activities performed by German universal banks, of banking activities and that Poland and the CSFR have declared their desire to join the EC in the future.

For the banking system to perform its credit allocation and corporate governance responsibilities effectively, it too will need to be regulated and supervised, unless one accepts the arguments of the pro 'free-banking' lobby (see e.g. Dowd, 1989). This raises the issues of who should monitor the 'monitors', or govern the 'corporate governors', and how should they be regulated and supervised (Mullineux, 1993; Lacoue-Labarthe, 1992).

Finally, it should be noted that the restructuring of SOEs is likely to lead to a considerable shedding of labour (reduction of hidden unemployment). If the unemployment levels are to be contained, new sources of employment need to be established. In the OECD countries in the 1980s job creation was fastest in the small and medium sized enterprise (SME) sector. A thriving SME sector is therefore crucial to a successful transition. The banks must therefore play a role in funding the SMEs created through 'small privatisation programmes', which typically take place at an early stage in transition. They must also provide 'seed corn' capital for business 'start-ups' and other venture capital, including that for management 'buy-outs' (or 'buy-ins'). Unfortunately, commercial banks have relatively low risk thresholds and can be expected to ration the supply of credit to the SME sector (Stiglitz and Weiss, 1981), especially given the highly level of uncertainty associated with the transition. Attention, therefore, needs to be paid to methods of providing loan guarantees to induce banks to lend to the SME sector. This is discussed further in the next section.

2) Restructuring the Banking System

2.1. The Desired Structure

In this section we assume, for reasons outlined above, that the objective is to establish a Germanic universal banking system to allocate capital and participate in corporate governance during the transition. Stock markets have already been established in Warsaw and Prague and their role will increase as shares are traded following the planned voucher or coupon based mass privatisation programmes. These markets cannot be relied upon to play a significant role in corporate finance or governance in the medium term, however, except in so far as the institutions created as a result of the mass privatisation programme have a role to play, alongside banks, in the governance sphere.

The Polish banking laws in fact permit the development of a universal banking system allowing banks to hold equity participations. The total limit of a bank's holdings in other institutions, including securities may not exceed 25% of its own funds. However, this proportion can reach the level of 50% in special cases approved by the president of the central bank, the National Bank of Poland (NBP). It should be also noted that holdings of Treasury bills and NBP bonds are exempted from this limit. The Polish regulations are tighter than the Second EC Banking Directive rules; which state that no credit institution may have qualifying holdings in an undertaking, other a than financial institution, that exceed 15% of its own funds and that the total amount of qualifying holdings may not exceed 60% of its own funds. However the Second Banking Directive states also that shares held temporarily during a financial reconstruction or rescue operation shall not be counted as qualifying holdings for the purpose of calculating limits mentioned above. Unfortunately such rules do not exist in the Polish banking bill. This should be recognized as a shortcoming, especially in the context of financial restructuring and privatisation of the banking sector in Poland.

The Polish banking law makes the central bank responsible for supervising the banking system and grants it independence with respect to the conduct and formulation of monetary policy. There is considerable debate amongst economists about the desirability of central bank independence, and about whether true independence can indeed be achieved. This will not be discussed further here, except to note that: advocacy of independence is currently in vogue, a number of countries have recently granted their central banks independence, and that it is enshrined in the 'Maastricht Treaty'. There is also considerable debate amongst central bankers about the desirability of combining monetary and supervisory responsibilities as opposed to allocating supervisory responsibility to a separate agency. Practices vary considerably (Mullineux, 1987; Pecchioli 1987) and the EC Monetary Committee is currently exploring such issues in relation to the supervisory responsibilities of the proposed EC central bank. The argument for combining them is that effective monetary control requires the intimate knowledge of the banking system gleaned from involvement in supervision (Federal Reserve Bulletin, 1984). Against this, the Swiss central bank pushed some of its supervisory duties onto the Swiss banking commission in the late 1980s in order to enable it to concentrate on its monetary responsibilities. The crux of the matter is the potential conflict between 'lender of last resort' and monetary control responsibilities. To contain the moral hazard created by extending lender of last resort support, the central bank would need to be involved in regulatory design and supervision (Mullineux, 1993). Central bank involvement can, however, be reduced if a regulatory system can be designed that relies on central bank intervention as a last, rather than a first, resort. Towards this end, risk-related deposit insurance and capital adequacy requirements, and prudential liquid reserve requirements will be required (Mullineux, 1993). These are contentious issues, however, and will not be discussed further here.

2.2 SME Finance and Credit Guarantees

SME financing appears to be a weakness in most financial systems and as a result state intervention is common. Banks exercise voluntary credit rationing due to self imposed risk thresholds in the face of limited information. These thresholds are likely to be quite low given the high level uncertainty in the transition economies. This problem will be compounded as a result of the macro-stabilisation programme which imposes monetary restraint and high interest rates; and by the aforementioned 'perverse' incentives facing banks which inherited bad debt problems, which biases their lending towards SOEs.

In the former GDR, banks have been induced to lend to firms being restructured by the Treuhandanstalt, the privatisation and restructuring agency, by the provision of generous (up to 100%) loan guarantees. Loan guarantees are also available via specially created funds. These are, distributed primarily by KfW, the state-owned investment bank (Mullineux, 1992d). It should be noted, that the kfw has been providing loan guarantees to banks lending to the SME sector in the 'West' Germany, throughout the post-war period.

In formerly centrally-planned economies, loan guarantees are probably a better way of inducing bank lending to the SME sector than offering central bank refinancing because of the need to break reliance of the banking system on central bank finance as part of the attempt to establish a 'hard macro-budget constraint'. The reduction of bank reliance on central bank refinancing is also likely to encourage the establishment of an effective interbank market.

In Poland a development bank (Polski Bank Rozwoju (PBR) was established in 1990 to oversee the development of the interbank market and the money markets. It also provides credit lines in foreign currencies for investment projects. There are also plans to establish the Polish Investment Bank formed on the basis of about 50 NBP branches. The capital of the bank is to reach the level of 500 billion zloty. There is no clear concept of the role to be played by the Polish Investment Bank. On the one hand it is to be formed with the aim of taking over all the remaining commercial activities of the central bank. On the other hand it is expected to deliver funds for activities which stimulate restructuring, changes in the ownership structure and to promote development of capital market. To make a significant impact an funding SME growth and start-ups,considerable outside funding will be required, perhaps via the EIB,the EBRD and the IFC (World Bank).

Thorne (1992) has suggested that private sector banks, including privatised SOBs, should concentrate on funding the private sector and the remaining SOBs should be forced to concentrate on lending to, and taking part in the restructuring of, SOEs, prior to their privatisation. Such a 'dual track' approach is potentially dangerous because it is likely to lead to a concentration of risks and may slow down the restructuring process. This is because many of the most viable firms currently remain in the state-owned sector and the currently privatised firms are predominantly SMEs, which have a greater chance of failing and are therefore higher credit risks. It would appear to be better to 'commercialise' banks as soon as possible and then to privatise them following their financial restructuring. This is the subject of the next sub-section.

2.3 Bank Commercialisation, Privatisation and Corporate Governance

Polish SOBs were 'commercialised', in the sense that they were subject to the direction of supervisory boards, in the last two years. Since then their lending behaviour seems to have become less perverse (Belka and Mullineux, 1993). Commercialisation coincided with the 'transition recession', which may have made banks and their clients more risk conscious and therefore cautious, and with the 'twinning' of Polish banks with Western banks. As well as learning good banking practices from their Western twins, the banks have also been 'learning by doing'.

Given this change of behaviour, the question arises: is bank privatisation necessary? The pro's and con's of privatisation in general have long been debated, but assuming that the balance of the argument lies with privatisation as a means of increasing competition and efficiency, the next step is to decide how banks are to be privatised. Here the problem is not so much whether flotation on the stock exchange or voucher distribution should be used, as how the bad debt problem is to be resolved so that banks can be privatised with positive net worth.

To the extent that the bad debt problem is an inheritance from the previous regime, it is the responsibility of the state and should be taken on to the budget (Begg and Portes, 1992). The debts should therefore be taken over and written down and should be replaced by government bonds to balance the banks' balance sheets. The banks should also be recapitalised to bring their risk-related capital asset ratios up to EC standards. Such a restructuring of banks is clearly costly and will be difficult to achieve at a time when the transforming country is also trying to bring its budget deficit under control (Mullineux, 1992a, b, c). To the extent that banks, through 'perverse' lending behaviour, have aggravated the problem in the early phases of transition, a complete bail-out may not be justifiable and would risk creating a moral hazard if banks were encouraged to expect further 'bail-outs', or access to cheap refinancing from the central bank, in the future.

In the former GDR, the Treuhand could count on the support of the established West German banking system and could concentrate on restructuring the SOEs. The privatisation agencies in Poland and the CSFR have so far concentrated more on planning mass privatisation, and less on restructuring prior to privatisation, than the Treuhand. This is probably a mistake, but the issue of whether restructuring (beyond commercialisation) should precede or succeed privatisation is a hotly disputed one. The privatisation ministries in Poland face the additional task of having to prepare banks for privatisation. To break the 'grid-lock', and enable banks to assist the privatisation ministry in the restructuring process and to allow them to perform their governance function vis a vis the private sector, banks must somehow be relieved of their burden. An effective regulatory and supervisory system and reduced reliance on central bank refinancing should help contain the moral hazard problem, but what else should be done?

In Poland a debt consolidation bank (DCB) should be established and banks should be re-capitalised. In Poland the 'stabilisation fund' originally provided for by the IMF to underwrite convertibility, but which remained unused for that purpose, could be used to assist in the financial restructuring of banks, which now nominally satisfy the Basle Ratios. The DCB should be allocated funds out of the budget in accordance with government priorities and supplementary funding should be sought from overseas given the high priority of bank refinancing. To the extent that the privatisation programme generates revenue, the state privatisation ministry could contribute funds to speed the process (Lipton and Sachs, 1990), as in the (Ex) CSFR.

One possibility is that banks could be encouraged to 'sell' loans to the privatisation ministry or the consolidation bank in return for state-backed bonds and/or equity in the state-owned firms which are also indebted to them at a 'price' designed to maintain balance sheet values. The equity participation of banks in their clients would encourage them to become more actively involved in the governance process. It might also make sense for the privatisation ministry to share and financial restructuring roles with the consolidation bank. The privatisation ministry would then be forced into a more active restructuring role, and it might be advisable for it to transfer its responsibilities to a semi-autonomous privatisation agency with well defined objectives, like the 'Treuhand' in Germany.

In connection with the privatisation process, consideration should be given to the extent to which enterprises should be allowed to build up equity participations in other enterprises, and banks in particular. Currently SOBs are partly owned by the state and partly owned by SOEs and many private banks have SOEs as their major shareholders. There has been considerable debate, particularly in the US and Italy about whether non- banks should be allowed to hold equity in banks. Ultimately the debate revolves around the importance of risks of 'contagion' and the possibility that lender of last resort support may have to be extended to companies owning banks if the banks themselves are to be protected. The solution lies in devising a system in which lender of last resort intervention is normally unnecessary. If banks are to be privatised at an early stage, however, then the SOEs are likely to end up as major shareholders since they are the major source of capital. This may complicate the governance relationships and also raises the risk that banks will be coerced into lending primarily to their major corporate (SOE and privatised) shareholders. To guard against this, and over concentration of lending and the associated risks in general, exposure or lending concentration rules have become more widespread in 'Western' banking systems. They are now enshrined in the EC regulations and in the Polish banking regulations.

Both Poland and the CSFR are pursuing voucher-based mass privatisation programmes. In Poland twenty state backed and Western expert managed national investment funds (NIFs) are to hold the shares and the vouchers will be used to purchase shares in these funds. Risks will therefore be diversified from the point of view of the investors and the funds will have a potential role to play in corporate governance, like institutional investors in 'Anglo- American' financial systems. Thus the extent to which an 'insider', as opposed to an 'outsider', system of corporate control develops may depend on the extent to which banks develop equity participations through debt for equity swaps. In the CSFR the investment funds have been established spontaneously and many banks have established their own funds. Thus banks will rapidly be involved as both lenders and fund managers in corporate governance and may therefore be expected to adopt an attitude similar to Germanic universal banks.

3. Recent Developments in Polish Banking

The activities of the Polish banks on the assets side of their balance sheets concentrates mainly on providing credit services. Only recently the largest banks engaged more actively in trading Treasury bills. Nevertheless lending still dominates the banking behaviour in Poland. But there are important differences in the behaviour of the 14 commercial state-owned and recently privatised, banks and newly created 'private' banks in the field of lending. Private banks concentrate almost exclusively on extending short-run credits for turnover purposes, whilst commercial banks are much more heavily engaged in long-run lending for investments.

Table 1: Structure of credits in 57 banks (end of October 1992)

Type of bank	Data n/a	Investment credit	Turnover credit
Commercial banks	3	11	11
Private banks	9	18	33

Source: Data from Gazeta Bankowa 52/1992, p.24

Out of a total of 57 banks on which data was available, information about structure of lending are not available for 3 commercial banks and 9 private banks. All private banks except one (Kredyt Bank) are engaged in turnover credit. Only 53% of banks granted investment credit. For the 17 banks which grant both type of credits, the value of investments credits exceeds the value of turnover credit only in the case of 3 banks. Moreover, in many cases private banks' engagement in investment credit is of marginal importance. The low level of investment activity and the high risk related to investment projects in the economy under restructuring and in transition could constitute a possible explanation of the bias of private banks toward turnover credit.

The behaviour of the 14 commercial banks shows differential trends. Data are not available in the case of Bank Handlowy, PeKaO SA and Bank Gospodarki ZywnoPciowej but it could be reasonably assumed that they are engaged in both types of lending. Data available for the remaining 11 'SOBs' indicate that total amount of investment credit (77 trillion zloty) significantly exceeds total amount of turnover credit (56 trillion zloty). It is worth noting that the financing of investment activity in Poland is dominated by a few large SOBs: PKO BP (housing industry), Powszechny Bank Gospodarczy (coal mining centre in Belchatow), and Bank Przemyslowo-Handlowy (automobile industry in Tychy). Powszechny Bank Gospodarczy made most use of the NBP refinancing credit, which accounts for 84% of total investment lending. In this context one should asses the last amendment to the banking legislation according to which credits with government guarantees are exempted from credit concentration limits. It is not surprising that credit concentration limits do not apply to the savings bank (PKO BP), which is heavily in debt in housing industry. It is also quite understandable that PKO BP and Powszechny Bank Gospodarczy did not publish their capital adequacy ratios. Further, in 1992 the SOBs and the largest 'private banks' increasingly engaged in trading securities.

Owing to liberal regulation concerning the formulation of new banks the number of banks has been growing rapidly. Up to the beginning of 1992 about 60 newly established banks belonged to the Association of Polish Banks. This number does not include the 14 'SOBs'. In 1992 growth was much slower due to more restrictive minimum capital requirements. In 1992 24 private banks exceeded the 70 billion zloty level of own funds required by central bank, and hance some rationalisation can be expected. The structural development of private banks is illustrated in tables 3 and 5 and the development of SOBs is illustrated in Tables 4 and 6.

Table 2.1: Portfolio diversification of private banks

Private banks	Loans in billion		Securities in billion	
	1991	1992	1991	1992
Kredyt Bank	591	949	3	133
Bank Posnania	180	466	0	5
BIG	1390	1478	284	5130
Gecobank	24	201	-	114
Bank Ochrony				
Srodowiska	237	972	-	103
Invest Bank	110	642	-	14
Agrobank	676	959	-	22
Bank Ziemi				
Radomskiej	91	176	1	14
GBPZ	-	33	-	10

Source: Data from Rzeczpospolita 58/1993

Table 2.2: Portfolio diversification of commercial banks

Commercial banks	Loans in billion		Securities in billion	
	1991	1992	1991	1992
Bank Handlowy	10259	15437	16079	5186
PeKaO SA	4152	6922	33694	46943
Bank Slaski	10165	11610	2983	7072
Bank Przemyslowo-Handlowy	11561	14315	693	4279
BGZ	29907	35686	0	0
PBK	10608	12645	1402	5191
Bank Pomorski	7089	8767	562	1521
Bank Zachodni	5863	6614	113	2289
Bank Gdanski	6687	6365	2657	4680
WBK	6614	7475	473	1978
PBR	265	1392	727	2819
BRE	3367	3442	26	1536
PBG	9987	14909	13	148
BDK	4801	5620	730	1719
PKO BP	40537	48517	7412	6883

Source: Data from Rzeczpospolita 58/1993

Table 3: The development of private sector (in billion zloty)

Bank	Own funds		Assets		Profits		Branches	
	'91	'92	'91	'92	'91	'92	'91	'92
total	1409	3588	11746	30319	409	523	75	158
including Kredyt Bank	210	350	1096	1986	21	n/a	3	10
Bank Posnania	48	277	234	873	5	8	1	3
BIG	143	312	3047	8563	70	92	4	6
Gecobank	20	237	41	617	2	23	0	1
Bank Ochrony Srodowiska	152	244	367	1614	23	70	2	15
Invest Bank	60	200	259	1007	1	2	1	13
Agrobank	81	160	1357	2057	24	8	9	15
Bank Ziemi Radomskiej	13	186	209	471	10	37	0	1
GBPZ	-	140	-	481	-	3	-	n/a
Cuprum Bank	50	126	172	725	10	25	1	4

Source: Data from Rzeczpospolita 52/1993

Table 4: Network Development (Commercial Banks)

Commercial Banks	Number of branches		Number of employees	
	1991	1992	1991	1992
Bank Handlowy	20	24	2495	2830
PeKaO SA	83	89	6917	7861
Bank Slaski	44	45	3590	4231
BPH	44	57	3959	5045
BGŻ	99	99	7907	8435
PBK	n/a	39	3420	3931
Bank Pomorski	42	48	2643	3219
Bank Zachodni	54	56	3187	3515
Bank Gdański	44	44	2878	3721
WBK	43	47	3155	3758
PBR	0	0	110	177
BRE	8	10	541	640
PBG	n/a	n/a	n/a	n/a
BDK	58	71	2524	2795
PKO bp	378	393	34560	37127

Source: Data from Rzeczpospolita 58/1993

Table 5: Network Development (Private Banks)

Private Banks	Number of branches		Number of employees	
	1991	1991	1991	1992
Kredyt Bank	3	10	265	540
Bank Posnania	1	3	156	185
BIG	4	6	324	515
Gecobank	0	1	36	78
Bank Ochrony				
Srodowiska	2	15	132	609

Table 5 (Continued)

Invest Bank	1	13	223	539
Agrobank	9	15	379	608
Bank Ziemi				
Radomskiej	0	1	77	126
GBPZ	-	n/a	-	n/a
Cuprum Bank	1	4	123	240

Source: Data from Rzeczpospolita 58/1993

Table 6: Development of state-owned commercial banks in Poland (in billion zloty)

Bank	Own funds		Assets		Profit	
	1991	1992	1991	1992	1991	1992
Total	26455	31447	411747	547628	20912	23207
Bank Handlowy	5914	7279	75264	85937	2951	8467
PeKaO SA	2872	3203	61095	87319	1003	880
Bank Slåski	2393	2584	19707	27660	1325	1750
BPH	1437	1712	20436	34741	898	1424
BGŻ	2446	2806	45535	56939	3013	718
PBK	1688	1702	20501	30105	1088	1858
Bank Pomorski	1203	1794	11562	19091	1376	664
Bank Zachodni	n/a	n/a	10846	14426	1048	818
Bank Gdański	1301	1422	14544	19459	471	1020
WBK	1365	1779	12924	19773	843	789
PBR	1018	1255	1664	5541	390	808
BRE	688	872	4981	7589	178	198
PBG	808	917	33910	25480	617	750
BDK	928	1243	8642	11198	940	465
PKO bp	3082	3751	75117	109959	4945	2797

Source: Data from Rzeczpospolita 58/1993

4. Restructuring of the Czech Banking Sector

4.1. From Mono-Bank to a Two-Tier Banking System

The process of restructuring of the Czechoslovak banking sector differs from the Polish case. The major differences are in the speed of privatization of the commercial banks and in recapitalization of the banks which helped them to built up loan loss provisions and reserves.

Until the end of 1989 the Czechoslovak banking sector was dominated by the State Bank of Czechoslovakia; the SBCS, as a one-tier bank, performed both the central bank and the most of deposit and credit operations in the commercial sector. The Czech State Savings Bank and the Slovak State Savings Bank which accepted deposits and gave personal credits to individuals completed the picture. In addition, there were several small specialized money institutions.

A modern two-tier banking system started in Czechoslovakia on 1January 1990 when the authorities transferred the commercial banking activities of the central mono-bank to three new commercial banks. These were Komercní banka (for the Czech Republic), Vseobecná úverová banka (for the Slovak Republic) and Investicní banka which took over the credit portfolio of federal long term investment projects and housing loans. These changes did not usher in competition because the two commercial banks operated in different Republics. Nearly all personal savings were further held by the two national savings banks and money market thus remained segmented. The first traces of real competition started soon afterward, when the central bank permitted the establishment of new private banks.

Since then the Czechoslovak banking system has undergone a rapid development. Act No. 21 on Banks and Savings Banks as of December 1989 and the revised Act No. 21 on Banks as of February 1992 enabled private entities to establish banks, savings banks and branches of foreign banks. The number of commercial banks quickly increased. In 1990 there were 14 banks, in 1991 38 banks and in 1992 60 banks and branches of foreign banks.

Table 7: Banking Institutions in Ex-Czechoslovakia and in the Czech Republic[1]

	1990		1991		1992		1993
	1/1	31/12	31/3	31/12	31/3	31/12	30/6
CSFR - total	7	23	30	39	43	61	
state financial institutions	6	6	7	8	4	3	
JSC without foreign participation	1	11	13	16	22	33	
CS banks partly foreign owned	-	5	5	6	8	11	
CS banks entirely foreign owned	-	1	5	9	9	9	
branches of foreign banks in the CSFR	-	-	-	-	-	5	
Czech Republic total	5	21	27	33	35	46	50
state financial institutions	4	4	5	5	1	1	1
JSC without foreign participation	1	11	12	15	19	25	24
CZ banks partly foreign owned	-	5	5	5	7	7	8
CZ banks entirely foreign owned	-	1	5	8	8	9	11
branches of foreign banks in the CR	-	-	-	-	-	4	6

JSC = Joint Stock Company

[1] Licenced commercial banks, including branches of foreign bank

Table 8

The Structure of Credit and Deposit Markets in the Czech Republic
(December 1992, in %)

	Credits	Deposits			
		Total	By clients	By Central Bank	By other banks
1. Big ("old") banks total	71.8	78.8	91.1	44.2	59.3
Commercial Bank	31.9	27.8	29.0	--	36.9
Investment Bank	13.1	10.4	6.4	43.4	8.4
Czechoslovak Trade Bank	11.0	9.1	8.9	0.8	14.0
Czech Saving Bank	15.9	31.4	46.8	—	—
2. Small ("new") banks total	14.2	11.3	7.1	11.0	23.5
Agrobank Praha	4.6	3.9	2.8	1.1	8.0
Bohemia Bank	0.8	0.6	0.9	0.4	0.0
Credit Bank Plzeň	0.9	0.8	0.2	1.7	0.0
Moravia Bank	0.2	0.4	0.3	0.1	0.0
Postal Bank	0.7	0.4	0.3	1.0	0.0
3. Consolidation Bank	14.1	9.8	1.8	44.8	17.2

Table 9 Credits extended by banks (in billions of CSK)*

	1989	1990	1991				1992			
			Q1	Q2	Q3	Q4[3)]	Q1	Q2	Q3	Q4
Total	583.6	640.2	656,0	667.3	695.6	755.7	743.5	780.0	828.5	876.9
Net credit to government	5.9	54.2[1)]	37.9	8.6	11.6[2)]	36.8[2)]	13.4[2)]	22.2	34.2[2)]	66.3[2)]
Net credit to National Property Fund	0.0	0.0	0.9	4.2	11.7	13.7	1.9	0.8	10.3	23.8
Credits to enterprises and households	577.7	586.0	619.0	662.9	695.7	700.0	715.3	746.1	788.9	814.7
Enterprises	530.8	536.0	567.8	611.3	642.6	644.6	659.0	690.2	726.0	748.3
Households	46.9	50.0	51.2	51.6	53.1	55.4	56.3	55.9	62.9	66.4
Credit in foreign exchange	...	...	...	...	...	5.2	12.9	12.5	15.7	19.7

*) End of quarter (year) data

1) Including the effects of devaluations in 1990

2) Including EC, World Bank and G-24 loans to government

3) Including debt-write off and bank recapitalization

Source: Financial Statistical Information, Czech National Bank

The banking system in the Czech Republic after the division of Czechoslovakia into the Czech Republic and the Slovak Republic consists of the central bank - the Czech National Bank - and commercial banks which from the standpoint of capital origin are structured as follows:

The banks in ex-Czechoslovakia developed mostly along the model of an universal type, providing for both commercial and investment banking activitieis. In accordance with the Law on Banks, commercial banks are entitled to acquire shares and stakes up to 10% of the capital of a non-banking institution. The total volume of bank's stakes in non-banking firms should not, however, exceed 25% of its own capital and reserves. To hold stakes exceeding these norms, prior consent of the Central Bank is required. These limits have remained unchanged in the Czech Republic.

4.2. Czech Banking Sector

In 1994 there is only one bank, Konsolidacní Banka, which is fully state-owned and the role of which has been to take over major bad loans from the past that were originally on the credit portfolios of large commercial banks. For this purpose Konsolidacní banka was established and capitalized from the proceeds of privatisation. This operation partially cleared the balance sheets of newly established large commercial banks Komercní banka, Investicní banka and Vseobecná úverová banka (Hrncír, M., Matousek, R., 1994).

The Czech banking system is still highly segmented and concentrated. But the anti-monopoly clause in the Banking Law requires banks to reduce their market shares to maximum 30 per cent by early 1995. Major adjustments are needed: the national savings bank control more than 90 per cent of savings in the market. Komer_ní banka in turn is responsible for about more than 40 per cent of credits. Although the total number of banks is high and possibly even excessive, the money market does not yet operate efficiently enough.

But the activities of the smaller banks are increasing rapidly, they continually increase their share of total bank capital and assets. They are beginning to provide a wider range of banking services and new banking products.

At the same time, the process of despecialization and integration of various "traditionally" separated financial circuits has been taking place, albeit slowly: commercial banks were increasingly engaged in deposit markets, including household savings, and in foreign exchange activities, while savings banks extended their lending activities to firms. (See Table 8 and 9). However, unlike functional integration, the existing territorial segmentation was even exacerbated by the split of the federal state into two political entities, the Czech and Slovak republics.

4.3. Role of the Banking Sector in Privatisation

In the first wave of privatisation, 8,5 million Czech and Slovak citizens (77 per cent of those eligible) participated in the voucher privatisation scheme, bidding for shares of about 1,500 enterprises worth an estimated CSK 300 bn. The second wave started in 1994 is separated by Republics: in Czech Republic it included about 800 enterprises worth about CSK 150 bn.

Participants to privatisation have placed about 72% of their investment points in more than 400 privatisation investment funds (PIFs) and the rest in the shares of individual companies to be privatized. The largest fund is run by the Czech Savings Bank with 9.3 per cent of all points. VUB, the state credit bank in Slovakia, controls the biggest fund in Slovakia. Ranked by size, the leading PIFs are listed below. The PIFs marked with "*" are nonbank funds.

Leading Privatisation Investment Funds in Czechoslovakia

Privatisation Investment Fund	Investment Points (in mill.)
Czech Savings Bank	800
*Harvard Capital and Consulting	640
VUB (General Credit Bank)	500
Investicní banka	450
Komercní banka	400
*Ceské pojistovny (former state insurer)	330
Creditanstalt	220
*First Slovak Fund	160
*First Privatisation Fund	120
Zivnostenská banka	120

Source: Central European, July/August 1992

As bank-controlled funds are not allowed to invest in the capital of other banks, Harvard Capital and Consulting (HC and C) fund has developed a powerful position within the banking sector. HC and C has bought

17.5 per cent of Komerční banka's capital and 13 per cent of the Czech Savings Bank's, the two largest Czech banks by assets.

The Czech Savings Bank, Investicní banka and Komercní banka of the Czech Republic, and Investicní rozvojová banka and Vseobecná úverová banka of Slovakia have all been (partially) privatized through the voucher programme. Civnostenská banka was privatized fully, with a majority stake being sold to BHF Bank and the International Finance Corporation. The foreign trade bank, Ceskoslovenská obchodní banka remains a joint stock company in which the Czech and Slovak National Bank hold a 50.5% stake.

The Investment Privatization Funds will have not only to monitor the companies on their portfolios but delegate their representants to the boards of the companies and provide functions of corporate governance. This way the banking sector tends to play a role similar to that in Germany while the role of "wild" take-overs and individual investors may be of minor importance. The corporate sector seems to be run by the banks more than by the stock exchange.

Aside from the management implications of privatisation, the process also indirectly affects bank asset quality. The main reason is that large state-owned enterprises lost state subsidies once they were privatized, which threatened viability of many of them. Commercial banks as creditors of the privatized companies will find themselves constrained when introducing financial discipline since the same companies are owned by the PIFs established and owned by the banks.

5. Future Developments in the Financial Sectors in Poland and the CSFR

After imposing more restrictive regulation and supervision on the banking sector one may reasonably assume that the banking sector in Poland will enter a period of rationalisation characterised by mergers and acquisitions. Simultaneously privatisation will, especially after the financial restructuring of SOBs and SOEs, progress more rapidly.

The creation of the EC internal market in financial services has been recognized as an important challenge by many non-member countries. The threat stems from two perhaps equally important sources. The first one is related to the possibility of building up a national financial market which is not compatible with standards adopted by in EC countries. The second challenge stems from the expected greater efficiency of institutions established within the Community. The dangers are recognized even by countries with very experienced and widely respected financial sectors such as Switzerland. The countries trying to shift from a centrally planned economy to a market economy should be particularly aware of these challenges, since all of them have inherited very immature financial sectors.

The establishment of efficient wholesale money and interbank markets is essential for the efficient allocation of capital (Mullineux, 1992a, b, c). Active steps should be taken to wean banks off central bank refinancing and the central bank or some other agency, should actively encourage the development of such markets. In Poland, the development bank has been given the responsibility of overseeing the development of the interbank market and the payments system.

The reason that the interbank market is crucial for efficient credit allocation is that it allows banks with a surplus of funds (shortage of lending opportunities) to lend to banks with a shortage of funds (surfeit of lending opportunities). This is particularly important, given the regional orientation of banks, because flows of funds between regions is likely to facilitate restructuring. Additionally, state-owned savings banks traditionally have a surplus of funds. These were previously deposited with the national bank and on-lent to SOEs. In Western banking systems, the savings banks also commonly have a surplus. This is often lent to commercial banks via interbank wholesale money markets; unless the savings banks have their own centralised institutions which can or lend the surplus funds (Mullineux, 1987).

REFERENCES

Basle Agreement (1988), "International Convergence of Capital Measures and Standard", Committee on Bank Regulations and Supervisory Practices, July,. Basle: Bank for International Settlements.

Begg, D. and **Portes, R.** (1992), "Enterprise Debt and Economic Tranformation: Financial Restructuring of the State Sector in Central and Eastern Europe", *CEPR Discussion Paper No. 695*, London: Centre for Economic Policy Research.

Belka, M. and **Mullineux, A.W.** (1993), "Hardening Micro Budget Constraints: Bank Behaviour and Corporate Governance in Poland". *Working paper, EC* (ACE) Project, International Finance Group: University of Birmingham.

Blommenstein H.J., Lange J.R. (1993), "Balance Sheet Restructuring and Privatisation of the Banks". *In: Transforming of the Banking System: Portfolio Restructuring, Privatisation and the Payment System.* Paris, OECD 1993.

Brainard L.J. (1991)

Carlin, W. and **Mayer, C.** (1992), "Restructuring Enterprises in Eastern Europe", *CEPR Discussion Paper No. 700,* London: Centre for Economic Policy Research.

Corbett, J. and **Mayer, C.** (1991), "Financial Reform in Eastern Europe: Progress with the Wrong Model", *Oxford Review of Economic Policy,* 7(4).

Diamond, D. (1984), "Financial Intermediation and Delegated Monitoring", *Review of Economic Studies,* 51.

Dowd, K. (1989), "*The State and the Monetary System*", London: Philip Allan.

Hrncír, M. and **Matousek, R.** (1994), "Banking and Financial Markets in Former Czechoslovakia and in the Czech Republic", Paper presented at conference Financial Reform in Central and Eastern Europe, Prague 1993.

Herr H. et al.: "A Strategy for Economic Transformation and Development in Eastern Europe." *De Pecunia,* vol. 3, Décembre 1991.

Lacoue - Labarthe, D. (1992), "Setting up a Safe and Sound Banking System in Central and Eastern European Economies", *International Finance Group Working Paper* (IFGWP-92-07), University of Birmingham.

Lampe, J.R. (ed.) (1992), "*Creating Capital Markets in Eastern Europe*", Baltimore, Maryland: The John Hopkins University Press.

Mullineux, A.W. (1987), *"International Banking and Financial Systems: A Comparison"*, London: Graham and Trotman.

Mullineux, A.W. (1992a), "Hard Budget Constraints, Credit Crunches, and Central Bank Independence", *University of Wales Business and Economic Review,* No. 8 (Jan/Feb)

Mullineux, A.W. (1992b), "Banking Privatisation and Restructuring in Poland", *University of Wales Business and Economic Review,* No. 9/10

Mullineux, A.W. (1992c), "Privatisation and Financial Structure in Eastern and Central European Countries", *National Westminster Bank Quarterly Review,* May, 1992

Mullineux, A.W. (1992d), "Privatisation and Small Business Financing in the U.K. and Germany: Lessons for Central and Eastern Europe", *Anglo-German Foundational Report,* August, London: Anglo-German Foundation.

Mullineux, A.W. (1993), "Bank Regulation, Uncertainty and Business Cycles", in: *Risk and Uncertainty in Economics: Essays in Honour of James L. Ford*", Forthcoming 1993/4, Cheltenham: Edward Edgar.

Pecchioli, R.M. (1987), "Prudential Supervision of Banks", Paris: OECD

Rybczynski, T.M. (1986), "The U.K. Financial System in Transition", *National Westminster Bank Quarterly Review*, November, 1986

Rybczynski, T.M. (1991), "The Sequences of Reform", *Oxford Review of Economic Policy*, 7(4), 1991

Stiglitz, J.E. and **Weiss A.** (1981), "Credit Rationing in Markets with Imperfect Information", *American Economic Review*, 71.

Thorne, A. (1992), "Reforming Finanical System in Eastern Europe: The Case of Bulgaria", Chapter 6, in: *Lampe* (1992)

Banking and Financial Markets in Former Czechoslovakia and in the Czech Republic*

Miroslav Hrnčíř and Roman Matoušek
Institute of Economics
Czech National Bank, Prague

Summary

The article evaluates the process of financial liberalization in former Czechoslovakia and argues why the banks are to play the key role in financial intermediation. Resulting both from the legacy of the past and from the impact of transition the phenomena of banks' undercapitalization and bad loans coupled with interenterprise arrears proved to be structural constraints in all transition economies. Though in the Czechoslovak case addressed by the policies since the early stage, they could be only alleviated, not solved. The evidence also showed a persistent lack of effective competitive pressure and only a very slow increase of new banks' market share, despite dramatic growth of banking institutions, including foreign ones. Nevertheless, compared to other transition economies, a substantial advance was achieved in privatisation and restructuring of banking institutions and in deregulation of

* Prepared for the conference "Financial Reform in Central and Eastern Europe," Prague, September 1993.

financial intermediation including interest rates. There was also a remarkable shift of credit allocation to the emerging private sector. The fundamental issue concerns the type and structure of the evolving banking system, the role of banks in the corporate governance and in the firms restructuring. While the adopted banking law allows for universal type of banks, the Czech banks remained as yet cautious in their engagement in the enterprise sphere. However, the investment privatisation funds established by financial institutions, and by commercial banks in particular, acquired a dominating stake in voucher privatisation. A special type of cross-ownership thus seems to be evolving, with potential benefits but also risk involved.

1. Introduction

The key importance of workable factor markets for the entire transition and for its ultimate success has been underlined by a number of observers since its early stages (Hinds M., 1990). These markets were effectively lacking under the former centrally planned economy framework, they form, however, the core of any market economy. It applies in particular to financial markets and to financial intermediation. The degree of efficiency in allocation and reallocation of savings to prospective users is of utmost importance for growth potentials of the given economy. Hence, the more flexible and rational allocation of disposable resources is mediated through the emerging financial markets, the better are the prospects for the given economy in transition.

Compared to the initial conditions, a substantial progress has been accomplished within the relatively short period of a few transition years since the end of 1980s. Referring to the group of Visegrad countries, i.e. Hungary, Poland, Czech and Slovak Republics, these countries can be claimed to have their financial and banking systems already closer to market framework. Nevertheless, even in these relatively most advanced transition economies the degree of functional efficiency and competitiveness in financial markets evidently lagged behind the demands and expectations.

The underdevelopment, weaknesses and constraints of factor markets in the emerging market economies (EMEs), and of financial markets in particular, came to the foreground in connection with the "real" economy developments. Compared to the reform scenarios and expectations the fall of economic activity was everywhere deeper and more protracted in the initial transition period, and the signals of economic recovery, though differentiated across individual countries, remained mostly only vague in 1992 and 1993.

Identifying the causal factors, both "insiders" and foreign observers pointed to the impact of the financial markets' constraints. "Savings that is urgently needed to lay the foundation for future growth is being wasted by banks' lending to loss-making enterprises". (Dittus P., 1993, p. 15). And Abel and Bonin conclude: "The failure of credit markets in the Central and East European countries is the primary reason for the stalled transition," (Abel I., Bonin J.P., 1993, p. 6).

Just the links and interactions between financial markets and the "real" economy developments, and not so much the state of financial markets per se became a matter of concern and discussion.

The constraining impact of the financial sphere on the economies of transition countries materialized in a number of ways, in particular due to

- misallocation of disposable savings, which was claimed to result especially from the traditional ties between old banks and state owned enterprises, at the cost of the newly emerging private firms and other more prospective users,
- rigidity and low functional efficiency of credit markets and banking institutions, associated with the lack of expertise, qualified personnel and distorted incentives, and coupled with the unsolved legacy of the past (banks' undercapitalization and bad loans in their portfolios). The interaction of these factors caused the spread between banks' lending and borrowing rates in EMEs too wide and the implied price of credits too high,
- lack of alternative sources of financing, in particular of long-term funds. Capital markets have been only emerging and remained as yet too limited and too thin to provide a real option. The long term savings continued to be scarce, both because of underdeveloped institutional framework and due to only gradually increasing range of marketed products.

If persistent, the identified defects and constraints of financial intermediation would represent a serious "comparative disadvantage" of EMEs. In such a case the prospects of their recovery and of sustainable growth would remain rather gloomy. Consequently, both external and domestic observers seemed to agree that financial markets and financial intermediation were the spheres where a further radical advance was most urgently needed. The "second" financial and banking reform thus appeared to be on the agenda (Lacoue-Labarthe D., 1993).

The discussion is concentrated in particular on banks and on their functional efficiency and stability. This reflects the emerging consensus that the banks are and should be the core of financial systems in the course of transition, and especially in its early stages (Mullineux A., Belka M., 1993). The relevant issue is therefore not whither banks, but what types of banks and what to change in their conditions, environment and incentives to secure a more satisfactory standard of financial intermediation in EMEs.

Should the established "old" banks continue to play their dominant role, providing their restructuring, privatisation and changed incentives (Dittus P., 1993) or should it be increasingly relied upon the newly emerging banks and their developments supported (Phelps E.S. et al., 1993) or better to "import" banking institutions from the West (Schmieding H., Buch C., 1992).

A related strategic issue is what type of banking system is to be aimed at in EMEs and what role the banking institutions could and should play in the "real" economy and in the corporate governance in the transition period. The universal type of banks, implying integration of commercial and investment banking, is increasingly given preference in the literature discussing transition economies (Saunders A., Walter I., 1991). This model is consistent with the trend in the EC countries as reflected in the 2nd EC Banking Directive which provided for a broad range of banking activities. Also the legislation in EMEs seemed to mostly follow the option of universal banking, as documented for example by the Polish and Czech banking laws.

Nevertheless, there are also significant risks and constraints implied in the adoption of universal banking in transition economies. Along with the arguments of general relevance, pointing to the moral hazard problem, potential conflict of interest and of monopoly position of conglomerate financial institutions in the economy, in the specific conditions of EMEs the given model could also imply the risk of keeping afloat non-viable firms. The re-emergence of such a "traditional" behaviour pattern would be just the opposite of what should be aimed at in the transition countries (Hare P., 1992).

Could and should be these issues discussed as parallel to all transition economies and, consequently, a common solution searched for?

On the one hand it is true that all the EMEs still have to cope with the common constraints inherited from the past as well as with those arising in the process of institutional changes and restructuring in the course of transition. In this respect the goals of the second financial and banking reform should also be mostly parallel in all EMEs.

At the same time, however, the transition economies of Central and Eastern Europe became much more differentiated compared with the conditions of the "first" financial reform when the two-tier banking systems were introduced. Also the policies addressing bad, non-performing loans, undercapitalization of banks and interenterprise arrears, to name just the dominant common structural constraints, widely diverged in the instruments used and in their timing even across relatively homogeneous group of Visegrad countries.[1] It follows, the reform options available for individual countries, their viability as well as their costs and benefits are increasingly related to the specific features and characteristics of a particular transition economy.

Against this background, the article examines the case of former Czechoslovakia and of the Czech Republic. It identifies the interrelated dimensions of their financial intermediation and financial markets' developments: structural constraints inherited from the past, institutional changes and the policies adopted. The pros and cons, benefits and costs of the Czech approach are evaluated compared to the other options. The article concludes with the discussion of the potential role of banks in the "real" economy and in corporate governance.

2. Legacy of the Past: An Unsolved Issue

The occurrence of bad loans, debt contract failures, interfirm arrears, bankruptcies and banking crises is certainly not confined to the EMEs. Just the recent recession of early 1990s provided a tough lesson on the impact of the "real" economy developments on the stability and soundness of even already well established financial and banking systems in a number of developed market economies. For example, the banking systems of Nordic countries were particularly hit by the evolving crisis (Nyberg P., Vihriäla V., 1993).

There were parallel factors affecting market and transition economies recently: both types of economies were exposed to a number of exogenous and endogenous constraints, including recession abroad as well as in the domestic economy, to external shocks, to the failed or asymmetric regulation. Despite these parallels, the nature, intensity and impact of debt contract failures in EMEs substantially differed from the situation in market economies.

2.1. What Made the Situation in the EMEs Specific?

The apparent distinguishing difference was a wider range of unfavourable factors affecting EMEs in the given time span, their intensity and time dimensions. Against predominantly "only" cyclical character of the recession in the

[1] For the identification and evaluation of the Polish policies and developments see Belka M., Pruski J., Raczko A., 1992; Bauc J., Grabowski B., Raczko A., 1992.

West, though more severe than the previous ones, these were mostly structural causes of the fall of economic activity in the EMEs.

However, the decisive difference affecting the developments in the EMEs seems to be the legacy of the past. This legacy included not only inherited bad loans and accumulated interenterprise arrears, but also institutional and behaviour legacy.

In the established regime of a "standard" market economy any firm has both positive and negative incentives to comply with the "code of behaviour" requiring, among other, to honour debt contracts at their maturity. Under the rules of the game, the options are in principle either adjustment or bankruptcy and exit. This is implied in the tradition, in behaviour habits and in the shared expectations, and such a behaviour code is supported by the established institutional and legal infrastructure.

Unlike market economies, these institutional and behaviour preconditions for maintaining and enforcing the market code of behaviour were mostly missing in the initial stage of transition in EMEs.

The increasing occurrence of debt contract failures and interenterprise arrears in EMEs were not "matched" by the corresponding actions, including bankruptcy procedures, against defaulting clients. In the given environment, neither banks nor suppliers were ready to initiate such procedures. Their apparent "passivity" in enforcing credit contracts (Begg D., Portes R., 1992) had, however,a number of interrelated grounds.

Because of the legacy of the developments under centrally planned framework, there was hardly any correlation between the "state of accounts" of individual firms and their "real" financial standing, and even less with their medium-term prospects. The existing non-transparent situation of individual firms made almost impossible any clear-cut distinction between their illiquidity and insolvency.

Given the extent of disarrays in payments flows and of overlapping claims and liabilities from the past, the suppliers could hardly ex-ante properly assess the payments moral and credibility of their clients. However, even more important proved to be the inertia of "traditional" behaviour pattern of state owned enterprises. They were accustomed to supply the goods without devoting proper care to the risk of failed payments. This tendency "to go on with the supplies" appeared even exacerbated under the pressure of the diminishing domestic and foreign markets in the beginning of 1990s. Many Czech firms, for example, were reported to continue their exports to the former USSR in 1991 in a "routine way" irrespective of the fact that the institutional framework of the COMECON trading was already phased out.

In a parallel way, the debtors' conditions and response were also controversial. On the one hand, a good deal of them were constrained by the payments arrears of their own clients. At the same time they were not induced to do their utmost to meet the obligations of the contracts. Some evidence has been accumulated that in the given environment even the firms which were neither insolvent nor illiquid deliberately joined for some time the "club" of overdue debtors, including private firms and joint-ventures. By not paying at maturity they in fact drew a cheap credit, cheaper than in commercial banks (if available at all).

The passivity of commercial banks in enforcing the credit contracts was also conditioned by their own fragile situation, given their sub-standard capital/assets ratios, substantial share of non-performing loans in the portfolios, along with initially non-existent or only rather limited loan-loss provisions (Lacoue-Labarthe D., 1993). As a result, the "old" commercial banks appeared to be dependent on the survival of their major clients.

The desirable institutional and legal framework, though differently advanced across individual EMEs, could be developed and made effective only gradually. In former Czechoslovakia only a step-wise approach was also adopted in the implementation of bankruptcy legislation. The bankruptcy law approved by the Parliament in autumn 1991 was to enter into force on October 1, 1991. The extent of its enforcement was, however, constrained by a "blocking" article, effectively allowing to start bankruptcy procedure only in the special case of "overindebtedness". Though scheduled for full applicability since autumn 1992, it was once more postponed until April 1993 and, at the same time, its provisions amended by the new reading in the Czech Parliament at the beginning of 1993. These amendments introduced a number of safeguards, including e.g. the institution of a three months grace period, aimed at avoiding "domino effect" and uncontrolled chain of bankruptcies.

The reasoning behind such a cautious approach was to reconcile the intensity of the given law's impact with the underlying institutional and economic conditions of the particular development stage. Despite the efforts to proceed with the privatisation process as quickly as possible, allocating a substantial role to the voucher scheme and giving thus the preference to the speed compared to its other dimensions, the large-scale privatisation proved to be inevitably a longer-term process. In the relevant period of 1992 and the beginning of 1993, the first wave of voucher privatisation was only under way, delayed compared to the scenarios.

Summarizing, the microeconomic foundations for a market economy regime and for enforcing its rules of the game have been mostly missing in the first transition phase. Moreover, the still underdeveloped infrastructure, including courts facilities, was seen as an important constraining factor. That's why the amendments to the bankruptcy law provided among other for the outside-court solutions. The aim was to give way to the bankruptcy procedures and to make effective the implied incentives, avoiding at the same time the unnecessary high costs, given the existing institutional constraints.

The specific features affecting the occurrence of debt-contract failures in the initial development stage of EMEs should be seen in the lacking microeconomic and institutional pre-requisites, which could secure both the incentives to adhere to the conditions of the contracts as well as the means to enforce them. In the given environment, the "old" bad loans and debt contract failures inherited from the past interacted with the "new" ones, arising in the course of transition itself.

These are also the reasons why bad loans and debt contract failures in EMEs, unlike market economies, became a widespread, mass phenomenon and acquired persistent, structural character, not only a cyclical one. As a result, the "disease" proved to be long-term and contagious one.

2.2. Undercapitalization of Banks, Non-Performing Loans and Interenterprise Appears in Former Czechoslovakia

In 1990, at the start of banking reform in former Czechoslovakia and when two-tier system was introduced, there were only 7 banks operating (against 55 registered towards the end of 1992 when Czechoslovakia was dissolved and 54 registered in the Czech Republic in September 1993, of which 50 commenced operations). All these 7 banks were undercapitalized and at the same time burdened with the inherited non-performing loans and/or credits extended at artificially low interest rates. Assessed by the international standards, they were all technically insolvent.

The two largest banks, Commercial Bank, Praha and General Credit Bank, Bratislava which took over the established network of the former mono-bank, started their activities at a rather unfavourable capital adequacy ratio (i.e. the ratio of own capital to assets) of only about 1 1/2 percent. The respective ratios of savings banks were even lower, around 1 percent.

These figures highlighted the fragility of the emerging banking system. The two mentioned banks formed the substantial part of the entire commercial banking, their combined share amounted to 68 percent of total bank credits and 25 percent on total deposits at the end of 1990.

However, the real situation was even gloomier, as there was hardly any reliable loan-risk classification applied at that time. According to the available estimates, after the start of the stabilization and liberalization programme in early 1991, about 1/4 of the outstanding loans could be qualified as either bad, non-performing loans or loans with high risk involved.

The non-performing and risky credits were not confined to domestic clients, a specific feature of ex-Czechoslovakia was a relatively high share of bad loans incurred in foreign trade deals. Though in nominal terms in a better shape than other commercial banks, the balance-sheets of Czechoslovak Trade Bank, a joint stock company, which in the past almost exclusively effected foreign exchange payments and deals, were also heavily burdened with questionable claims. These were mostly linked to various forms of bilateral trading and to government credits extended in the past.

The initial situation of emerging banking sector in former Czechoslovakia was therefore not particularly sound. The capital /assets ratio of the existing banks with mostly inherited portfolio from the mono-bank institutions was not only far from meeting the international standards, but it appeared also significantly less favourable with respect to the Polish and Hungarian conditions.[2] The banks' undercapitalization, coupled with uncertainty about the real performance of a substantial share of their portfolios inevitably implied severe constraints on the functional capabilities and behaviour of existing commercial banks, in particular with respect to the defaulting clients.

The deficiencies in the banking sphere has been in the post-communist countries interrelated with the increasing burden of interenterprise arrears. Irrespective of the concrete conditions and policies of individual countries, their nominal volume surged in the first "stabilization stage" of transition.

The interpretation of these developments was, however, far from being unambiguous. On the one hand, there were apparently some parallel features with trade credit which is quite common in market economies. Referring to its dimensions in developed market economies the argument was raised that, at least to some extent, the proliferation of interenterprise indebtedness in the EMEs was a spontaneous correction to the previous conditions under which trade credits were not officially allowed (Begg D., Portes R., 1992).

However, the type of monitoring and the criteria used were not capable to distinguish "voluntary" and "involuntary" forms of indebtedness and to draw

---

[2] In Poland high inflation rates of 1989 and 1990 effectively eroded real value of the former enterprise debts. This may explain that a substantial deterioration of capital/assets ratio was reported to have taken place only afterwards (Compare: Poland, OECD Survey, 1992).
In Hungary, the "norm" of 8 percent risk weighted capital/assets ratio recommended by BIS was at the beginning of 1990s targetted already for 1993, as indicated by Hungarian sources.

a dividing line between them. The interenterprise arrears mushroomed in the given time span under the pressure of deep recession, of restrictive stance of macroeconomic policies and diminishing sales in both domestic and foreign markets. Consequently, they were apparently mostly of an "induced" character. As such they differed from the institution of trade credit, interfering with the "rules of the game" and with the market type code of behaviour.

In former Czechoslovakia, the volume of interenterprise arrears has been increasing with some ups and downs since the early 1970s. Substantial increases were registered in 1981-82 and again in 1987, i.e. in periods when the monetary authorities tried to tighten credit policies.[3]

An unprecedented sharp increase has developed since the second half of 1990. As follows from Table 1, the mentioned trend even accelerated in the course of 1991 and at the beginning of 1992.

At the end of 1991, the identified sum of interenterprise indebtedness amounted to CSK 170 bn, i.e. to 1/4 of total banks' credits extended to enterprises. 4,723 firms (from the total of 11,043) e.i. 43 percent, showed payments arrears to other firms.

The data in Table 1 include the split into the "primary" and "secondary" indebtedness. Primary arrears or primary indebtedness is identified as the state in which an enterprise's overdue payables are greater than its overdue receivables. The secondary indebtedness or secondary arrears includes all its overdue payables

Table 1: Interenterprise arrears in former Czechoslovakia (in bn CSK, end period)

	Inter-enterprise		indebtednes	Number of firms	
	Total	Primary	Secondary	Total	Indebted
June 1989	16.3	-	-	-	-
December 1989	6.6	3.2	3.4	1,522	460
June 1990	14.5	7.8	6.7	4,728	727
September 1990	24.9	12.4	12.5	5,566	1,106

[3] For the data on interenterprise arrears in former Czechoslovakia in the period 1982-1990 see Hrnčíř M., Klacek J., 1991.

Table 1 (Continued)

December 1990	47.8	20.0	27.8	4,827	1,651
March 1991	76.7	27.1	49.6	7,388	2,766
June 1991	124.3	35.0	89.3	8,201	3,587
September 1991	147.2	36.0	111.2	9,109	3,960
December 1991	170.7	37.8	133.0	11,043	4,723
March 1992	170.5	35.9	134.5	n.a.	n.a.
June 1992	165.2	37.8	127.4	n.a.	n.a.
September 1992	154.6	35.3	119.3	n.a.	n.a.

Source: Financial indicators, Federal Ministry of Finance[*)]

The data on interenterprise indebtedness were based on two different sources:

- bank data were only available until March, 1991. Since then, with the changes in payments regime, banks have not been obliged any more to accept bills for payments against an enterprise, given insufficient funds on its account with the particular bank. As a result, the bank data ceased to reflect the entire volume of payments in arrears,
- since the first quarter of 1991 until September 1991, the available official source are enterprise data as collected by Ministry of Finance. After this date the official institutions, including Statistical Office, as well as the banks discontinued the publicly available evidence on enterprise indebtedness. All data referring to later periods are based only on estimates, sample surveys and expert evaluations.

which could be covered by its overdue receivables.[4] As follows from Table 1, since the beginning of 1991, i.e. since the start of macroeconomic stabilization and liberalization programmes, the increases of interenterprise arrears were due to its secondary form, i.e. due to the increasing clients' failures to honour their obligations to suppliers at maturity.

---

[4] The data represent the cumulative amount of liabilities of firms in payments arrears, the asset counterpart is not identified. It follows, the respective amount of outstanding liabilities does not imply the corresponding overhang of liabilities of the Czechoslovak economy as a whole vis-a-vis the rest of the world.

Though unprecedented, the identified trend of interenterprise arrears was much less dramatic in real terms, when corrected for price level increases.

Table 2: Nominal and real changes in interenterprise arrears (in bn CSK)

Year	Producer Price Index[1)]	Increase [+] (Decrease [-]) of interenterprise arrears	
		Nominal[2)]	Real[2)]
1990	117.1	+41.2	+35.2
1991	154.8	+122.9	+79.4
1992	108.4	-15.1[*)]	-13.9[*)]

1) As against previous year
2) As against December of previous year
*) September 1992

As already mentioned, there are no consistent official data on interenterprise arrears covering the recent period. This is in particular due to the extensive institutional and ownership changes taking place which precluded the prolongation of the former time series. At the same time, in the changing conditions the relevant issue shifted to the developments of overall indebtedness of all economic agents, and not only of its interenterprise segment.

The estimates of such a wider coverage of indebtedness in former Czechoslovakia identified its volume around CSK 300 bn in 1992, while for the Czech Republic alone in the range of CK 170-220 bn (compare Ptáček J., 1993).

With respect to the interenterprise arrears only, the available evidence seemed to suggest - with all the reservations to the respective data - that since the second half of 1992 their volume in the Czech Republic was not increasing any more, not even in nominal terms, showing rather some tendency to contract. Nevertheless, its extent coupled with bad loans in banks' portfolios continued to be potentially serious destabilizing factor.[5]

---

5 The issue of interenterprise arrears has been extensively discussed in Hungary as "queuing" (Estrin S., Hare P., Suranyi M., 1992). I. Abel reported that the amount of interenterprise credits in Hungary increased at the end of November 1991 to HUF 160 bn (extending on 1,017 enterprises). According to the author, this sum only included payments arrears above HUF 25 million. Those non-recorded arrears were estimated to amount to HUF 168 bn as of July 1991 (Abel I., 1992). Despite such an extent of the arrears, the situation was reported to change dramatically with the introduction of new bankruptcy law in 1992. The "queuing" ceased to be a major issue.

2.3. Options in Coping with the Legacy of the Past

In coping with the legacy of centrally planned economy in principle two alternative strategies could be adopted:

a) to draw a clear dividing line with the past at the early stage of transition, i.e. to eliminate monetary overhang and to clean the balance-sheets of banks and firms once they were still only parts of the all-comprising state sector,

b) to postpone the principal solution to the privatisation phase and to the follow-up restructuring of the privatised enterprises.

The former approach addresses the inherited stock first, aiming to avoid its distorting impact on the emerging flows.

The latter one, on the other hand, leaves the accumulated stock untouched, relying on partial corrections via flows and on "muddling through" until privatisation takes place.

The companies' results in the past, their balance-sheets, profits and liabilities had hardly any correlation with their current "standing" in the changed conditions and even less with their potentials. The merit of the strategy eliminating inherited financial liabilities at the very beginning of transition was therefore seen in the "levelling of the grounds", with the assumption that once not locked-in, both banks and enterprises could proceed in accordance with rational criteria and incentives, addressing the present problems instead of being absorbed and constrained by the consequences of the distorted past.

This was also the rationale behind the former approach. Its conclusions underlined the importance of banks' balance-sheets cleaning and re-capitalization (Brainard L.J., 1991). The sooner they are accomplished, the better are the prospects for economic recovery.

The crucial constraint of this approach was the dominance of the state ownership in both banking and non-banking institutions at the start of the transition. It made any write-off and re-capitalisation subject to risk of an unchanged behaviour pattern and of an early re-emergence of the former ills.

At the same time it also implied the moral hazard problem once it would not be perfectly clear that the bail-out was strictly once-for-all measure.

Within the framework of the mentioned approach a number of options have been suggested, including currency reform, general or partial debt cancellation, debt "socialization" via some form of debt swaps: debt (bad) for debt (good), debt for equity, debt for bonds, debt for savings.

Though intensively discussed in literature, neither the option of currency reform (suggested e.g. by Herr H., et al., 1991, apparently with some reminiscence on the favourable follow-ups of the German monetary reform of 1948), nor the general cancellation of the old debts or their transformation via some form of debt swaps have been adopted in any transition economy.

The comparative advantage of the latter approach was the link between privatisation and implementation of re-capitalization and financial restructuring. Privatisation, though not panacea solving alone the issue of corporate governance, provides for a clear identification and enforcement of property rights and for the changed incentives in both banks and enterprises. In the course of time, more and more observers highlighted this link as a necessary pre-requisite for success (See e.g. Begg D., Portes R., 1992).

The drawback of this approach was the implied time span of "policy vacuum" in dealing with the debts and bad loans accumulated in the past. Given their impact on the flows not alleviated, the volume of bad loans was likely to increase and the occurrence of debt contract failures further disseminated. The resulting risk was the increased destabilization of payments flows and a worsened payments moral in the interim period. The longer such a period, the higher the costs incurred.

2.4. "Stock" Versus "Flows" Policies in Ex-Czechoslovakia and in the Czech Republic: A Pragmatic Compromise

Czechoslovak authorities initially did not foresee any "interference" at all into the inherited stock of enterprise liabilities, until at least the first wave of voucher privatisation was over.

This stance was based on the assumption that a quick mass-scale privatisation can be and will be accomplished, in particular through voucher scheme. At the same time, the potential "interim" measures such as the efforts to change incentives of the management, "commercialisation" of the state firms and their transformation into legally separate entities were not considered capable to harden the state firms' budget constraint and, accordingly, the government did not intend to resort to them in any considerable extent.

However, the prolonged privatisation horizon compared to the initial expectations, as well as the emerging constraints in the flow of funds and the increasing disarray in financial intermediation prompted the authorities to implement a number of interim pragmatic measures.

The initial policy stance notwithstanding, ex-Czechoslovakia took the lead among transition economies in correcting the legacy of the past. The steps effected included in particular:

(I) The Establishment of Consolidation Bank

Consolidation Bank, a form of recovery agency, was founded by the Ministry of Finance and the Central Bank in March 1991 with the assignment to manage the state's long term assets. Its immediate role was, however, to take over "perpetual credits for inventories" from the balance-sheets of commercial banks.

These special "credits" (extended without any fixed maturity and at an artificially low interest rate fixed at 6 per cent) supplanted firms' funds confiscated by the government's budgetary authorities in the early 1970s. As its first big "deal" Consolidation Bank took over substantial part of these credits, amounting to CSK 110 billion, i.e. to almost 1/5 of the total bank credits then extended to enterprises and households.

The transfer was relatively easy to effect as it concerned in principle only two banks, Commercial Bank, Praha and General Credit Bank, Bratislava and, besides, the perpetual credits for inventories as a "special class" could be easily sorted out. Though the whole volume of these credits could not be labelled "bad loans" (part of them has been afterwards already recovered by the Consolidation Bank), the move contributed to clean balance-sheets of the mentioned banks.

Only later on Consolidation Bank extended its activities on the "normal" non-standard (classified) loans. Unlike the above identified mass shift, commercial banks had to negotiate their transfer from the balance-sheets on case by case basis and to arrive to an agreement on the discount in the deal, incurring thus some nominal losses. To support these activities, Consolidation Bank was recapitalised by the National Property Fund, drawing on the proceeds from privatisation.

(II) Recapitalization of Commercial Banks

Though discussed from the start of transition, the decision to recapitalize "big" commercial banks which took over their portfolios from the former mono-bank system was taken by the authorities only in October 1991, i.e. almost two years after the introduction of two-tier system. Financed from the privatisation proceeds, the amount of CSK 50 billion (i.e. equal to about 8 per cent of all bank credits to enterprises) was allocated for banks' recapitalization and write-offs through debt-for-bond swaps.

A part of the sum (CSK 12 billion) was earmarked to increase the banks' own capital, and the major part (CSK 38 billion) was given for write-offs of non-performing loans. The aim the banks were expected to follow was to write-off liabilities of such firms which, according to the banks' appraisal, had a good chance to survive given the bail-out and the given bank would be ready to extend them new credits.

The bonds allocated for the swap should be repaid from the privatisation means or, alternatively, exchanged for the equities in the privatized companies.

(III) Netting Out Companies' Bilateral and Multilateral Arrears

Commercial Bank, and later on specialized institutions, including private ones, took the initiative to net out mutual overdue obligations of enterprises. Though of some impact, the netting activities had also their constraints. They could address only the symptoms of the problem, and not its causes. Moreover, they increasingly interfered with the companies' policies and preferences. With regard to these drawbacks, the "obligatory" netting of the mutual overdue obligations was discontinued in the second half of 1993.

The impact of the above identified steps aimed to cope with the inherited bad loans and payments arrears appeared to be rather ambiguous. Controversial are also its assessments.

The measures taken were only resorted to under the growing pressure and targetted just to alleviate the most sensitive constraints emerging. Moreover, they were adopted and executed as an induced "deviation" from the government's policy stance which linked the principal solution only with privatisation.

Not getting rid of it, the "stock" continued to be a constraint, and its impact on "flows" did materialize in the follow-up period. Being feeded-in by the side-effects of the stabilization policies and by both external and domestic shocks, the credit contract failures and interenterprise arrears persisted on a mass scale. The intensity of bad debt problem remained unrelieved. This would evidently develop even if, instead of only partial solutions, a more radical clean-up of banks' portfolios and entire cancellation of all past debts were effected.

Table 3: Risk Credits, Reserves and Provisions of the Banking Institutions in the Czech Republic

	12/92	3/93	6/93	9/93
Credits total[1)]	571.4	597.9	631.8	654.4
Risk credits total	110.0	133.8	139.7	149.4
of which				
(i) temporary illiquid claims	62.5	70.0	24.2[+)]	28.1
(ii) sub-standard and non-performing loans	47.5	63.8	115.5[+)]	121.3
of which				
- non-performing loans	21.4	14.0	35.2	40.8
% share of risk credits on total credits	19.3	22.4	22.1	22.8
Reserves	45.3	49.9	54.5	61.1
- reserves against losses	16.5	19.6	23.7	28.8
- banks reserve funds (from profits)	28.8	30.3	30.8	32.3
Loan-loss provisions	11.5	11.5	11.4	11.4
% share of reserves and provisions on risk credits	51.5	45.9	47.1	48.5

[1)] Bank credits to firms and households extended in domestic currency, in CK bn

[+)] The shift in the relative weight between the first and second sub-category of risk credits in the second quarter of 1993 was due to the changed classification. As the similar corrections in classification were made also earlier, the significant one in the third quarter of 1992, the data for the individual types of risk credits are not consistent in the time series. On the other hand, thanks hanks in particular to the obligatory external auditing of banks' accounts, the reliability of the available data has been increasing.

Source: Czech National Bank, own calculations

As follows from Table 3, the volume of risk credits, i.e. classified, non-standard loans amounted in the Czech Republic in 1993 to more than 1/5 of total banks' credits extended to firms and households in domestic currency, and this share tended to increase further in the course of the year.

Such a share, i.e. in the range of 1/5 to 1/4 of total bank credits, was often referred to by external observers as the figure representing the volume of non-performing loans in Czechoslovakia. Blommenstein and Lange e.g. in the OECD study quoted 21% (Blommenstein H.J., Lange J.R., 1993). The assessment of the real extent of bad, non-performing loans in transition economies could be hardly precise and unambigous, given all the qualifications as for data classification and evaluation. Nevertheless, the concept of risk credits, as used in the Czech banking statistics, should cover all the types of classified loans, of which bad, non-performing loans are only one, the "worst" sub-category.

From the point of view of the "stock" approach, the measures taken were only partial, compromised and, moreover, delayed. To avoid moral hazard problem, the banks' re-capitalization should be "once-for-all" action. As only a partial solution was effected, there was a risk implied that the re-capitalization will have to be repeated.

On the other hand, the steps to correct for the legacy of the past were taken at an earlier stage compared to other EMEs and, while not solving the problem, they evidently alleviated its intensity. It seemed to be important particularly in the case of former Czechoslovakia where, unlike some other transition economies, relatively lower inflation rates had not eroded so much the weight of the past debts compared to the current ones.

3. The Quest for Functional Efficiency and Stability of the Banking System

The properties which should be secured in any financial and banking system can be grouped into two dimensions: functional efficiency and safety and stability. As discussed by Saunders and Walter, all the systems in Western market economies, however differentiated in their forms they may be, seek to secure simultaneously static (allocational) and dynamic efficiency (in financial innovations and in accelerated rates of capital formation) and, at the same time, safe and sound financial intermediation (Saunders A., Walter I., 1991).

The main driving force for the enhancement of functional efficiency is definitely competition. Not so much in the Marshallian, but rather in the Schumpeterian sense, i.e. what matters are the incentive aspects of workable, contestable competition. If weak and too constrained, the functional efficiency is not likely to advance. If too tough on the other hand, it may become destructive in its pressure on profit margins and capital, with the resulting chain of bank crises and/or bails out, in each case undermining the stability of the entire banking system and the public confidence.

The assessments of the financial markets in EMEs more or less unanimously highlighted the absence of effective competitive pressure (see e.g. OECD Survey on Czech and Slovak Federal Republic, 1991; Schmieding H., Buch C., 1992; Corbett J., Mayer C., 1991). The evidence for this conclusion was provided, among other, by the existence of banks' high nominal profits, in the early stage of transition sometimes even super-normal (however artificial they could be in reality). High profit margins co-existed with the persistently low standard of banking services, with only gradual extension of the range of products offered to the clients, with overstaffing and high operating costs of the "profitable" banks. As the main source of these profits was the spread between the banks' borrowing and lending interest rates, the argument was that these spreads could be maintained significantly higher than the customary 1-2 percent on competitive money markets of developed economies just because of the low competitive pressure.

Notwithstanding, despite technical insolvency of most existing banks according to the international standards and despite the dramatic fall in economic activity in all transition economies, the banking sector seemed to be stable in the initial stage of transition. The grounds for such a stability could be, however, only temporary. Because of the continued state "umbrella" in the banking institutions, low competitive pressure and almost no occurrence of bankruptcies in the "real" economy, keeping the entire business sector "afloat", the banks were not exposed to the real tests.

However, though differentiated across individual countries, the policies and developments initiated in the first transition stage started to work towards enhanced efficiency in both "real" and financial spheres. The state authorities were increasingly "relieved" from their previous ownership functions, privatisation programmes were initiated, competitive pressure gradually became stronger and the occurrence of companies' bankruptcies increased. As a consequence of the changes, the inherent fragility of the former "stable" banking system was revealed. The ensuing developments and the policies aiming at increased efficiency inevitably eroded status quo. To cope with the changed conditions and to comply with the targets of prudential regulation, the banks were induced to increase the allocations for reserves and for loan-loss provisions. This explains, why despite a tougher competitive pressure the interest spreads continued to widen in transition economies rather than to narrow (for ex-Czechoslovakia and the Czech Republic compare Table 4; for the data on Hungary see Abel I., Szekely I.P., 1993) and, at the same time, banks' profits margins showed a decreasing tendency (according to the International Accountancy Standard (IAS) they turned mostly to the red).

It follows, the "stability" of financial and banking systems which came into existence after the first wave of reforms was rather constrained, not sustainable, and linked with low competitive pressure and low functional efficiency. The established balance was thus of a "bad equilibrium" type. The challenge of the transition was to accomplish the shift from the "bad equilibrium" to a "better" one.

3.1. The Shift in the Challenge: From Macroeconomic Stabilization to Microeconomic Adjustment

At the very start of transition, former Czechoslovakia adopted shock-like approach to macroeconomic stabilization and to price, foreign trade and foreign exchange liberalization. At the same time, it launched the programme of a mass privatisation, including privatisation of banking institutions. Though delayed compared to the initial aspirations, the steps implemented along this programme pushed the country well ahead in the process of institutional and ownership changes, both in "real" and financial spheres.

However, after passing from the stage of "macroeconomic stabilization and liberalization" to the "adjustment and consolidation" stage with the dominant institutional and microeconomic developments, the policies adopted a more gradual, step-wise pattern. The aim of both the government and the Central Bank was to maintain the balanced course of their policies with the advance in privatisation and in microeconomic and institutional adjustment. As it turned out that, unlike macroeconomic stabilization and liberalization, to make institutional and ownership changes effective required a longer time period, the policies had to become more evolutionary and "gradualistic".

As discussed in section 2.4., a pragmatic, step by step approach was followed in coping with the legacy of the past and in working out the bad debt problem. The "old" banking institutions co-existed with the "new" ones and the solution was seen in their privatisation and internal restructuring coupled with the increasing competitive pressure from both foreign and newly created banks, rather than in some forms of their dismantling or discontinuity. A relatively wide time scope was also set for meeting the norms of prudential regulation. The Central Bank, while anxious to apply the standards recommended by the Basle Committee for Banking Supervision and Practises as soon as possible, i.e. to set the required capital/assets ratio at 8 percent, risk weighted, had to account for the constraining factors, in particular the starting conditions of "old" banks. The 8 percent target was only made obligatory for new entrants i.e. for those starting banking activities after January 1, 1991. The "old" banks were granted a transitional adjustment period with the following interim targets:

- at least 4.5% by the end of 1991;
- 6.25% by the end of 1993; and the final target of
- 8 per cent not later than the end of 1996.

Assessing the situation towards the end of 1993, the respective interim target was likely to be adhered to by "old" banks.

3.2. Benefits and Costs of the Implemented Policies

A number of positive features in the financial and banking developments in the Czech republic can be linked to the adopted type of policies:

- there were no significant discontinuities in the bank lending to enterprises and households,
- "old" banks got into a substantially better shape compared to the initial stage when they all were technically bankrupt. Provided with the sufficient time for adjustment, they could improve their capital/assets ratios and to create previously lacking reserves and loan-loss provisions to be better "equipped" to cope with the threatening clients' bankruptcies,
- the spread between lending and borrowing interest rates was maintained at a relatively moderate level.

As a consequence of the adopted pragmatic "step by step" approach and "evolutionary" policies in the institutional and microeconomic spheres, the adjustment costs, including the costs of debt contract failures and payment arrears, have been widely spread, both in time and across individual types of economic agents.

To identify and evaluate the implied costs, two concepts should be relevant:

- direct or "real" costs, i.e. the costs which must be ultimately born by concrete economic agents in one way or another,
- "opportunity" costs, including indirect ones, i.e. the costs implied in the given strategy and policies compared to those which would be incurred in alternative options.

As for the direct costs, the "price" for payments arrears and for the bad, non-performing loans was paid for by the "sinners" themselves only to a minor extent in the period 1990-1993. Apart from the cases of the "administratively" implemented dismantling or closing down of several state enterprises and apart from the limited number of concluded bankruptcy procedures against minor firms in 1993, the implied costs were mostly "socialized", passed over on other economic agents. This was effected via various channels:

a) the proceeds from privatisation were drawn upon to cover partial recapitalization of commercial banks burdened with the legacy of bad loans from the past
b) subsidy provided to enterprise sector via negative real interest rates
c) large borrowing-lending spreads in interest rates
d) drawing on the state assets and budgetary means, as well as on the Central Bank's funds.

It follows, the costs were "distributed" among a wide range of subjects: households as savers, general public as tax-payers and recipients of the privatisation proceeds, the firms which were duly meeting the terms of their debt contracts and of other obligations.

Subsidy provided to enterprise sector via negative real interest rate

As follows from data in Tables 4 and 4a, in the period since the start of the transition in 1990 the values of real interest rates fluctuated from highly negative to positive ones. Though the extent and frequency of nominal interest rate's adjustments significantly increased compared to the previous period, the main cause of real interest rate's fluctuations were varying rates of domestic inflation. Accordingly, four sub-periods can be identified in the years 1990-1993:

- from mid 1990 to mid 1991: surging price level and mostly highly negative real interest rates
- from mid 1991 to the third quarter of 1992: price level stabilized and positive real interest rates prevailed
- second inflationary wave at the end of 1992 and at the beginning of 1993: real interest rates turned again to negative values
- from the second quarter of 1993 onwards: the tendency back to positive real interest rates.

Compared to mostly repressed inflation under the former centrally planned framewok, open inflation accelerated since the second half of 1990. The impact of the inflation proper (i.e. of core inflation) was, however, mixed with the impact of "corrective" price changes administered by the authorities, with the once-for-all institutional changes such as sweeping price liberalization at the beginning of 1991 and the reform of tax system, including the introduction of value-added tax at the start of 1993.

Summarizing the experience of the period 1990-1993, real interest rates acquired positive values when inflation was relatively low, and negative ones when inflation rate accelerated. This conclusion coincides with the lessons learned elsewhere: in the conditions of regulated interest rates and underdeveloped credit markets, the determining factor for real interest rate values was the extent of price level increases.[6] The mentioned outcome also reflected the policies of the Central Bank. In the high inflation period the Bank's discount rate signalled that the surging price level should be considered only a temporary phenomenon. In the opposite situations, when inflation rate decreased to almost zero level, the discount rate policy reflected the still inherent inflationary pressures.

Though the inflation record of the former Czechoslovakia and of the Czech Republic in the years 1990-93 was more successful than elsewhere in the EMEs, the data suggest that the real interest rates, especially on deposits, were negative for protracted time spans. It refers in particular to the first

[6] Though both credit volume limits for major banks and obligatory interest rate ceilings were phased out in the course of 1992, the developments of interest rates and their pattern continued to be under the impact of the legacy of the past and reflected the rigidity and underdevelopment of money and foreign exchange markets. The credit contracts concluded in the past e.g., significantly affected the recorded level of long term interest rates, deviating their average from what could be expected a rational pattern of interest rates.

Table 4

Lending and Borrowing Interest Rates of Commercial Banks (average)

Czechoslovakia

	1989	1990				1991				1992			
		I.	II.	III.	IV.	I.	II.	III.	IV.	I.	II.	III.	IV.
Credits (lending rates)	5.7	5.4	5.4	5.6	7.6	14.7	15.1	14.2	13.9	13.4	13.7	13.6	13.3
Deposits (borrowing rates)	2.5	2.6	2.6	2.8	3.3	7.6	8.2	8.6	8.0	8.6	6.9	6.6	6.6
Margin	3.2	2.8	2.8	2.8	4.3	7.1	6.9	5.6	5.9	4.8	6.8	7.0	6.7

Czech Republic

	1992				1993								
	I.	II.	III.	IV.	1	2	3	4	5	6	7	8	9
Credits (lending rates)	13.9	13.4	13.4	13.2	13.7	14.2	14.4	14.6	14.8	14.8	14.3	14.2	13.8
Deposits (borrowing rates)	7.9	6.7	6.1	6.3	6.8	6.9	7.2	7.3	7.5	7.0	7.0	7.0	7.0
Margin	6.0	6.7	7.3	6.9	6.9	7.3	7.2	7.3	7.3	7.8	7.3	7.2	6.8

Source: Czech National Bank; Financial Statistical Information

Table 4a

Inflation Rates in Former Czechoslovakia and in the Czech Republic

Czechoslovakia

	1989	1990				1991			
		I.	II.	III.	IV.	I.	II.	III.	IV.
CPI[1)]	1.4	2.4	5.4	13.0	17.5	40.9	49.2	49.5	53.6
CPI[2)]	1.4	3.4	3.9	14.1	18.4	54.7	68.5	56.3	52.7

	1992											
	1	2	3	4	5	6	7	8	9	10	11	12
CPI[1)]	1.0	1.5	1.8	2.3	2.7	3.0	3.9	4.5	6.4	8.5	10.5	11.5
CPI[2)]	23.3	15.7	10.8	9.4	7.7	6.2	6.9	7.4	9.1	11.4	11.9	11.5

Czech Republic

	1993											
	1	2	3	4	5	6	7	8	9	10	11	12
CPI[1)]	8.5	9.9	10.6	11.2	11.7	12.1	12.9	13.7	15.3	16.6	17.2	...
CPI[2)]	21.2	21.9	21.9	21.8	21.8	21.8	21.3	21.4	20.9	19.9	17.9	...

1) in % against December of the previous year

2) in % against the same period of the previous year

Source: Monthly Statistics of the Czech Republic

months of 1991 and, to a lesser extent, to the beginning of 1993 as well. It implied a substantial resource transfer from creditors to debtors. As the overhelming share of savings was generated by the households, while the major part of credits was contracted by the enterprises, households extended a substantial "hidden" subsidy to enterprises. In this way the savers, i.e. mostly households, extending via credit-contracts subsidy to debtors, i.e. mostly firms, were also paying for the costs of their payments arrears and of debt contract failures.

Large borrowing-lending margins

The extent and the consequences of the borrowing-lending margins proved to be a controversial issue in transition (Begg, D., Portes R., 1992). On the one hand, the drawbacks of the large spreads were evident: a tax was in fact imposed on both savings and investment at a time when incentives to increase savings were vital for restructuring and economic recovery of transition countries. This argument therefore called for as small margins as possible, excluding to use them as a means of coping with the "stock" problem.

However, the other side of the coin was the stability and credibility of the entire banking system. The Central Bank found itself in a contradictory position: on the one hand, in the interest of the credibility of the banking system it motivated commercial banks to build-up reserves and to channel a large part of their profits into loan-loss provisions. At the same time it used the forms of moral persuasion and "window guidance" to make the large banks to narrow gradually their spreads.

An "acceptable" compromise seemed to develop, avoiding both the dramatic increases in the spreads and the banks' failures as well. As follows from Table 4, the average spread increased to 5-6% in 1991 and 1992 and fluctuated around 7% in the second half of 1992 and in 1993. Though higher than in most developed market economies, it was, however, significantly lower and more stabilized than in other transition economies, including Hungary and Poland, and also lower than elsewhere in the periods of economic reforms (as demonstrated e.g. in the case of Chile).[7]

Though to some extent evidently still the "price" for persisting low efficiency, the interest rate margins enabled the banks' reserves and loan loss provisions to be augmented to a more satisfactory level (compare Table 3).

---

[7] To make an international comparison of the margins consistent, the nominal data should be corrected for differentiated inflation rates in individual countries. Though to a lesser extent, also in real terms the average margin appeared relatively narrower in the Czech Rerpublic compared to other EMEs.

Nevertheless, extensive debt contract failures and the implied bank risk made the "price" of credit higher than it could be otherwise. The burden was thus shared by the debtors who do pay and do honour their obligations, and also by those who would contract credits provided their cost was lower.

The identified strategy of "spreading the costs" made them more manageable and allowed for gradual adjustment to take place. Nevertheless, the apparent pros of any policies must be confronted with the cons. It could be argued that the opportunity costs of the adopted policies included such constraints as the often highlighted symbiosis of old banks and state enterprises (Dittus P., 1993, Phelps E.S. et al., 1993), the slower pace of restructuring than expected and the persisting bad-debt issue, low competitive pressure and only slowly increasing role of new banks. However, to identify these deficiencies as opportunity costs of the implemented policies, their causal links would have to be established and other option proved as both viable and less costly.

4. Conclusion

Czechoslovak banks were restructured into a two-tier system only at the beginning of 1990, the move coincided with the start of radical transition. Both Hungary and Poland effected this change earlier, in 1987 and 1988 respectively. Being a late-comer to the institutional building, former Czechoslovakia faced considerable constraints at the start of transition compared to Hungary and Poland: unlike these countries, it was not possible to draw on the already established two-tire type banking network and on the legislation and prudential regulation already in force.

However, being a late-comer also implied that "big" banks were mostly installed as separate entities only with the start of political and economic reforms. These "old" banks therefore were not much older than the "new" small private ones. Besides, starting their activities in reform environment and with the prospects of being included in the forthcoming first wave of voucher privatisation, with changed incentives and with mostly newly recruited management, the behaviour pattern, policies and preferences of "old" banks in principle have not diverged from those of "new" banks. As the experience showed, in the course of transition the dividing line among Czech banking institutions could be increasingly identified not between the "old" and "new" ones, but rather between the well and bad managed and operating banks. Nevertheless, while the number of operating banks appeared possibly already too high for the Czech market, the bi-polar pattern of big and small institutions persisted with the apparent lack of medium-size banks.

Due to including banks into the first wave of voucher scheme privatisation, former Czechoslovakia made a substiantial advance to change ownership forms of banking institutions. While all the existing banks were state owned at the beginning of 1990, three years later there was only one banking institution in the Czech Republic, Consolidation Bank, entirely state owned, apart from the Central Bank. However, the state has retained a significant stake of around 43 percent in most "old" banks (the big four), privatised via voucher scheme. This concept of "partial" privatisation, however controversial, seemed warranted in the conditions. On the one hand it provided the opportunity to the monetary authorities to apply some"window guidance" in the liberalized but still rather non-competitive and imperfect money markets. On the other hand a certain state "umbrella" was desirable, given only gradual overcoming of the initial technical insolvency of the privatised banks.

The Law on Banks (No. 21/1992) provided for universal type of banking, integrating both commercial and investment banking activities. The discussion of the advantages and constraints of universal type of banks versus separated commercial and investment banking is related to the strategic issue: what should be the role of banks in the "real" sector and in the corporate governance in EMEs.

Though not necessarily implying the "German" model of banks' role in non-financial sector, the universal type of banks does create pre-requisites for such an approach. Banks, while extending credits and holding equity at the same time are in a better position, due to intimate insider information, to manage the developments of the firm, exercise control over the projects and investments and, having interest in long term profitability, to smooth the periods of financial distress. For the specific conditions of EMEs seems to be of particular importance that universal banks could have a strong position to enforce early restructuring of enterprises, short of bankruptcy situation.[8]

Though with some limits, the legal framework in the Czech Republic made possible for the banks to hold equities of non-banking companies.[9] These limits were not as yet, however, effective limits. Rather, banks were discouraged by the non-transparent situation of companies and by the unset-

---

[8] "Taking into account present-day conditions in the east European region, the paper argues that one class of mechanisms, namely, outsider control by banks and other financial intermediaries, is well- designed to promote enterprise performance, while some of the other mechanisms, such a stock market or foreign investment, will not be strong enough in the near future, if ever, to be a major source of outsider governance." (Phelps E.S., et al., 1993, p.38).

[9] In accordance with the Law on Banks, commercial banks are entitled to acquire shares up to 10 % of capital of a non-banking institution. The total volume of their stakes in non-banking firms should not, however, exceed 25% of their own capital and reserves. To hold stakes exceeding these norms, the prior consent of the Central Bank is required.

tled, fluctuating ratios of share prices. In the circumstances, the risk of trading bad debt for bad equity was relatively high. Besides, when co-owners of the firms which turn bankrupt, banks are in much less favourable position vis-a-vis other creditors in recovering their assets.

At the same time, the Investment Privatisation Funds (IPF) founded by banks and other financial institutions became owners of a substantial share of property privatised in the first wave of voucher scheme. According to the data, about 72 percent of "points" have been assigned to IPFs, of which 10 top funds collected more than a half (i.e. about 40 percent of all voucher-points in the first wave). From these 10 top funds 9 were founded by commercial banks and other financial situations (Mullineux A., Pruski J., Klacek J., 1993). Via this intermediation the bank-oriented model of corporate control may ultimately develop.

The behaviour, preferences and activities of IPFs, especially of those who have attracted substantial portions of voucher-points, are of crucial importance. The distribution of shares which developed from the first wave is mostly considered as more or less optimal. Both the potential extremes, i.e. too dispersed and too concentrated ownership did not happen. Though there are differences among the IPFs and a number of them evidently will not survive (the process, including mergers, was already under way), the available evidence points to the determination of considerable part of them to become active proprietors, to exercise ownership function meaningfully and to demonstrate some entrepreneurial spirit.

However, there are many potential constraints. Quite a number of IPFs have at present a rather wide portfolio, which could be hardly manageable in an active way of overseeing the respective companies. At the same time, the conflict between the short-term interests and liquidity pressures may interfere with the intention to be long-run investors.

The key issue of the impact on corporate behaviour and governance is still to be resolved.

REFERENCES

Abel, Istvan, *Company Management and Capital Market Development in the Transition*, Conference Paper, Leuven, 1992

Abel, Istvan and **John P. Bonin**, "Financial Sector Reform in the Economies in Transition: On the Way to Privatizing Commercial Banks", forthcoming in Székely Istvan and John P. Bonin (eds.) *Development and Reform in Central and Eastern Europe*, London, Edward Elgar, 1994

Abel, Istvan and **Istvan P. Szekely**, "Market Structures, Competition and Innovation in the Hungarian Banking System", forthcoming in Székely István and John P. Bonin (eds.) *Development and Reform in Central and Eastern Europe*, London, Edward Elgar, 1994

Bauc Jaroslaw, Grabowski Boguslaw and **Raczko Andrzej**, *The Transition Programme of the Polish Banking System*, The University of Birmingham, International Finance Group, 1992

Begg, David and **Richard Portes**, *Enterprise Debt and Economic Transformation in Central and Eastern Europe*, CEPR Discussion Paper No. 695, 1992

Belka, Marek, Pruski Jerzy and **Raczko Andrzej**, *The Evolution of the Polish Banking System and EC Regulatory Standards*, The University of Birmingham, International Finance Group 1992

Blommenstein, Hans J. and **Jean R. Lange**, "Balance Sheet Restructuring and Privatisation of the Banks", in *Transforming of the Banking System: Portfolio Restructuring, Privatisation and the Payment System*, Paris, OECD 1993, pp. 13-33

Brainard, Lawrence, "Strategies for Economic Transformation in Central and Eastern Europe: the Role of Financial Market Reform", in Blommenstein, Hans and Michael Marrese (eds.) *Transformation of Planned Economies: Property Rights Reform and Macroeconomic Stability*, Paris, OECD, 1991, pp. 95-108

Corbett, Jenny and **Colin Mayer**, "Financial Reform in Eastern Europe: Progress with the Wrong Model", *Oxford Review of Economic Policy*, 7, 4, 1991, pp. 57-75,

Dittus, Poter, "Finance and Corporate Governance in Eastern Europe", May, mimeo, 1993, forthcoming in Fischer B. (ed.) *Investment and Financing in Developing Countries*, Nomos Verlagsgesellschaft, Baden-Baden

Estrin, Saul, Hare Paul and **Marta C. Surany**, "Banking in Transition: Development and Current Problems in Hungary", *Soviet Studies*, 44, 1992, pp. 785-808

Hare, Paul, "The Assessment: Microeconomics of Transition in Eastern Europe", *Oxford Review of Economic Policy*, 7, 4, 1991

Herr, Hansjörg, Tober, Silke and **Andreas Westphal**, "A Strategy for Economic Transformation and Development in Eastern Europe", *De Pecunia*, 3, 3, Décembre 1991

Hinds, Manuel, *Issues in the Introduction of Market Forces in Eastern European Socialist Economies*, World Bank Seminar Paper, Laxenburg, IIASA, March 1990

Hrncír, Miroslav and **Jan Klacek**, "Stabilization Policies and Currency Convertibility in Czechoslovakia, *European Economy*, Special Edition No. 2, 1991, pp. 17-39

Lacoue-Labarthe, Dominique, *The Second Banking Reform in Transitional Central European Economies: An Assessment*, Conference on Financial Reform in Central and Eastern Europe, Prague, September 1993

Mullineux, Andy and **Marek Belka**, *Hardening Micro Budget Constraints: Bank Behaviour and Corporate Governance in Poland*, The University of Birmingham, International Finance Group, 1993

Mullineux, Andy, Pruski, Jerzy and **Jan Klacek**, *Privatisation and Bankng Sector Reform in Poland and the Czech Republic*, University of Birmingham, September 1993

Nyberg, Peter and **Vesa Vihriäla**, *The Finnish Banking Crisis and Its Handling*, Bank of Finland, Discussion Papers No. 15, 1993

OECD Economic Survey of the Czech and Slovak Federal Republic, Paris, 1991

OECD Economic Survey of Poland, Paris, 1992

Phelps, Edmund S., Frydman, Roman, Rapaczynski Andrzej and **Andrei Shleifer**, *Needed Mechanism of Corporate Governance and Finance in Eastern Europe*, EBRD Working Paper, 1, March 1993

Ptácek, Jicí, *Insolvency of the Part of the Czech Enterprises and the Possibilities of Its Solution*, (in Czech), Prague, Institute of Economics, Czech National Bank, Research Report No. 9, 1993

Saunders, Anthony and **Ingo Walter**, "Reconfiguration of Banking and Capital Markets in Eastern Europe", *The Journal of International Securities Markets*, Autumn 1991

Schmieding, Holger and **Claudia Buch**, *Better Banks for Eastern Europe*, Kiel Discussion Paper No. 197, Kiel, December 1992

Analysis of Changes in the Banking Sector in 1992*

Andrzej Raczko
Institute of Economics
University of Lodz
41 Rewolucji 1905r
90-214 Lodz,
Poland

Summary

This paper analysis the changes of the Polish Banking sector in 1992. Emphasis is placed on the ways in which the Polish National Bank (NBP) intended to remodel current structure of banking sector. Before the details of new NBP policy are discussed the current situation of the Polish banks is described.

In the first part the main sectors of the Polish banking sector are presented. The second part is devoted to comparative analysis of main indicators of financial position of leading banks from different sectors. In the final part particular attention is paid to the causes which determines NBP's policy in 1992.

---

* Financial Reform in Central and Eastern Europe. (ACE) Project No. ERB 4012 PL 900 69.

1. Introduction

Reforms of the Polish banking sector initiated in 1989 have changed the structure of Polish banking system. Firstly, the nine commercial banks were established on the basis of the former regional NBP (National Bank of Poland) branches. Secondly, a very low capital limit and income tax breaks caused of launching foreign banking sector. Thirdly, new banking law led into spontaneous development of a new private commercial banks' sector (see Jaworski 1993, Daniluk 1992).

Presented paper aims to show how deep were the changes of the banking structure. In the first part the leading banks of main sectors of banking system are described. The second part is devoted to a comparative analysis of principal indicators demonstrating economic position of leading banks from different sectors. The results present in this part will be helpful in explanation of changes of the Polish National Bank's (NBP) policy which intention is remodeling current structure of banking sector (see Gronkiweicz-Waltz 1992). The last part focuses on the causes of these NBP's corrections observed in 1992.

2. The Structure of the Polish Banking Sector

2.1 State-Owned Banks

This sector of so called "big fourteen" state-own banks is not homogeneous and consists of two groups:

- state-owned commercial banks,
- state-owned specialized banks.

One of the primary goals in 1989 was to transfer the bank's commercial services for state-own enterprises from the NBP to newly established commercial banks. Nine commercial banks were created on the strength of the government's decree of 11 April 1988. The state-own "nine" commercial banks are as follows:

- Bank Slaski in Katowice,
- Powszechny Bank Kredytowy in Warsaw,

- Bank Przemyslowo-Handlowy in Cracow,
- Bank Gdanski in Gdansk,
- Bank Zachodni in Wroclaw,
- Wielkopolski Bank Kredytowy in Poznan,
- Pomorski Bank Kredytowy in Szczecin,
- Bank Depozytowo-Kredytowy in Lublin,
- Powszechny Bank Gospodarczy in Lodz.

These banks were branched off from the NBP network. In the first year each of them operated on different part of Poland although formally they might operate all over the country. After two years all of the nine commercial banks built network of branches which covers not only a single region. They quickly expanded services for different types of economic items and obtained position of universal banks. The main field of banking operations for these nine banks are still credits for large industrial enterprises (nine banks granted 38% of total sum of loans in 1992). It is one of the causes of bad debts problem which limits the expansion of nine commercial banks (see Bogu- szewski 1992).

In the period of 2-3 years the nine commercial banks will be privatized by public offer. The first, Wielkopolski Bank Kredytowy has been privatized in Spring 1993.

The banks from the second group (state-owned specialized banks) were established before Polish reforms and each of them performing a specialized function.

Bank Handlowy focuses on the servicing of foreign trade transactions. The bank nearly monopolizes financing imports and long term loans to finance exports. In 1991, Bank Handlowy serviced about 80% of Polish exports and 70% of imports. Together with Polish central bank, Bank Handlowy takes part in the management of Poland's official foreign exchange reserves. It has 18 domestic branches, a branch in London and holds shares of foreign banks: Bank Handlowy Int. (Luxembourg), Centro Internationale Handelsbank AG (Wiena), Mitteleuropaische Handelsbank AG (Frankfurt). His role has been limited since a permission to perform foreign currency transactions was extended for big commercial banks and foreign banks in Poland.

Powszechna Kasa Oszczednosci (PKO BP Savings Bank) is the largest bank in SwolaSw, operating in 365 branches and more than 12,000 agencies. Before reform it mainly collected money of households and granted loans for consumers. In 1988 PKO BP was excluded from NBP's structure and obtained status of universal bank but it still has State organizational entity with the president appointed by the Prime Minister. The strong side of this bank is the biggest network and the experience in handling of millions household savings accounts.

Bank Polska Kasa Opieki SA (PKO SA) has a long tradition in foreign currency operations for households and private industry sectors. It played parallel role to PKO BP collecting small foreign currency deposits from households. Now it is state-own bank (98.65% of shares is held by the State 1.35% by PKO BP) with wide range of services like international and domestic trade finance, insurance services etc.

Bank Gospodarstwa Krajowego was established in 1924 but it was closed in 1948. The bank was re-activated in 1989 and fulfilled special tasks, it arranged the issue, sale and repurchase over 60% of Polish internal debt. Bank also conducts universal banking operations but it is very limited by small size of bank's own capital.

Bank Gospodarki Zywnosciowej (Bank for Food Economy or BGZ) was created in 1975 for financial services of the state owned agriculture and food production sector. This bank has mixed state-cooperative ownership, 51% of shares are owned by State, 49% by small cooperative agriculture banks. BGZ cooperates with most of the cooperative banks which are its shareholders. Now, BGZ does not only specialize in the servicing of agriculture sector it has a license to conduct foreign-exchange transactions and universal bank's services.

2.2 Specialized Banks Created by State with A Minority Share of Foreign Capital

Among the specialized banks playing important role in Polish banking sector are banks which were established as a state-own and then privatisated with assistance of foreign banks or new created banks on the initiative of Polish state institutions in which foreign financial institutions are shareholders.

Bank Rozwoju Eksportu (Export Development Bank) was established in 1987 and its main tasks was to offer foreign currency for state controlled export projects. In 1992 it was privatisated by public offer. Among shareholders are foreign investors (2% of the shares were bought by Austrian Girokredit). The bank is still granting export-oriented investments credits and operate as an intermediary institution for World Bank credit lines.

Two other banks: Bank Inicjatyw Spoleczno-Ekonomicznych SA (BISE - Socio-Economic Initiative Bank) and Polski Bank Rozwoju SA (PBR - Polish Development Bank) were created after 1989. The BISE was set up in July 1990 on the initiative of the then Labour Minister, Jacek Kuron. The aid in its establishment was given by the French bank, Caisse Centralle de Credit Cooperatif. The capital contributed by that bank was small (7% of the joint stock capital), on the other hand the assistance of that bank in the organization of the BISE's activity was very important. The BISE specializes in granting high risk credits intended mainly for aiding the development of small and medium-sized business. Credits are financed from the bank's own capital and from the credit lines opened under the agreement signed by the Polish and French governments on financial support for Polish-French firms acting in Poland.

The second of the enumerated banks, the Polski Bank Rozwoju SA was set up on the strength of the Polish government decision of July 1990. It was intended to become a mover of novel activities in three areas: in the nascent capital market, in the interbank money market and in area of investment credits. As regards the third element, the PBR was to ensure the financing of investment credits on the basis of foreign credit lines. It started to grant credits from the credit lines of the World Bank and the European Investment Bank. It acted in the framework of the so-called apex system, i.e. it was a refinancing bank acting through a system of intermediary banks (it used a network of over 20 intermediary banks). The specific nature of its activity required that it should have international credibility and that is why attempts were made to attract renowned shareholders. As a result of the conducted negotiations, the new issuance of shares was bought by:

- the French bank Credit National,
- the Austrian bank Oesterriche Invetitionskredit AG
- the Italian banking institution Istituto Mobiliare Italiano.

The effected issuance resulted in the following joint stock ownership structure:

- 74.6% the Treasury
- 19% the Agency for Industrial Development
- 6.4% the above named foreign shareholders.

2.3 Foreign Banks

As I have already mentioned, by setting a very low minimal own capital limit (USD 6 million) and income tax breaks (for banks which started to operate before the end of 1991) it was counted that foreign banks would take considerable interest in the Polish banking market. In reality, a sector of small-sized foreign banks was established. The foreign banks are as follows:

1. AmerBank SA
2. CitiBank SA
3. Creditanstalt
4. International Bank in Poland
5. ING Bank
6. Raiffeisen Centrobank
7. Polish-Canadian St. Stanislaw Bank.[1]
8. Societe Generale.

The list does not include the Pierwszy Komercyjny Bank (First Commercial Bank) in Lublin established by David Bogatin, for it was taken over by Polish stockholders as result of the declaration of insolvency of Bogatin' s firms in Poland and commercial banks with a minority share of foreign capital (Pier-wszy Polsko-Amerykanski Bank SA in Crocow, Solidarnosc-Chase DT Bank in Gdansk[2], Gospodarczy Bank Wielkopolski SA, Polish- American Mortgage Bank).

Most of the listed foreign banks were established or are controlled by foreign banks:

Name of bank	Main share holders
AmerBank	Bankers Trust Co.
Citibank	Citicorp.
Creditanstalt	Creditanstalt Bankverain

[1]The Polish-Canadian St. Stanislaw Bank was established on the initiative of the Polish Catholic church.

[2]Solidarnosc-Chase DT Bank SA in Gdansk, was set up thanks to the initiative of the Solidarity Union and the money of Mr. Chase from the USA. This bank, however, is not controlled by the Union.

Table (Continued)

Internationale Bank in Poland	ABN-AMRO, Credit Lynnais Credit Lunnais Banca Commerciale Itl.
ING Bank	ING Group
Raiffeisen Centrobank	Raiffeisen Zentralbank
Societe Generale	Societe Generale

Source: Gazeta Bankowa no. 42/92, 25/93

The enumerated banks fulfill specific functions in the Polish banking system. Having access to the advanced banking communication system SWIFT they concentrated on such banking services as foreign exchange services (documentary credits, clean payments) and foreign exchange credits and guarantees. For example, AmerBank services only 800 accounts belonging to firms and 1,750 individual accounts, Creditanstalt services 330 and 1,7070 accounts respectively (the figures for end-August 1992). Credit activity was largely concerned with short-term foreign currency credits. The level of the granted credits indicates the wish to gain medium-sized firms with a considerable share in foreign trade (a minimum credit amounts to US$ 100,000). The above foreign banks do not establish a network, and most of them are seated in Warsaw. As regards their size and scope of activities, these banks resemble rather foreign branches. (Technically, such a function is fulfilled by branches of the ING Bank and Societe Generale in Warsaw).

The main reason for the small inflow of foreign banking capital lies in the still upheld opinion about Poland as a high risk country. Hence banking investments are made in two ways: foreign investors either buy shares in state-owned banks functioning under international agreements (e.g. BISE and PBR) or set up small banks concentrated on specific activity. The second, more common case is concerned with establishment of banks with small capital, modest technical equipment and a small number of employees. Such banks have small costs and at the same time they are competitors for Polish banks in foreign currency services and foreign currency credits which the Polish banks are not willing to grant owing to the exchange rate risk.

The above characteristics of the banking sector points out that banks established jointly with foreign capital play a marginal role in the Polish banking system.

2.4 Private Commercial Banks

In the beginning of the Polish banking reforms were established very liberal criteria of issuing operating licenses to new banks. As a result 85 banks received operating licenses during two years. More of them belong to private banking sector. In the sense given in the 1989 Act on Banking Law "privately owned" banks have status of joint stock company which shareholders are economic items (not State)[3]. It seems that the fast development of the private sector will limit the dominating role of the state banks, this view will be discussed in the last part of paper. Among the private-own banks two play leading role, there are: Bank Incjatyw Gospodarczych SA (BIG) and Kredyt Bank SA.

BIG was established in June 1989. The bank offered not only typical banking services but organized the floatation of, and trading in clients' securities. BIG was the first bank in Poland which launched own brokerage office and organized the secondary shares market. In 1991, BIG joined the VISA international credit card system. It was pioneer bank which introduced yearly bonds very convenient form of placement for large sum of money for big firms.

Kredit Bank was established in August 1990 as a really private bank, 51% of shares was held by 11 private firms and individuals, 49% by state-own companies. The bank obtained full banking license including permission for foreign currency operations. It maintains traditional banking services (handles enterprise accounts in zlotys and foreign currency, accepts deposits from them and granting credits) and additionally offers financial consultancy services. Kredyt Bank SA joined the VISA system as well.

The size, experience and economic results show that both banks BIG and Kredyt Bank may successfully compete with state-own commercial banks. Their position in Polish banking system is confirmed by memberships of the Warsaw Stock Exchange and National Clearing House.

3. Synthetic Analysis of Main Banking Sectors

The analysis carried out below serves to grasp the differences among banking sectors. The analysis was made on the basis of data for December 1992. The data are concerned with all the (14) banks of the state sector, (BRE, BISE and PBR are presented separately), five leading foreign banks

[3]It means that bank which 100% of shares belong to state-own firms is private bank.

and with 18 selected banks of the private sector (there are over 70 banks in the private sector). Of the private banks those were selected which have been acting for at least two years and show an appropriately high increase in their own capital and assets, in other words they are banks which will maintain their position on the banking market in Poland.[4] The basic data of selected banks are in Table 1.

3.1 Capital Adequacy

The analysis of the structure of liabilities shows at once the share of banks' own capital in total liabilities. This share is markedly lower in the case of state banks, a particularly low indicator was recorded by the five oldest state banks (Table no. 2). What accounts for this phenomenon is the difference in the way in which the state and private sectors developed. State banks were already in existence at the time the new banking legislation was introduced, i.e. they had a fully-fledged networks of branches, regular customers. The introduction of the Banking Law in 1989 forced the government to provide the existing state banks with appropriate own capital. It was counted that they might be provided with small funds, for they would increase their own capital quickly through accumulation of some of the profits. The accumulation process was checked in 1991 and 1992 because banks had to amass reserves for unpaid credits (e.g. in the first three quarters, there was only a 4- percent increase in the funds of the "nine" banks).

It was different in the case of private banks. They ad to amass an appropriate own capital first in order to obtain a license and next they started to organize their banking activity. Hence they were bound to have a large share of their own capital in total liabilities. This indicator can be regarded as the degree to which a given bank succeeded in developing its activity. The surveyed group gives examples of banks with high shares of own capital (the BISE, Bank Ziemi Radomskiej) as well as examples of banks with relatively low shares (BIG, Bydgoski Bank Komunalny, Gornoslaski Bank Gospodarczy). The latter group comprises banks which were quick in developing their activities.

---

[4]It should be noted that the analysis does not take into account the entire sector of small cooperative banks which mostly service Polish agriculture owing to the present process of their mergers into banks with larger own capital.

3.2 Structure of Deposits

The share of non-banking sector's deposits in total liabilities is similar in the two analyzed sectors with two exceptions (Table no.2). This index is relatively low - which is understandable - in the case of private banks with high own capital shares (BISE, Bank Ziemi Radomskiej). This index is also very low in the case of two state banks: Bank Handlowy and BRE, which results from the specific nature of their activities. The two banks service foreign currency payments and documentary transactions, hence the high share of liabilities to other banks in total liabilities.

From the viewpoint of types of deposits (sight deposits and term deposits) it is apparent that term deposits are preferred by private banks (Table no.3). This phenomenon can be accounted for as follows. It is easier for small private banks to plan and control liquidity when they have term deposits rather than sight deposits.

Table 1: Capital (K), Total assets (A) and gross profit (Π) in mld zl

No	Name of the bank	K	A	Π
1	BANK SLASKI	2583	28954	1749
2	POWSZECHNY BANK KREDYTOWY	1394	29153	1858
3	BANK PRZEMYSLOWO-HANDLOWY	1709	32234	1421
4	BANK GDANSKI	1135	18985	1708
5	BANK ZACHODNI	1327	14426	786
6	WIELKOPOLSKI BANK KREDYTOWY	1943	19147	566
7	POMORSKI BANK KREDYTOWY	1485	16356	540
8	BANK DEPOZYTOWO-KREDYTOWY	929	11095	213
9	POWSZECHNY BANK GOSPODARCZY	917	25484	638
10	PKO	540	109891	2797
11	PEKAO	3185	94822	745
12	BGZ	1706	56939	646
13	BANK HANDLOWY	6277	84029	6756
14	BANK GOSPODARSTWA KRAJOWEGO	91	341	39
15	BANK ROZWOJU EKSPORTU	693	7589	198

Table 1 (Continued)

16	BISE	98	254	14
17	POLSKI BANK ROZWOJU	1255	5541	808
18	AMERBANK	196	1324	42
19	CITIBANK	158	2093	125
20	CREDITANSTALT	86	772	22
21	INTERNATIONALE BANK IN POLAND	315	2173	4
22	RAIFFEISEN CENTROBANK	111	2366	137
23	BIG	260	8564	92
24	KREDYT BANK	333	1986	11
25	BANK ROZWOJU ROLNICTWA	112	1538	56
26	AGROBANK	160	2057	8
27	BYDGOSKI BANK KOMUNALNY	45	1936	25
28	BANK ZIEMI RADOMSKIEJ	159	392	37
29	WSCHODNI BANK CUKROWNICTWA	126	1401	22
30	INTERKRAKBANK	70	753	5
31	GLOB	65	214	2
32	BANK WLASNOSCI PRACOWNICZEJ	67	220	5
33	MEGABANK	88	384	2
34	BYDGOSKI BANK BUDOWNICTWA	52	740	13
35	BANK STAROPOLSKI	102	1341	4
36	GORNOSLASKI BANK GOSPODARCZY	82	1738	31
37	BANK POCZTOWY W BYDGOSZCZY	72	366	11
38	BANK PREZEMYSLOWY W LODZI	46	231	12
39	BUDBANK	49	317	37

Source: Based on data from Gazeta Bankowa no 8/93,18/93

Table 2: Capital/assets (K/A) and deposits/liabilities (D/L) ratios

No	Name of the Bank	K/A	D/L
1	BANK SLASKI	8.9	76.4
2	POWSZECHNY BANK KREDYTOWY	4.8	63.9
3	BANK PRZEMYSLOWO-HANDLOWY	5.3	50.6
4	BANK GDANSKI	6.0	63.1
5	BANK ZACHODNI	9.2	76.8
6	WIELKOPOLSKI BANK KREDYTOWY	10.1	56.8
7	POMORSKI BANK KREDYTOWY	9.1	60.8
8	BANK DEPOZYTOWO-KREDYTOWY	8.4	52.0
9	POWSZECHNY BANK GOSPODARCZY	3.4	24.8
10	PKO	0.5	70.6
11	PEKAO	3.4	68.1
12	BGZ	3.0	35.5
13	BANK HANDLOWY	7.4	17.6
14	BANK GOSPODARSTWA KRAJOWEGO	26,7	27.6
15	BANK ROZWOJU EKSPORTU9.1 33.3		
16	BISE	38.5	42.1
17	POLSKI BANK ROZWOJU	22.6	21.1
18	AMERBANK	14.8	50.1
19	CITIBANK	7.5	66.3
20	CREDITANSTALT	11.1	60.0
21	INTERNATIONALE BANK IN POLAND	14.5	2.2
22	RAIFFEISEN CENTROBANK	4.7	38.2
23	BIG	3.1	64.0
24	KREDYT BANK	16.8	54.8
25	BANK ROZWOJU ROLNICTWA	7.3	66.4
26	AGROBANK	7.0	51.5
27	BYDGOSKI BANK KOMUNALNY	2.3	55.5
28	BANK ZIEMI RADOMSKIEJ	40.6	37.2
29	WSCHODNI BANK CUKROWNICTWA	9.0	47.5
30	INTERKRAKBANK	9.3	66.2
31	GLOB	30.5	52.8
32	BANK WLASNOSCI PRACOWNICZEJ	30.5	50.5
33	MEGABANK	22.9	31.0

Table 2 (Continued)

34	BYDGOSKI BANK BUDOWNICTWA	7.0	27.7
35	BANK STAROPOLSKI	7.6	61.4
36	GORNOSLASKI BANK GOSPODARCZY	4.7	89.4
37	BANK POCZTOWY W BYDGOSZCZY	19.6	63.4
38	BANK PREZEMYSLOWY W LODZI	19.9	57.5
39	BUDBANK	15.5	60.3

Source: Calculation based on data from Gazeta Bankowa no 8/93
25/93

Table 3: Sight deposits/total deposits (DS/D) ratio

No	Name of the bank	DS/D
1	BANK SLASKI	41.5
2	POWSZECHNY BANK KREDYTOWY	64.2
3	BANK PRZEMUYSLOWO-HANDLOWY	48.5
4	BANK GDANSKI	53.8
5	BANK ZACHODNI	40.5
6	WIELKOPOLSKI BANK KREDYTOWY	50.0
7	POMORSKI BANK KREDYTOWY	37.0
8	BANK DEPOZYTOWO-KREDYTOWY	40.3
9	POWSZECHNY BANK GOSPODARCZY	54.5
10	PKO	34.9
11	PEKAO	29.5
12	BGZ	27.6
13	BANK HANDLOWY	61.9
14	BANK GOSPODARSTWA KRAJOWEGO	-
15	BANK ROZWOJU EKSPORTU	-
16	BISE	38.3
17	POLSKI BANK ROZWOJU	-
18	AMERBANK	-
19	CITIBANK	-
20	CREDITANSTALT	-
21	INTERNATIONALE BANK IN POLAND	-
22	RAIFFEISEN CENTROBANK	-
23	BIG	8.3
24	KREDYT BANK	30.6

Table 3 (Continued)

25	BANK ROZWOJU ROLNICTWA	16.7
26	AGROBANK	19.4
27	BYDGOSKI BANK KOMUNALNY	24.7
28	BANK ZIEMI RADOMSKIEJ	17.9
29	WSCHODNI BANK CUKROWNICTWA	9.6
30	INTERKRAKBANK	9.6
31	GLOB	23.9
32	BANK WLASNOSCI PRACOWNICZEJ	66.4
33	MEGABANK	1.6
34	BYDGOSKI BANK BUDOWNICTWA	12.6
35	BANK STAROPOLSKI	1.6
36	GORNOSLASKI BANK GOSPODARCZY	24.3
37	BANK POCZTOWY W BYDGOSZCZY	21.4
38	BANK PREZEMYSLOWY W LODZI	30.2
39	BUDBANK	13.5

Source: Calculation based on data from *Gazeta Bankowa* no 8,25/93

Table 4: Refinancing credit - total deposits (REF/D) ratio.

No	Name of the bank	REF/D
1	BANK SLASKI	10.6
2	POWSZECHNY BANK KREDYTOWY	10.5
3	BANK PRZEMUYSLOWO-HANDLOWY	17.0
4	BANK GDANSKI	9.6
5	BANK ZACHODNI	0.3
6	WIELKOPOLSKI BANK KREDYTOWY	0.6
7	POMORSKI BANK KREDYTOWY	10.8
8	BANK DEPOZYTOWO-KREDYTOWY	4.9
9	POWSZECHNY BANK GOSPODARCZY	60.1
10	PKO	0.3
11	PEKAO	0.0
12	BGZ	11.5
13	BANK HANDLOWY	0.0
14	BANK GOSPODARSTWA KRAJOWEGO	-

Source: Calculation based on data from *Gazeta Bankowa* no 8/93

Table 5: Percentage of households' deposits in sight deposits (DSH/DS) and in term deposits (DTH/DT).

No	Name of the bank	DSH/DS	DTH/TD
1	BANK SLASKI	19.8	77.6
2	POWSZECHNY BANK KREDYTOWY	8.4	49.5
3	BANK PRZEMUYSLOWO-HANDLOWY	8.3	69.3
4	BANK GDANSKI	12.8	76.1
5	BANK ZACHODNI	21.7	79.6
6	WIELKOPOLSKI BANK KREDYTOWY	10.9	74.9
7	POMORSKI BANK KREDYTOWY	18.6	83.6
8	BANK DEPOZYTOWO-KREDYTOWY	18.5	79.8
9	POWSZECHNY BANK GOSPODARCZY	10.6	57.9
10	PKO	63.3	96.5
11	PEKAO	83.1	94.7
12	BGZ	45.4	53.8
13	BANK HANDLOWY	5.6	19.0
14	BANK GOSPODARSTWA KRAJOWEGO	-	-
15	BANK ROZWOJU EKSPORTU	0.0	0.2
16	BISE	8.7	1.3
17	POLSKI BANK ROZWOJU	-	-
18	AMERBANK	-	-
19	CITIBANK	-	-
20	CREDITANSTALT	-	-
21	INTERNATIONALE BANK IN POLAND	-	-
22	RAIFFEISEN CENTROBANK	-	-
23	BIG	1.2	13.1
24	KREDYT BANK	0.0	0.0
25	BANK ROZWOJU ROLNICTWA	3.5	61.3
26	AGROBANK	2.6	56.0
27	BYDGOSKI BANK KOMUNALNY	1.3	81.5
28	BANK ZIEMI RADOMSKIEJ	49.0	67.4
29	WSCHODNI BANK CUKROWNICTWA	2.9	92.4
30	INTERKRAKBANK	2.1	11.3
31	GLOB	0.0	24.6
32	BANK WLASNOSCI PRACOWNICZEJ	0.5	8.9
33	MEGABANK	0.0	14.7
34	BYDGOSKI BANK BUDOWNICTWA	0.2	43.7
35	BANK STAROPOLSKI	13.1	97.6

Table 5 (Continued)

36	GORNOSLASKI BANK GOSPODARCZY	5.7	71.8
37	BANK POCZTOWY W BYDGOSZCZY	0.0	89.3
38	BANK PREZEMYSLOWY W LODZI	3.0	44.8
39	BUDBANK	0.0	11.8

Source: Calculation based on data from *Gazeta Bankowa* no 8,25/93

Firstly, owing to a small number of their branches, private banks are not able to amass a large number of small individual sight deposits. Secondly, sight deposits of large firms cause too big a degree of concentration, which threatens with a temporary loss of liquidity.

The second feature distinguishing the state sector from the private sector is access to refinancing credit. (Table no 4) Refinancing credit serves to finance central investment projects and is accessible to the "Nine" banks and the BGZ. Because the refinancing credit rate is the lowest of all the rates at which banks obtain resources, a share of refinancing credits in deposits allows banks to achieve a higher profitability rate. This is of importance for state banks. An extreme case is the Powszechny Bank Gospodarczy, in which resources obtained thanks to refinancing credit account for over 60% of all deposits.

The structure of deposits proves interesting if the division into deposits made by households and by firms is adopted (Table no. 5). A characteristic feature is a low share of households in sight deposits with the exception of two banks: PKO SA and PEKAO. Owing to its large network of branches the former offers the very popular individual current accounts, and the latter amasses individuals' foreign-exchange deposits on current accounts. In most banks, households' deposits are largely the source of term deposits. However, there are exceptions to this rule. In the case of the state sectors, these are two banks specializing in foreign-exchange operations, namely Bank

Handlowy and the BRE. In the private sector, there are several such banks. The main reason is the deposit policy pursued by some private banks. Owing to a small net of branches, these banks do not seek to attract small deposits but concentrate on obtaining considerable sums of money by adopting a high minimum payment level and the principle of individual interestrate negotiations with the customer. This kind of policy is conducted by such banks as BIG, Interkrakbank, Megabank and Bank Wlasnosci Pracowniczej. Another reason for the prevalence of term deposits may lie in the specific nature of activity. The BISE is a good example. Set up to promote small and medium-sized business, it amasses mostly corporate resources. A similar example is provided by the Budbank, which services construction firms.

3.3 Structure of Loans

The structure of assets is largely indicative of character of banking activity. In the case of the nine state-owned commercial banks established after the division of the NBP, the share of credits in total assets shows clearly that these are credit banks (Table no. 6). The situation is similar in the case of the BGZ, BRE and PKO SA banks. On the other hand, the PEKAO bank has a very low share of credits in total assets. This bank specializes in foreign-currency services for individuals, and hence the slight number of credits given by it.

Private-sector banks vary greatly in share of credits i total assets. There are banks specializing in credit-giving activity such as Wschodni Bank Cukrownictwa and Bank Rozwoju Rolnictwa, which deal with giving credits to the agricultural and food industries. At the opposite extreme there are such banks as BIG or Bank Staropolski, which deal to a small degree with credit activity. Their areas of activity cover interbank operations and investment in securities.

The structure of credits shows that turnover credits are dominant (Table no. 7). In the case of the state sector, investment credits have a prevalent share in those of the "nine" banks which make considerable use of refinancing credit earmarked for central investment projects. Such banks are the Powszechny Bank Gospodarczy and the Bank Przemyslowo-Handlowy. A dominant share of investment credits was recorded in the case of the PKO SA and BRE Banks (the latter is the main source of foreign currency credits). With a couple of exceptions, private sector banks grant circulating credits. The exceptions are the BISE bank, which - as was already mentioned - serves to develop medium-sized and small business, and the Kredyt Bank SA.

Analyzing the credit activity it is worth noting a small role played by discount credit (Table no. 6). This credit is tiny in both the sectors. The share of discount credit is noticeable only in banks servicing the agricultural sector. This is exemplified by the BGZ in the case of state banks and by the Wschodni Bank Cukrownictwa in the case of private banks. In both these instances, discount credits are given on the basis of bills of exchange with which firms make payments for purchases of agricultural products.

Table 6: Credit-assets (C/A) and discount credit-credit (CD/C) ratios

No	Name of the bank	C/A	CD/C
1	BANK SLASKI	40.7	0.8
2	POWSZECHNY BANK KREDYTOWY	41.4	0.5
3	BANK PRZEMUYSLOWO-HANDLOWY	41.1	0.7
4	BANK GDANSKI	34.1	0.8
5	BANK ZACHODNI	37.8	0.9
6	WIELKOPOLSKI BANK KREDYTOWY	50.1	0.7
7	POMORSKI BANK KREDYTOWY	53.2	0.3
8	BANK DEPOZYTOWO-KREDYTOWY	35.3	-
9	POWSZECHNY BANK GOSPODARCZY	58.6	0.0
10	PKO	44.2	0.0
11	PEKAO	8.1	-
12	BGZ	66.7	4.9
13	BANK HANDLOWY	18.5	-
14	BANK GOSPODARSTWA KRAJOWEGO	51.0	-
15	BANK ROZWOJU EKSPORTU	45.8	4.4
16	BISE	61.1	-
17	POLSKI BANK ROZWOJU	25.2	-
18	AMERBANK	29.8	-
19	CITIBANK	16.6	-
20	CREDITANSTALT	13.4	-
21	INTERNATIONALE BANK IN POLAND	6.2	-
22	RAIFFEISEN CENTROBANK	11.1	-
23	BIG	17.3	0.4
24	KREDYT BANK	45.4	-
25	BANK ROZWOJU ROLNICTWA	68.8	1.5
26	AGROBANK	43.1	0.0
27	BYDGOSKI BANK KOMUNALNY	41.6	0.2
28	BANK ZIEMI RADOMSKIEJ	44.4	-
29	WSCHODNI BANK CUKROWNICTWA	80.1	34.5
30	INTERKRAKBANK	60.2	0.9
31	GLOB	29.3	-

Table 6 (Continued)

32	BANK WLASNOSCI PRACOWNICZEJ	28.1	-
33	MEGABANK	56.6	2.5
34	BYDGOSKI BANK BUDOWNICTWA	55.7	-
35	BANK STAROPOLSKI	15.3	3.0
36	GORNOSLASKI BANK GOSPODARCZY	40.0	4.1
37	BANK POCZTOWY W BYDGOSZCZY	21.5	-
38	BANK PREZEMYSLOWY W LODZI	55.7	-
39	BUDBANK	54.3	2.2

Source: Calculation based on data from *Gazeta Bankowa* no 8/93

Table 7: Investment credit/total credit (CI/C) and turnover credit/total credit (CO/C) ratios.

No	Name of the bank	CO/C	CI/C
1	BANK SLASKI	65.6	34.4
2	POWSZECHNY BANK KREDYTOWY	49.0	33.2
3	BANK PRZEMUYSLOWO-HANDLOWY	39.9	59.3
4	BANK GDANSKI	71.2	23.7
5	BANK ZACHODNI	87.7	11.5
6	WIELKOPOLSKI BANK KREDYTOWY	88.5	11.5
7	POMORSKI BANK KREDYTOWY	81.0	19.0
8	BANK DEPOZYTOWO-KREDYTOWY	86.5	13.5
9	POWSZECHNY BANK GOSPODARCZY	20.2	80.0
10	PKO	13.8	84.0
11	PEKAO	-	-
12	BGZ	-	-
13	BANK HANDLOWY	-	-
14	BANK GOSPODARSTWA KRAJOWEGO	-	-
15	BANK ROZWOJU EKSPORTU	25.4	74.6
16	BISE	2.7	97.2
17	POLSKI BANK ROZWOJU	-	-
18	AMERBANK	-	-
19	CITIBANK	-	-
20	CREDITANSTALT	-	-
21	INTERNATIONALE BANK IN POLAND	-	-

Table 7 (Continued)

22	RAIFFEISEN CENTROBANK	-	-
23	BIG	100.0	0.0
24	KREDYT BANK	-	52.3
25	BANK ROZWOJU ROLNICTWA	98.1	0.4
26	AGROBANK	96.4	3.6
27	BYDGOSKI BANK KOMUNALNY	71.2	24.0
28	BANK ZIEMI RADOMSKIEJ	99.6	0.4
29	WSCHODNI BANK CUKROWNICTWA	65.5	-
30	INTERKRAKBANK	99.1	-
31	GLOB	100.0	0.0
32	BANK WLASNOSCI PRACOWNICZEJ	100.0	0.0
33	MEGABANK	-	-
34	BYDGOSKI BANK BUDOWNICTWA	78.2	22.5
35	BANK STAROPOLSKI	95.3	1.7
36	GORNOSLASKI BANK GOSPODARCZY	100.0	0.0
37	BANK POCZTOWY W BYDGOSZCZY	84.3	-
38	BANK PREZEMYSLOWY W LODZI	78.2	21.8
39	BUDBANK	84.7	15.3

Source: Calculation based on data from Gazeta Bankowa no 8,25/93

3.4 Interest Rates

The interest rates demanded by the state sector differ significantly form the rates demanded by the private sector only in the case of sight deposits (Table no. 8). This is connected with the initial state of things in 1989, when most firms had their current accounts in state banks belonging to the "nine". Seeking to take over some of the corporate sight deposits, private commercial banks had to offer better terms. Let's note that two state banks, the BRE and PEKAO SA banks, acted in the same way.

It is hard to notice any differences in the level of interest rate on term deposits and credits. Such differences are not noticeable when the entire state and private sectors are analyzed. They become noticeable only when the level of interest rates in a given region is examined (Table no. 9). Then it is apparent that private banks offer deposits on better terms than state banks. As regards the rate of interest on credits, the analysis of base rates does not show any significant differences. Differences can be noticed only in the credit-awarding procedure, where private banks show greater elasticity in interest-rate negotiations.

Table 8: Interest rates of: sight deposits (rs)
one year deposits (rt), credit prime rate (rc), overdue debt penalty (rp)

No	Name of the bank	rs	rt	rc	rp
1	BANK SLASKI	6	40	42	60
2	POWSZECHNY BANK KREDYTOWY	6	44	40	65
3	BANK PRZEMUYSLOWO-HANDLOWY	5.5	52	42	-
4	BANK GDANSKI	6.5	46.5	46	80
5	BANK ZACHODNI	6	45	42	-
6	WIELKOPOLSKI BANK KREDYTOWY	7	46	47	80
7	POMORSKI BANK KREDYTOWY	6	48	47	75
8	BANK DEPOZYTOWO-KREDYTOWY	6	44	45	-
9	POWSZECHNY BANK GOSPODARCZY	6	46	44	80
10	PKO	6	38	48	96
11	PEKAO	16	44	38	80
12	BGZ	5	45	45	80
13	BANK HANDLOWY	8	40	41	60
14	BANK GOSPODARSTWA KRAJOWEGO	4.5	43	-	-
15	BANK ROZWOJU EKSPORTU	10	41	48	100
16	BISE	9	44	43	-
17	POLSKI BANK ROZWOJU	-	35	-	-
18	AMERBANK	10	40	50	-
19	CITIBANK				
20	CREDITANSTALT	10	40	-	-
21	INTERNATIONALE BANK IN POLAND	-	-	-	-
22	RAIFFEISEN CENTROBANK	-	-	-	-
23	BIG	15	43	44	100

Table 8 (Continued)

24	KREDYT BANK	10	39	41	-
25	BANK ROZWOJU ROLNICTWA	10	46	54	81
26	AGROBANK	10	46	48	100
27	BYDGOSKI BANK KOMUNALNY	12	50	50	90
28	BANK ZIEMI RADOMSKIEJ	9	50	46	90
29	WSCHODNI BANK CUKROWNICTWA	12	47	55	-
30	INTERKRAKBANK	10	53	48	96
31	GLOB	14	47	53	100
32	BANK WLASNOSCI PRACOWNICZEJ	9	51	46	-
33	MEGABANK	11	48	52	70
34	BYDGOSKI BANK BUDOWNICTWA	12	43	48	90
35	BANK STAROPOLSKI	12	48	42	80
36	GORNOSLASKI BANK GOSPODARCZY	6	48	46	80
37	BANK POCZTOWY W BYDGOSZCZY	8	50	45	100
38	BANK PREZEMYSLOWY W LODZI	15	42	48	-
39	BUDBANK	12	46	40	100

Source: *Gazeta Bankowa* no 8/93

Table 9: Interest rates of: Sight deposits (rs) one year deposits (rt) (LODZ region)

Name of the bank	rs	rt
POWSZECHNY BANK KREDYTOWY	6	44
BANK PRZEMUYSLOWO-HANDLOWY	5.5	52
WIELKOPOLSKI BANK KREDYTOWY	7	46
BANK DEPOZYTOWO-KREDYTOWY	6	44
POWSZECHNY BANK GOSPODARCZY	6	46
PKO	18	38-42
PEKAO	6	44

Table 9 (Continued)

BGZ	5	43
BANK HANDLOWY	12	40
BANK ROZWOJU EKSPORTU	10	41
BIG	10	45
KREDYT BANK	8	44
BANK ROZWOJU ROLNICTWA	10	46
AGROBANK	5-24	50
BANK PREZEMYSLOWY W LODZI	15	42
Invest-Bank	10	48
Lodzki Bank Rozwoju	10	48
Bank Spoldzielczy Rzemiosla	12	48
LTK-Bank	10	50

Source: *Gazeta Lodzka* 12 Jan.1993.

3.5 Banks' Credit Policy

The analysis of the development of the Polish banking sector leads to a conclusion that disregarding the technological backwardness connected with the lack of appropriate telecommunications and computer networks, Polish banks have mastered the basic rules of operation in a market economy: what is meant here is the ability to control the bank's liquidity (see Zukowski 1992) and to adopt an appropriate interest rate policy in order to attract deposits. It is their credit policy that gives rise to much concern. There are many reasons behind this state of things. Firstly, in the centrally planned economy, the investment process took place outside the banking sector. Secondly, the stock market in its current development stage cannot take over the function of a channel through which the investment process might proceed. Thus, this process has to proceed through the banking system. Thirdly, a high inflation level and the structural changes taking place at present cause considerable difficulties with evaluations of creditworthiness.

Taking the above into account, the state bank sector was considerably limited in its credit decisions. Credit limits were administratively imposed on those banks. It turned out that the scale of crediting was reduced by means of administrative instruments but no appropriate investment project selection mechanism was put forward. As a result, the phenomenon of bad debts began to mount. Table no.10 shows the share of bad debts in state banks in December 1990, 1991, 1992. As it can be seen, bad debts in some banks rose by several times in the course of 1991. The situation called for fast intervention: banks were obliged to amass reserves for bad debts (Table no. 11). An essential matter, however, was to force banks to pursue a cautious credit-giving policy. Did the symptoms of such policy occur in 1992?

After the three quarters of 1992, the share of bad debts accounted for 24.6% of total credits[5], and doubtful credits and loss for 27.6% of credits. Banks amassed reserves to cover the losses, and the amount of the reserves covered 20.8% of bad debts.

Thus, the growing phenomenon of bad debts was checked. The problem is whether this resulted from banks' better evaluations of corporate creditworthiness (see Pietruszynski 1993) or from other factors. The currently collected statistical material does not permit an unequivocal answer. Nevertheless, our analysis should allow for three factors:

- a relative decline in the credits granted,
- the credit crowding out effect by government expenditure financed by means of treasury bonds,
- improvement in the level of economic activity.

The first of the factors became noticeable in mid-1992, when the allot ed credit limits were not used in full by some of the "nine" banks.

Table 10: Bad debts/total credit ratio (BD/C)

No	Name of the bank	BD/C		
		1990	1991	1992
1	BANK SLASKI	2.1	9.7	18.2
2	POWSZECHNY BANK KREDYTOWY	9.8	35.7	31.7
3	BANK PRZEMUYSLOWO-HANDLOWY	2.2	6.4	7.5
4	BANK GDANSKI	16.1	23.8	18.0
5	BANK ZACHODNI	4.9	16.2	49.1
6	WIELKOPOLSKI BANK KREDYTOWY	1.7	17.9	25.8
7	POMORSKI BANK KREDYTOWY	10.9	19.0	40.6
8	BANK DEPOZYTOWO-KREDYTOWY	2.7	23.5	37.8

[5] The share of bad credits in the "nine" banks was similar and amounted to 22.1%.

Table 10 (Continued)

9	POWSZECHNY BANK GOSPODARCZY	2.8	6.8	7.8
10	PKO	-	9.2	22.9
11	PEKAO	-	-	-
12	BGZ	8.4	17.9	19.8
13	BANK HANDLOWY	-	-	37.1
14	BANK GOSPODARSTWA KRAJOWEGO	-	-	-

Source: Data from *Gazeta Bankowa* no 32/92

Table 11: Reserves for bad loans (RESD) and bad debts (BD) (December 1992, mld zl)

No	Name of the bank	RESD	BD	RESD /BD
1	BANK SLASKI	1140	2210	51.6
2	POWSZECHNY BANK KREDYTOWY	924	4012	23.0
3	BANK PRZEMUYSLOWO-HANDLOWY	745	1076	69.2
4	BANK GDANSKI	936	1145	81.7
5	BANK ZACHODNI	665	3191	45.2
6	WIELKOPOLSKI BANK KREDYTOWY	1271	1925	30.0
7	POMORSKI BANK KREDYTOWY	1742	3561	20.8
8	BANK DEPOZYTOWO-KREDYTOWY	304	2125	14.3
9	POWSZECHNY BANK GOSPODARCZY	238	1172	20.3
10	PKO	-	14166	-
11	PEKAO	2735	-	-
12	BGZ	966	7072	13.7
13	BANK HANDLOWY	4897	5769	84.9
14	BANK GOSPODARSTWA KRAJOWEGO	21	-	-

Source: data from *Gazeta Bankowa* no 18/93

Thus, it was the first case ever that credit expansion was checked by banks themselves, without administrative control. There are two processes behind this phenomenon. The first of them seems to be a better creditworthiness evaluation by banks. This is corroborated by the stabilization of the situation of enterprises having no creditworthiness and a steady fall in the number of enterprises losing creditworthiness (Table no. 12) Banks already gathered sufficient information to evaluate firms' reputation, thanks to which firms were divided into those which lost creditworthiness and those which were still credit worthy. The cessation of credits to the former enterprises should be viewed as crucial to the reduction in credit expansion. The question is how banks used the spare resources which resulted from their reduced credit activity (see Daniluk 1993b). This phenomenon is accounted for by the second of the processes: increased purchases of treasury bonds in connection with the financing by the government of the budget deficit (see Rajczyk 1992). It is, however, hard to say what was the cause and what was the effect in this process, i.e. whether banks were investing money in treasury bonds of necessity, i.e. because of the surplus of resources produced by their cautious credit policy or whether it was the other way round: the abundant supply of bonds bearing good interest was encouraging banks to reduce their credit activity. It will be possible to resolve which of these possibilities is more likely by analyzing the prices of treasury bonds on the secondary market after the original issue of treasury bonds expires (Table no. 12.).

The third factor, an improvement in the economic activity level, had the smallest influence on the decline in bad credits. Firstly, the size of production growth is so small that it can hardly be considered a durable trend (Table no.12). Secondly, the financial results are better than those recorded at the beginning of the year, yet they are still far from satisfactory. In other words, enterprises' standing was not improved significantly.

Table 12:

Months	B/A	pb	X	pi	GNP
91.12	15.3	-	2880	4.8	81.3
92.01	16.2	45.6	3100	3.2	96.6
92.02	17.8	46.4	3947	2.9	90.0
92.03	17.9	46.5	4144	3.5	98.8
92.04	18.0	46.3	4258	3.4	104.5
92.05	18.8	46.0	4317	3.4	102.5
92.06	17.9	45.7	4388	3.3	107.6
92.07	18.6	42.9	4450	3.3	109.6
92.08	18.6	42.6	4474	3.3	106.8

Table 12 (Continued)

92.09	18.4	42.4	4497	3.0	113.1
92.10	18.7	42.0	4550	3.2	109.4
92.11	19.2	40.5	4546	3.1	112.9
92.12	15.6	41.6	4448	2.1	114.6

Securities/assets ratio (B/A),
Average profit of 3 Treasury bills (pb)
No of firms without credit-worthines (X),
Profitability rate (pi),
GNP index (the same month of previous year = 100)

Source: NBP Information bulletin 11/12, 13 1992

4. Changes in the Banking Sector Transformation Policy

It could be observed that the NBP gave preference to state banks in its policy in 1992. The possibility of giving licenses to new banks was limited; in accordance with the resolution of the Polish Parliament, the minimal limit of the bank's own capital was raised to 70 billion zlotys. At the same time, certain banking services (e.g. foreign currency services) were reserved for banks with their own capital of PLZ (Polish zloty) 105 billion. The fact that state banks were given preference found its expression in the way in which the Krajowa Izba Rozrachunkowa (KIR - National Clearing House) was established. It is to substitute for the present system of interbank settlements. The KIR was set up in the form of a joint stock company, with banks as its shareholders. The banks making up the "big fourteen" and an insignificant number of private banks were allowed to share in this company. Thereby the banks being outside the system of the Krajowa Izba Gospodarcza (National Economic Chamber) will be forced to conduct their interbank settlements through their own accounts in a bank which is a member of the Chamber (see Struzynski 1993). The banks not belonging to the National Clearing House will incur two kinds of costs:

- the quality of their services will decline, for the time of many banking operations will be extended as a result of the necessity to clear through the account in the bank belonging to the National Economic Chamber,

- the costs of banking operations will rise, for the banks will have to pay the bank in which they have their clearing accounts for the operations made in these accounts (see Oldakowski 1993).

The third factor clearly pointing to the discrimination of the private bank sector is the fact that these banks were not covered by the Act on Financial Restructuring of Enterprises. This Act created procedures allowing banks to partly resolve the problem of the existing bad debts. On the one hand, it permits settlement procedures - advantageous for the bank - between the bank-creditor and the enterprise-debtor. On the other hand, the Act allows banks to exchange bad debts into 0-interest government securities. In this case, although the banks have no ensured possibilities of getting the interest, they have the possibility of recovering the invested capital. The exclusion of private banks constitutes a significant factor discriminating these banks (see Parafinowicz 1993, Groszek 1992).

The fourth element which will lower the competitiveness of private banks is connected with new regulations on cheque turnover. Cheques up to certain amounts can be cashed immediately, whereas under the new regulations each cheque may be cashed after its coverage in the account is checked. Large state banks having a large number of branches interconnected by a computer network will still be able to cash their clients' cheques at once. On the other hand, small banks will have to cash cheques in the time-consuming cheque collection (see Chenczke 1992b).

As the above shows, the degree of competitiveness of private banks has been falling in relation to state banks. It is worth adding that state banks already were in a privileged position:

- they had access to the cheapest source of financial means, i.e. to refinancing credits of the NBP (see Borys 1992),
- savings deposits were guaranteed by the government (see Chenczke 1992a).

It is worth asking the question: Why did a change take place in the Polish banking sector transformation policy? The experience gained in 1989 and 1990 pointed to a far-reaching demonopolization of the banking sector: 9 banks were set up from the regional NBP branches, very liberal bank-licensing regulations, including regulations on establishment of banks jointly with foreign capital, were introduced. It seemed that the Polish way of development of the banking sector would consists in a fast expansion of private banks, which would result in domination of privately owned commercial banks in Poland (see Kantecki 1993). What is more likely at present is a scenario of sharp selection of private banks and gradual privatization of the fourteen state banks through sale of their shares on the stock exchange.

Let's repeat the question once more: Why has the NBP been abandoning the liberal bank-licensing policy and giving clear preference to state-owned banks? There were many reasons for this. It was thought that liberal regulations concerning the issuance of licenses for foreign banks in Poland would attract foreign capital. In practice, the foreign banks opened in Poland have a relatively small capital, and their activity is confined to specific sphere of banking services (the functions fulfilled by foreign banks in Poland are discussed in greater detail in the next section). The liberal bank-licensing regulations and a relatively low minimal capital limit caused a fast increment in the number of banks (see Solarz 1993), for it turned out that of all the financial institutions such as banks, pension funds, insurance funds and unit trusts, banks were the easiest to open in Poland. As a result, a number of small banks were set up but they were not able to accumulate their own capital fast enough. As of 30 September 1992, 51 banks had their own funds below the required PLZ 70 billions.

It also turned out that lack of professional management and failure to observe the safety norms (prudential regulations) threatened a number of banks with bankruptcy (Jaworski 1993). The General Banking Supervision Inspectorate turned out to be unable to exact the fairly strict safety norms. In accordance with the Polish Parliament's resolution of 5 June 1992 on assumptions of monetary policy, state banks established before 1989 have to maintain their Cook ratios at the level of 8%, while the remaining banks have to keep this indicator at a higher level. As of 31 December 1992, 19 banks failed to achieve the specified level, and in the case of 8 of them the Cook ratio was negative. Disregarding the problem of inadequacy of the capital of the banks forming the big fourteen (this problem was connected with providing these banks with small capital at the time of their establishment), what matters here is the information that in 8 cases the Cook ratio was negative. This means that eight banks have negative own funds, and thus these banks should go into bankruptcy.

The growing number of banks in financial difficulties is a clear reflection of the accrual of negative own funds. They amounted only to -341 billion zlotys in 1991. In 1992, a rapid increase was recorded in that figure: -1,986.9 billion in March, - 2027.7 billion in June, - 8003.7 billion in August. The undertaken countermeasures allowed this level to be decreased to -5,187.9 billion zlotys in September.

For the sake of public trust in the banking sector, the banks were not declared bankrupt, but other solutions were looked for. In one case, the bank on the edge of bankruptcy was taken over by one of the largest private banks in Poland (having lost its liquidity, the Lodz Development Bank was bought out by the BIG, and in a separate agreement, the NBP guaranteed an appropriate aid packet for the buying bank). In the case of the second bank in which the bank's own funds did not cover its losses, a special commissioner board was appointed. Both these cited cases as well as the earlier events connected with the banking aspect of the ART B scandal showed that the banking supervision was not able to detect earlier enough and prevent the cases of prudential regulation breach. This state of things encourages the NBP to eliminate banks which potentially are unable to guarantee compliance the banking safety norms in the future.

Another reason for the restriction of the development of the banking sector lies in the credit policy. The signed letters of intent to the IMF imposed on Poland the necessity of strict control over the supply of bank credit. 1991 showed that the volume of credit should be controlled by means of administrative methods. Credits limits were assigned to the 14 state banks. It was not possible to exceed these limits even when the bank had a surplus of liquidity, for the resources sold in the interbank market by a state bank to a private bank were included into the limit of the state bank. A fast expansion of the private bank sector would preclude the possibility of administrative control by means of credit limits or the credit supply. For this reason, the restriction of the development of private banks was in the interest of effective control by the central bank of the volume of credit. Even though 1992 showed that the volume of credits could be regulated by the central bank by means of an appropriate policy of interest rates, it still turned out that the NBP was not able to affect an improvement in the quality of the credit portfolio. Credits in the irregular situation accounted for 24.6% of total credits. Unpaid credits accounted for 57.9% of all credits in irregular situation, difficult obligations accounted for 17.5% and doubtful and disputable obligations for 24.6% of all credits in the irregular situation. It is worth underlining here that the quality of the credit portfolio was similar for private and state banks (in the case of state banks, credits in the irregular situation accounted for 22.1% of total credits).

The arguments for the restriction of the development of private banks were provided by the financial results in 1992 (see Kokoszczynski 1993). Profitability - as was expected - fell by half in comparison with 1991. It amounted to 14.6% in the first quarter, to 12% for the first half-year, to

15.5% for the three quarters. and to 11.3 for the whole year. A closer analysis of profitability provides interesting information. The big "fourteen" achieved a profitability level of 13.3% (12.8% profitability rate, was recorded by the 9 banks established in 1989 from the regional NBP branches). Private banks recorded a loss, their profitability was -2.6%. Their negative profitability level was connected with the total loss of over 4,000 billion zlotys which occurred in 19 private banks.

Also the other economic indicators showed a lower efficiency level of private banks in comparison with state banks. In 1992 the costs increase for 44.8% and in the big 14 banks to 41.7%. Private banks had rate of costs' growth 70.9%.

The average ratio between the interest received by banks and the interest paid amounted to 124.8%. State banks recorded a higher level of this index (131.0) and in the case of private banks it was below 100%, to be more specific 92.5%.

Profitability of loans understood as the obtained interest to the total value of loans averaged 36.5% for all the banks, and this index was equal to 40.1% in the case of the state banks and to a mere 36.1% in the case of private banks.

The facts quoted above indicate that the expansion of the state banks was checked and if no significant changes are effected private banks will undergo a process of selection and will be shoved into the background of the banking activity in Poland.

REFERENCES

1. **Boguszewski P.**, (1992) "Wybrane problemy dzialalnosci kredytowej banków w okresie transformacji gospodarki", *Bank i Kredyt* no 10-12 pp.1-5
2. **Borys G.**, (1992) "Przekształcenia mechanizmu refinansowania bankow przez bank centralny", *Bank i Kredyt* no 7-9
3. **Chenczke T.P.**, (1992a) "Gwarancje dla wszystkich", *Bank* no 2 pp.18-21
4. **Chenczke T.P.**, (1992b) "Komu potrzebne sa polskie banki?", *Bank* no 3 pp.52-54
5. **Daniluk D.**, (1992) "Nowe prawo bankowe", *Bank* no 2 pp. 8-11
6. **Daniluk D.**, (1993) "Limity koncentracji kredytów i innych wierzytelnosci jako warunek budowy bezpiecznego portfela kredytowego banku", *Bank i Kredyt* no 2 pp.9-12

7. **Gronkiewicz-Waltz H.**, (1992) "Polski System Bankowy", *Bank* no 1/1992 pp.12-13
8. **Groszek M.**, (1992) "Banki a restrukturyzacja przedsiebiorstw", *Bank* no 3 pp.20-24
9. **Jaworski W.L.**, (1993) "Regulacje banku centralnego a biezaca sytuacja i perspektywy rozwoju bankowosci komercyjnej", *Bank i Kredyt* no 5-6 pp.27-32
10. **Kantecki A.**, (1993) "Problemy i kierunki rozwoju sektora bankowego w Polsce", *Bank* no pp.29-31
11. **Kokoszczynski R.**, **Wyczanski P.**, (1993) "Sytuacja finansowa bankow a finansowanie procesow wzrostu", *Bank i Kredyt* no 5-6 pp.38-43
12. **Oldakowski T.**, (1993) "KIR dla wszystkich", *Bank* no 4 pp.9-10
13. **Parfiniewicz A.**, **Zebrowski J.**, (1993) "Rola banków we wdrazniu programu restrukturyzacji finansowej przedsiebiorstw i banków" *Bank* no 5 pp.25-27
14. **Pietruszynska K.**, (1993) "Zdolnosc kredytowa podmiotów gospodarczych przyczyny jej utraty i odzyskiwania (1990-1992)", *Bank i Kredyt* no 4 pp.22-26
15. **Rajczyk M.**, (1992) "Dlaczego kredyt karleje?", *Gazeta Bankowa* no 44 pp.1-7
16. **Solarz J.K.**, (1993) "Docelowy model polskiego systemu bankowego", *Bank* no 2 pp.10-15
17. **Struzynski A.**, (1993) "Rozliczenia miedzybankowe - stan obecny i perspektywy", *Bank i Kredyt* no pp.30-33
18. **Zukowski P.**, (1992) "Miedzybankowy rynek pieniezny w Polsce", *Bank i Kredyt* no 3 pp.2-6

Discussant's Comments on Mullineux and Belka; on Mullineux, Pruski and Klacek; and on Hrncir and Matousek

Clas Wihlborg

The system for corporate governance stands at the center of a well-functioning market economy. It has not received the attention it merits in discussions of transition problems for the formerly planned economies. The organizers of this conference deserves great credit for addressing not only important but very urgent issues.

Rules for corporate governance determine the rights and the incentives of owners and other suppliers of financial resources such as banks. A well-functioning governance structure enables "control" over firms' resources to change hands, when these resources are used inefficiently. Such a change in "control" may involve a change in ownership through hostile or friendly take-overs or a change in management.

Designing an effective corporate governance structure from scratch is nearly impossible because the legal framework underlying the structure is complex and it involves a variety of laws and rules for financial institutions, securities markets, corporate charters, management's rights and responsibilities, labour relations and competitive behaviour. The understanding of the incentive effects for those controlling corporate behaviour of the complex system of rules is not well-understood but these effects have become a fruitful and rapidly expanding area for economic research.

A few basic principles of effective corporate governance structures have gained wide-spread agreement. For example, it is notoriously difficult to obtain effective mechanisms for control of management behaviour with state-ownership. The government or the state as an owner can fire a badly performing management team but it cannot fire itself when its objectives start veering away from wealth-maximization on behalf of the owners. Thus, for longer run effectiveness wide-spread private ownership with mechanisms for changes in ownership in response to incentives based on wealth-maximization is necessary.

A second principle for effective corporate governance is that effectiveness can be achieved under alternative institutional arrangements for financial markets. The Anglo-Saxon, the Japanese and the German system are very different but they are all reasonably well-functioning systems. Cultural industrial, and regulatory factors seem to combine to determine the specific set of efficient rules in any one country.

A third principle is that in most countries banks have played a very important role in corporate governance during the development stage and they continue to play a large role in small and medium sized firms with little access to securities markets. The central role of banks is derived from their incentive to monitor management and firm performance, and their power to force reorganization and/or restructuring by with-holding loans.

From the above principle it follows that if banks are to perform their monitoring- and control roles efficiently over the longer term, their management teams must work with incentives consistent with wealth-maximization on behalf of their owners. Thus, there is a very strong case for banks to be privately owned and subject to change in ownership and management structure. Furthermore, there are grave dangers associated with strong guarantees and insurance systems for those supplying financial resources to banks. In addition, there are dangers associated with privatization without solving the bad debt problem, because risk-taking incentives becomes too great when banks' net worth is low.

The paper by Mullineux and Belka (MB) is written in the spirit of the above principles for corporate governance and the role of banks. The banking sector is crucial for providing the "micro-budget constraint" on corporations preventing waste of resources but in order to perform this role banks must be subject to the same type of micro-budget constraint.

Unless banks individually are subject to micro-budget constraints, then there is no well-functioning macro-budget constraint with the consequence that inflation remains high. Thus, the macro- and the micro budget constraints go hand in hand in transition economies.

While the focus of much of the debate about economic policy in transition economies has been on macroeconomic stabilization - the macro budget constraint - this conference and in particular this session shifts the focus to the micro-budget constraint on banks and corporations as a precondition, not only for economic growth in the longer term, but also for macroeconomic stabilization.

As is clear from my comments so far I am in agreement with the spirit of the MB-paper. Besides addressing the principles discussed so far, the paper provides a look at Polish attempts at substituting a set of governance rules for banks for a fully recapitalized and privatized banking system. There are some attempts at recapitalization while "commercialization" substitutes for privatization, and bankruptcy procedures should induce improved financial discipline in corporations. "Commercialization" implies that banks' and corporate boards are assigned explicit commercial objectives as if owners were private individuals.

The MB-paper points to difficulties of inducing banks to work as truly private institutions imposing strong micro-budget constraints on the state-owned enterprises. The authors refer to lack of skill, lack of incentives in the form of, for example, executive compensation, and the existence of workers' councils as impediments to effective commercialization as well as to effectively functioning privatized banks.

In my opinion there is too much emphasis in the debate on bankers' inexperience, lack of good credit-evaluation system, and poor accounting and information system. These factors are often seen as an argument for going slow with privatization. This argument can be turned on its head. The incentive to develop skills and information systems would be strengthened by privatization since having owners of banks with wealth at stake provides a very strong inducement for the owners to ask themselves what they need to know more about. Although mistakes will occur, one should not underestimate peoples' ability to find solutions to their information problems. The learning process depends on economic incentives. There is a danger with privatization before learning has taken place if governments continue guaranteeing the liability side of the banks, and if the net worth of the banks is low or negative. Thus, it is essential to combine the privatization with debt-restructuring as well as a credible policy shift away from insurance of suppliers of funds to the banking system. In other words, I am very sceptical about deposit insurance schemes in transition economies. Such schemes can possibly be afforded by richer countries where economic efficiency need not be such a dominant policy objective. The deposit insurance schemes represent most likely a policy of "consumer protection" rather than a requirement for an effective payment system. There exists substantial evidence that periods of "free banking" have not been characterized by contagious bank runs.[1]

MB also touch upon the method of privatization in their rich paper. They refer to the free rider problem in monitoring by owners if ownership is widely dispersed. In Poland, the creation of a limited number of large funds in which people own shares, alleviates this problem while the Czech scheme implies less concentrated ownership. I believe that the fear of excessively widespread ownership is unfounded as long as the right to trade equity is not restricted. If there are substantial gains from concentration, it can be expected that funds will be created and individuals will appear with incentives to buy large amounts of equity in individual firms. Thus, it is a mistake to let endless debates about methods of privatization delay the process, when the problem caused by the lack of hard micro budget constraints requires urgent attention.

I agree with MB that allowing banks to own equity as in Germany increases the likelihood that a strong, monitoring owner emerges. For this no regulation is necessary but governments should rather avoid regulation of banks along the Anglo-Saxon model. Thus, the debate about the alternative "models" for bank-lending and banks' equity holding is superfluous. Lack of restrictions on banks' asset choice leaves the choice of "model" to the market. The Anglo-Saxon model is not the free-market model for banking as is commonly thought.

The Mullineux, Pruski and Klacek (MPK)-paper covers grounds similar to those covered in the MB-paper. The spirit is in line with the principles outlined above with a few additions.

MPK suggest government guarantees for funding of small and medium sized companies. There is some evidence that such firms have born the brunt of a credit crunch on the macro level in combination with a lack of micro constraints on state-owned enterprises. There is certainly a case for guarantees as long there is no limit to the credits given the large state-owned enterprises. I am less sure the case remains after privatization, and after the creation of a banking system able to impose the budget constraint on small firms. Allowing the banks to own equity in firms should also help increasing the supply of credit to viable small and medium sized enterprises.

MPK also point to the need for bankruptcy procedures to be legislated. This type of legislation seems to be high on the agenda in many transition economies. However, I wonder how such procedures can become effective if the micro budget constraint is imposed on firms. A wave of bankruptcies is likely to swamp the judicial system for years. Long delays in bankruptcy procedures can become a problem for banks that often are not willing to lend to firms unless they know that assets can be claimed with reasonable speed and certainty. Collateral is made meaningless in many developing countries by banks' uncertainty about their ability to claim collateralized assets.

This discussion implies that when banks' balance sheets are cleaned, the initial wave of bankruptcies by firms responsible for the bad loans must be removed from the system in order not to clog it up. This wave of company failures must be handled by a separate authority.

I would also like to question whether elaborate bankruptcy procedures are required in the initial stages of a market economy. It would seem that banks are in the position to take over distressed firms at a low price by refusing new loans. Thereafter, the banks would have responsibility for resolving disputes about claims from different stakeholders. Such non-legislated procedures may not minimize "agency costs" but it is important that governments and parliaments do not create legislation that they lack the legal capacity to implement.[2]

More important, from the point of view of a functioning banking system willing to lend to viable projects, is that property can be used as collateral against loans. This is especially important for loans to entrepreneurs and it requires that title to property is clearly defined and transferable.

The paper by Hrncir and Matousek (HM) provides a picture of progress towards privatization and the imposition of hard micro budget constraints in the Czeck Republic. They point towards the same kinds of problems as in the Polish case discussed in the papers referred to above. The Czeck government has neglected the bad debt problem and continued to build-up of inter-enterprise arrears.

HM discuss the economic and political forces in a transition economy that contribute to making the problem both hard to solve and of increasing urgency. They point to the lack of procedures for enforcing credit contracts and the incentives of existing state owned banks and enterprises to delay a resolution of the problem.

The authors also raise the potential moral hazard problem caused by the writing off of large amounts of debt. This problem implies that when large amounts of debt are forgiven it is necessary to impose the micro budget constraint for the future with credibility. Banks and firms must have the incentive to claim repayment of loans and the legal system must have credible means for enforcing contracts.

The result of the combination of economic and political forces is that no strong policy initiatives are taken for fear of consequences in the form of wide-spread unemployment. The costs of this "muddling-through" policy is high, however, in terms of inflation and severe misallocation of existing resources as well as of new savings. It is hard to see a slow resolution of the problem without substantial risk that it becomes increasingly hard to solve. Unless the hard microbudget constraints are imposed incentives to build up debt in wasteful firms and projects remain. Vested interests in the current situation tend to increase in strength with time so that both economically and politically, the problems of inflation and unnecessarily low growth rates become hard to solve.

REFERENCES

Cappie and **Wood** (1991), *"Unregulated Banking: Chaos or Order*?" Edited by Forrest Capie and Geoffrey H Wood London: Macmillan

Eliasson, G. and **C. Wihlborg** (1993), "Developing a Minimum Legal Framework for Economies in Transition", *Report to the ICC.*

Mullineux, Pruski and Klacek on Banking Reform: Comment

Frank C Wykoff
Pomona College, Claremont, California

The central banks of Poland and the Czech Republic are accomplishing remarkable feats in the transition to market economies. They are fortunate at this juncture to receive this thoughtful paper from three experts on financial market structures. Mullineux, Pruski and Klacek (MPK) provide an excellent guidepost along the road towards institutional financial health.

When Soviet tanks withdrew from central Europe in 1989, the Poles and Czechs began dismantling their communist' controlled central planning structures in order to construct institutions that would nurture development of an economy driven by decentralised decisions that respond to market determined price signals. In this very constructive paper, MPK argue that the transition is unlikely to succeed unless accompanied by compatible reforms in monetary institutions. The old regime of central controls must be replaced by a more flexible and forward looking financial system conducive to the development of a private market economy. Crucial to this system is a structure of flexible market-determined interest rates upon which various lenders base their choices. A flexible market system of interest rates assures that financial resources, like real resources responding to market signals, will flow to their most desired social uses.

MPK present tables in parts 3 and 4 showing that, by the end of 1992, considerable progress on monetary reform had already been made in both countries. Each has not transferred commercial banking out of the central bank creating a two tier Western style system. Each country has encouraged the creation of many private banks. The central bankers concentrate on traditional central bankers' responsibilities: management of the payments system, supervision and regulation of the commercial banks, implementation of monetary policy, and execution of exchange rate policy.

Much, of course, remains to be done. Most lending for investment is still made by very large state-owned banks, and the principal recipients of loans are still the old, large state-owned enterprises rather than emerging small and medium size enterprises which undoubtedly represent these countries' futures. In Poland, for example, 84% of total investment lending was made by Powszechny Bank Gospodarczy in the coal mining center of Belchatow. In the Czech and Slovak Republics the two national savings banks control 90% of savings in their respective markets. Thus state owned banks would appear to hold 80% to 90% of all financial assets, and these banks are run by bureaucrats who cut their teeth under the old guard. Can one expect such individuals, operating in such an institutional setting, to encourage the transition away from the old regime towards decentralized, competitive markets? As if these entrenched legacies of communism do not present transition problems enough, the large banks also find themselves enmeshed in a complex web of financial transactions with former failing, large state-owned enterprises. These tie-ins take the form of bad debt instruments, that, non-performing assets on the banks' balance sheets.

MPK suggest ways to enhance appropriate development of a competitive banking system that will look forward to transition to private markets rather than try to prop up old state enterprises. Who better to provide such advice? MPK are expert in monetary theory and in modern European monetary institutions, including knowledge of European Community standards. One is a Pole and one a Czech, both keenly aware of the recent history of their countries and their legacies as well as of the successes and difficulties of recent reform efforts. The advice proffered is forward looking and wise, and I have little doubt that the central banks will adopt most suggestions as soon as politically feasible. In addition to the direct economic rewards of a better working, more market sensitive banking system, many of the proposals dovetail with requirements of the European Community, so that the new governments will come closer to qualifying for full EC membership. It is impressive and gratifying to see the European Community help their neighbours develop the technical and organizational skills and structures necessary for conversion to healthy private markets.

Two main themes underlie MPK's advice on monetary reform. First, the new democracies can choose from among two central banking models, the German universal model or the Anglo-American model. Second, the bad debt still on bank balance sheets from the old regime is resulting in a kind of market failure in which the banks that have the most financial resources (large, old and state-owned), continue to lend money to large, old, failing state-owned enterprises in order to protect the banks' own solvency as well as, possibly, the bankers' jobs. The old largestate-owned banks would be at risk of collapse should the old state-owned enterprises fail. Rather than continuing to pour funds into decrepit state-owned enterprises, banks, MPK argue, should start to provide financial capital to emerging private enterprises.

On the choice of central banking model, the authors endorse the German universal over the Anglo-American. The authors do not seem to take this recommendation very seriously, though, in the sense of putting up a strong argument in its favour. The point out that the essential difference between the two models is that the universal bank has greater "inside control" of corporations than the American-Anglo in that the universal bank actually involves itself directly in the governance of its corporate clients whereas the American-Anglo exercises less control so that governance of corporations depends more on "outside" monitoring by capital markets via stockholders of the corporation.

I essentially agree with this description, universal banks are more tightly involved in corporate decisions than their American-Anglo counterparts. This, however, does not mean that American-Anglo banks rarely involve themselves deeply in corporate policy. While the central bank itself does not, commercial banks actively engage in close scrutiny of corporate conduct when bank money is at stake. This is done through very carefully drafted and detailed contracts that contain frequent check points and that permit close monitoring. If corporations fail to meet an obligation along the way, then penalty fees are charged by the banks who have lent the money to the corporation.

Nonetheless, as the authors point out, the choice of model is controversial, MPK's rather half-hearted argument seems to rest on the historical short-sighted investment behaviour of the American-Anglo system in the eighties. This observation seems a bit misguided to me. In the U.S. at least, in the eighties real inflation-corrected interest rates were very high by historical standards. They were closer to 10% than to the normal 3% levels of the sixties and seventies. Does one really want to argue that firms in this environment should invest for the long haul? I think not, because it would have been difficult to find many projects that could have covered a ten percent rate of return.

In my view, the choice of system should depend upon industrial organisation arguments and upon the nature of the economy the bankers are going to be financing. In addition, I would consider issues related to political economy. Certainly, universal bank has been successful for Germany. The ability to coordinate plans for large firms in concentrated economic sectors simultaneously with the financial planning for the economy has made for a formidable economic competitor. But, why stop here? The Keiretsu system in Japan, even more tightly interwoven with family connections and cross fertilization between banking giants and integrated conglomerates, has been successful for Japan too. Here the linkages between financial considerations and corporate conduct are even tighter, I would argue, than in Germany, almost dynastic in nature. Why not this model?

During relatively stable periods of consistent growth, such centrally organized banking-commerce arrangements can indeed work very well. But how well do they respond to destabilizing, recessionary shocks, or to the need for radical restructuring? The U.S. economy has recently undergone, and continues to undergo, just such a radical restructuring. This restructuring has been going on for fifteen to twenty years now. Great corporate giants, U.S. Steel, Chrysler, General Motors, IBM and others have fallen on difficult times. They have been forced to shrink their work forces, curtail investment, replace top management, and still have lost market share. Meanwhile, entirely new industries, in telecommunications, computer software and hardware, genetic engineering, and so forth have blossomed in their place. These new industries are populated by many small and medium size enterprises rather than by giants. Would a highly centralized universal banking system, run by directors who also serve on the boards of the old giants, have had the will and capacity to accept such revolutionary change? Or, rather would they have prevented this massive reorganisation and resisted the inevitable forces of trade and technology? Adaptation to change is an advantage of less concentrated banking regimes.

My guess is that the economies of the emerging democracies may well reflect this recent American experience with many small and medium size firms, and that such a system may better be served by a more remote, flexible and disinterested central bank and banking system.

Perhaps as an American, I am more sensitive to the political economy arguments favouring the American-Anglo capital market oriented central bank model than are my European friends. The federal Reserve System, the U.S. version of a central bank, is a relatively diffuse monetary authority with limited supervisory authority over commercial banks and with no official direct involvement in the non-bank sector. This design and arrangement reflects primarily political considerations; namely, a long standing American mistrust of placing too much power in any one place, especially in the hands of central bankers. With their control of funds, banks have a good deal of power as it is. With their rules governing commercial bank balance sheets, central bankers have even more power. Does one really want to vest them with direct control in the non-banking business sector as well?

Concern about concentrations of power are not only related to possible abuse but to the extent of damage that can be done when mistakes are made by persons in concentrated power positions. In light of recent history of central control in Poland and the Czech Republic, I need to hear some very strong arguments before I would endorse a German unified model. In my personal judgment, diffusion of power and multiple checks and balances, while cumbersome, serve as important political buffers against abuse of power. Still, as the authors point out, this is controversial territory and a judgment call is required.

The second theme of the paper concerns the problem of the bad debt held by the major banks in Poland and the Czech Republic. The presence of these bad debts presents the authors with their most compelling argument for recommending additional banking reform. Though they do not quite say so explicitly, MPK are clearly concerned that the big banks, who hold the vast majority of assets, and who are still state-owned, are much too stingy with loans to the emerging private sector. They attribute this stinginess to excessive risk aversion, old habits, and so on. This is all true, but their most compelling argument is that the state-owned banks are protecting the bad debt on their own balance sheets by propping up their old friends, the large stateowned enterprises, with new loans. The bankers continue to fund these dinosaurs because the banks hold much of the bad debt issued by them and turning them away would be tantamount to admitting the bankers' own culpability under the previous regime. Furthermore, making loans to new, small firms is not only risky but a different activity for which old bankers are poorly trained.

I agree with MPK that these practices of the large, commercial banks vitiate the prospects for growth of the private sector. This represents a serious social concern. The banks are choking off new firms and throwing more good money after the old bad money already poorly invested in the dinosaurs. Banks, once an enterprise is failing, should withdraw funds almost immediately. Bankers in the U.S. for instance would not wait long to withdraw funds, downgrade credit lines or renegotiate loans if they were to suspect trouble, because they know that every investment dollar must be forward looking not backward looking. To profit maximizing firms all relevant costs are in the future, and poor investments made last year never justify the use of current funds. MPK are quite correct, the central banks need to find some way to induce commercial banks to alter their lending activity more toward new private firms and lend to the old enterprises only when the latter have a promising future.

Perhaps I can take a cut at fleshing out this argument. The bad debt from the old centrally planned regimes reflects errors made in the past that should not be allowed to have any influence on contemporary financial allocations. Consider, for instance, a worker in the old regime working in a factory for whom planners invest pension earnings into the state-owned bank. He expects to retire on his accumulated funds held in the bank on a state provided pension. When his funds entered the bank, back in say the early eighties, they were invested by the bank in a stateowned enterprise. If the state-owned enterprise had in turn invested these funds wisely, it would have hired physical capital, workers, energy and materials with these funds, combined these productive inputs in a process that would have generated products of value. In compensation for these valuable products, the state-owned enterprise then would have earned a rate of return on its investment which could be used to pay back the bank with a rate of return that in turn would have lead to growth in the real earnings power of the worker's pension fund.

Unfortunately, not all state-owned enterprises were sufficiently wise, honest, or careful with investment funds and production plans. Without either the lash of competition or the discipline imposed by a profit-driven banker, too many state-run enterprises squandered real resources back in the previous regime and wasted the workers' pensions. The key now is to recognize that the real economic resources lost, which are represented by today's bad debts,were incurred earlier when the state-owned enterprises produced shoddy products or unwanted goods and thus wasted the real capital, real labour, real energy, and real materials. These mistakes essentially prevent the enterprises from paying off their loans today which prevents the state-owned banks from honouring today's pension claims of former workers.

But the real resource waste occurred back in the old regime, and this happened because it was pathologically inefficient. The day Soviet tanks pulled out, the damage had already been done. Pension funds had already been squandered. In reality both the bank assets (loans issued to the old state enterprises) and its liabilities (deposits of former workers) today are worth much less than book value. No amount of contemporary finagling can change that unfortunate reality. Pensions and savings that Polish and Czech citizens thought were in their bank accounts are not there in a very real sense. Because the old regime failed to produce useful products with real resources, current financial obligations cannot be met. One hesitates to be blunt, but the fact is some large central European banks are essentially bankrupt. Bad assets mean that liabilities, promises to the public, cannot be honoured! No politician likes to deliver such bad news, but nonetheless the citizens' bank accounts are not fully matched by viable assets.

Given this reality, what can be done now? In other words, what is now the least costly policy for dealing with this sad reality? First, any policy should prevent the residual paper legacy of past errors from contributing to any additional waste of real resources. The main goal of monetary arrangements must now be to assist the proper allocation of real resources today among competing demands. There are two possible impediments to a successful policy. One is political. How does one announce to the public the negative legacy of former mistakes? Pension claims cannot be honoured, because banks are bankrupt. Neither the government nor the banks can meet social obligations made by the previous inept and corrupt regimes. Since bad news is politically hard to deliver, this impediment is an important consideration. Second, today's sound commercial and financial institutions should not be damaged by any new policy.

In principle one solution would be to invite an outside team of foreign auditors answerable to the central bank, but independent of the bank, to evaluate the balance sheets of banks in order to determine their net worth. Those that are bankrupt would then be restructured so that their uncovered liability claims would be honoured by the central bank at a ratio which reflects the audited value of the asset side of the balance sheet. This process would have no real goods' consequences, except the cost of the audit, and would make explicit the poor quality of old bank deposit accounts. Politically this should be easier to do sooner than later. MPK call for early action on the bad debt problem, precisely because one does not want the public to blame the new leaders and new system for this hangover from socialism. The now-sanitized banks would be responsible for all financial decisions hence forth, subject to central bank supervision and inspection. Depositors who can choose from among competing banks, given limited deposit insurance, will restrain bank lending practices, and the profit motive and bank stock value will help to balance bank policy between return and risk.

MPK stress that these countries deal with the problem "at an early stage in the transition". They advise the government to take over the bad debt. Elected officials may need some "foreign accounting experts" though to provide political cover for this process, because they do not have the resources to take over all the bad assets without at the same time acknowledging the poor quality of the corresponding bank liabilities. Thus MPK also recommend formation of a "debt consolidation bank" to recapitalize banks using funds from privatisation earnings and from IMF stabilization funds. They also suggest that bad loans be swapped with the state enterprises in exchange for shares in the enterprises.

This idea is sound, but one must be confident that such swaps will result in sound forward looking valuations of the enterprises' prospects rather than consisting merely of shuffling bad paper. To the extent that new sources of funds from the IMF, other international agencies and from privatization funds, are not adequate to cover the bad debt instruments on the asset side of bank balance sheets, bank liabilities must be retired by the central bank in some type of exchange. This would honestly inform the public of the deleterious impact on their savings of mistakes by old central planners.

Subject to this caveat, then, I find MPK's suggestions wise and constructive. The government, central bank and commercial banks will all enhance their credibility and stability by creating a clean break from the past. The sooner the central bankers find a way to remove the bad debt problem, the sooner the commercial banks under their care can begin to lend money to promising future ventures which will help in the socially desirable market driven allocation of real resources.

---

1. See Kevin Dowd. Reviews free banking-periods in his book. The bank runs during the 30s can be explained by misguided central bank behaviour.

2. See Eliasson and Wihlborg (1993) for a more elaborate discussion.

Part III:

Bank Regulation and Supervision and Lessons from China

The Prevention of Bank Runs in Eastern Europe:

Lessons from the West[*]

Daniel Goyeau
University of Poitiers
and
Amin Tarazi
University of Limoges

Introduction

In eastern european countries, now that the stabilization phase is over, the lack in a wide genuine financial market but also in an efficient banking industry constitutes the main obstacle to the transition process towards a market economy. It can be argued that the issue of a great amount of equity necessary to the privatization programme requires the development of a wide capital market. However such a strategy would obviously be more costly and slower than the reliance on bank credit to some extent[1]. It seems that leaving the potentially rare amount of equity to banks which could thereby participate to the development of the private real sector and grant loans may be a more efficient solution (Lacoue -

[*] Prepared for the Conference on Financial Reform in Eastern Europe (EC-ACE Project), Prague, 2-3 September 1993.

[1] For an assessment of the benefits and costs of both financing strategies in an economy in transition see Lacoue-Labarthe (1993).

Labarthe (1993)). Moreover, this type of strategy may appear more interesting because bank equity is in general invested in a more diversified asset portfolio than an individual firm's equity thereby less risky for investors specially in a transition economy. Also banks appear to be more able to ensure the financing of newly created firms. As a whole, in a transition economy, a broadly intermediated financing of the real sector seems to be the only solution to be considered.

However, it is clear that the banking systems established in centrally planified economies are not capable of ensuring their financing function in market oriented economies. Banking reforms implemented untill now have not allowed the emergence of an efficient and competitive market industry. For instance in Poland the state bank was split into 9 banks specialized in given activities and regions (only two in czechoslovakia) and the entry conditions were freed for the banking sector. As a result numerous new private banks emerged on the banking market. However state commercial banks still dominate the market holding nearly 92% of total bank assets (Raczko (1993)). Moreover the current policy of the central bank of Poland tends to encourage the development of state commercial banks (limitations on the issue of new licences, increase in the amount of minimum capital requirement, restrictions to be admitted to the national clearing house...). As noted by Raczko (1993) it seems that in the near future what is more likely is a sharp selection of private banks and a gradual privatization of the state banks. If that should be the case it then seems clear that the banking system can reach a given level of competitiveness and efficiency only if specialization is limited to some extent and if the rules imposed by the central bank are smoothened. Also in order for private newly created banks to be able to compete with the former large state banks merger and takeover operations may have to be encouraged to some extent.

One of the issues that then arises is relative to the soundness and the safety of the banking system as a whole. The first factor of instability concerns the runs that can be experienced by banks specially in fragile newly and weakly founded market economies as transition economies. The problems experienced in western economies suggest that this should be taken as a matter of serious concern.

As a matter of fact in order to ensure the stability of the banking system it is currently widely recognized that a credible either explicit or implicit deposit insurance system is a first order necessity. Apart from providing safety for bank customers (depositors) the deposit insurance system achieves the key goal of preventing bank runs. Runs are a potential problem because the assets of banks are relatively illiquid while their liabilities are short and are used as money (Diamond and Dybvig (1983)).

From a macroeconomic perspective a run on a failing or illiquid institution is perceived as negative because it potentially endangers the whole banking system by spreading (Domino effect) on other institutions (Paroush (1988)).

The social costs related to bank failures can be extremely high. Indeed one of the major roles of banks in imperfect capital markets is the production of information on lenders and borrowers (Leland and Pyle (1977), Diamond (1984)). In other words banks can be considered as essentially solving information asymmetries problems among borrowers and lenders. Moreover this monitoring function of banks is enhanced because of the close relationships with customers and also because banks simultaneously manage the assets and the liabilities of these customers. If the stock of information produced cannot be transmitted and thus if it is lost because of bank failures the cost of intermediation may become consequently higher (Bernanke (1983)). The result is a deficiency of the banking system and social costs that cannot in this case be countered ex post with conventionnal monetary policy instruments.

The major problem is thus to prevent bank runs either on illiquid or on insolvent banks. Indeed if the bank is only illiquid (that is experiences only transitory problems) a run by unsufficiantly informed depositors can cause the bank to fail. If the bank is already insolvent then the run while justified can increase the cost of failure since illiquid assets would have to be sold at an underpriced value.

While preventing bank runs is a necessity the question that arises is relative to the optimal rules that can be implemented to prevent them. If the presence of a credible lender of last resort who would support illiquid institutions could seem to be sufficient the only way to dampen any incentive towards runs is the existence of a credible deposit insurer. While a broad and explicit form of deposit insurance exists mainly in the USA in most OECD countries private or public agencies insure deposits up to a limit while the rest is implicitly publicly insured [2] (i.e. France with major banks being nationalized).

---

[2] Note that in the USA the insurance agency that is the FDIC (Federal Deposit Insurance Corporation) officially only ensures deposits up to $100 000. However in practice depositors are most of the time repaid in full.

Country (nature of insurer)	Coverage	Premium financed
Belgium (public)	BEF 500 000	yes
France (banks)	FF 400 000	no
Germany (banks)	30% of Capital	yes
The Netherlands (banks)	Dfl 35 000	no
U.K. (public)	75% of deposits up to £ 20 000	yes
Spain (mixed)	Ps 1500 000	yes

Source: Baltensperger and Dermine (1987 (b)) and Peccioli (1987) cited by Dermine (1988)

Concerning most eastern european countries, at present, deposits in state banks are insured by the governement but no system exists for private banks. While those private banks do not currently issue a great amount of deposits or at least now deposits they may encounter severe difficuties in the more or less near future with the privatization process.

However in the currently existing systems in most OECD countries while able to limit bank runs, deposit insurance potentially creates another problem related to insurance that is moral hazard effects. Because they are insured either explicitly by a private or public insurance corporation or implicitly by the government, banks can be encouraged to increase the riskiness of their activities thereby increasing their risk of failure and generating social costs. Indeed as long as the pricing of the premium charged by the insurer is computed on a fixed rate basis the heightening of risk taken by banks does not lead to higher costs of funds since insured depositors will not require a higher return on their deposits. Thus whereas uninsured institutions generate costs due to potential bank runs, insured ones generate costs because part of the potential failure costs are to be paid by the taxpayer. The problems encountered with deposit insurance in western countries potentially hold for eastern countries as far as the state insured banks are concerned and will obviously arise sharply when a given insurance system is implemented for private banks.

To counter the moral hazard effects related to deposit insurance, regulators went on regulating the banking industry very closely. However since the step towards deregulation taken in the late seventies in the USA or in the early eigthies in other countries, the only tools remaining in hand of the authorities are those which are commonly called prudential rules. Since directly regulating the structure of banking activities was of no matter anymore authorities enforced more stringent rules to constrain the strategic behaviour of banks. The main reaction to counter moral hazard incentives was to increase capital standards in the banking industry and since the late eighties at an internationally coordinated and more sophisticated level (Cooke ratio) (BIS (1987)).

However the effectiveness of capital regulation on the actual riskiness of banks that is on their behaviour has widely been argued (Kahane (1977), Blair and Heggestad (1978), Koehn and Santomero (1980), Kim and Santomero (1988), Rochet (1992).

Also the directly observable severe losses endured by the FDIC (Federal deposit insurance corporation) in the USA since the late eighties has opened a great debate aiming to reform the current system (see table).

	1988	1989	1990
FDIC Losses (Billion $)	4.2	1	4.7
Premium (% of deposits)	0.08	0.12	0.19

Source: *Revue Banque*, April 1991

In fact those losses occured despite a tremendous increase in the value of the premia charged. Therefore the extent of the crisis in deposit insurance has been perceived with such seriousness that the contributions to propose reforms of the system have recently significantly risen in number.

The aim of this paper is to draw lessons from the experience of current protective and prudential rules. The effectiveness of the prudential rules enforced to limit the social costs related to moral hazard behaviour are assessed as well as the reform proposals for deposit insurance.

A formal analysis of the moral hazard incentives of banks induced by deposit insurance is first presented (part one). One way to solve this induced effect is to impose a more stringent capital requirement (part two). Another way consists in increasing market discipline by rearranging the deposit insurance system (part three). Stress will be put on the particular frame that fits best economies in transition towards a market adjustment mechanism.

Deposit Insurance, Moral Hazard and Risk

Deposit Insurance, Moral Hazard and Risk

The effect of deposit insurance on the behaviour of banks and mainly on risk considerations has been widely analysed by economists specially in the case of the USA. The current debate concerning the reform of the insurance system due to the crisis experienced by the FDIC has lead to multiple developments.

Consider the simplified following bank balance sheet at time 0:

A_0	C_0
	D_0

where A_0 stands for bank assets, C_0 is bank capital (equity) and D_0 represents bank deposits. All amounts are economic values.

Without bankruptcy possibility the market value of deposits would be $D_0 = D_0^{rf}$ (riskless deposits value or historical book value). When bankruptcy is possible the market value of deposits D_0 is less than the value of riskless deposits D_0^{rf}. However if bank deposits are insured the value of deposits for depositors remains unchanged that is equal to D_0^{rf}. The situation can be summarized considering that depositors hold two types of claims: one on the bank and the other on the insurer (see Sharpe (1978)).

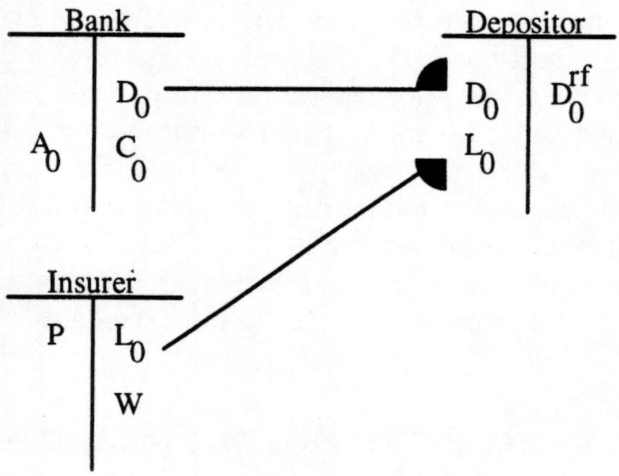

Depositors consider their deposits riskless that is of a value equal to D_0^{rf}. For the bank the value of deposits is D_0 in any case. The difference L_0 (= D_0^{rf} - D_0) represents the present value of the insurer's liability.

When failure occurs the situation can be represented as follows:

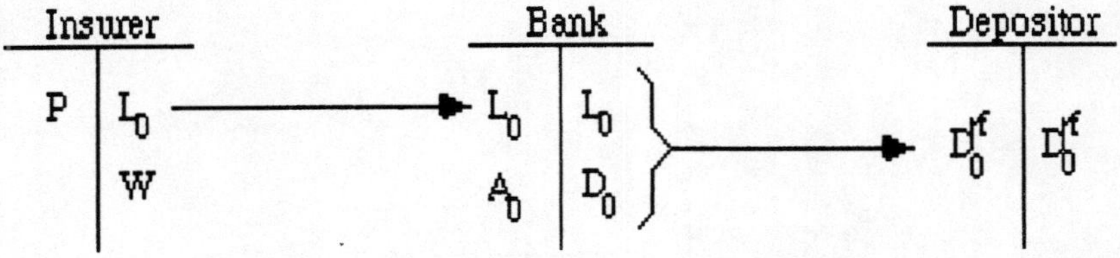

where P is the premium paid by the bank to the insurer and W the insurer's net worth.

In fact when deposits are insured the bank receives L_0 from the insurer. Thus to avoid a negative net worth ex-ante the insurer has to charge a premium that is at least equal to his liability that is L_0.

As shown by Merton (1977) the guarantee provided by the insurer can be considered as a put option written by the insurer allowing the bank to sell its assets at a strike price equal to the value of deposits D_T^{rf} (at maturity T). Specifically, at time T:

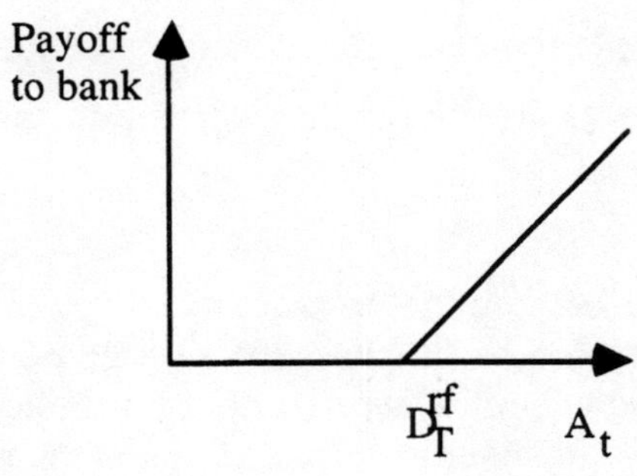

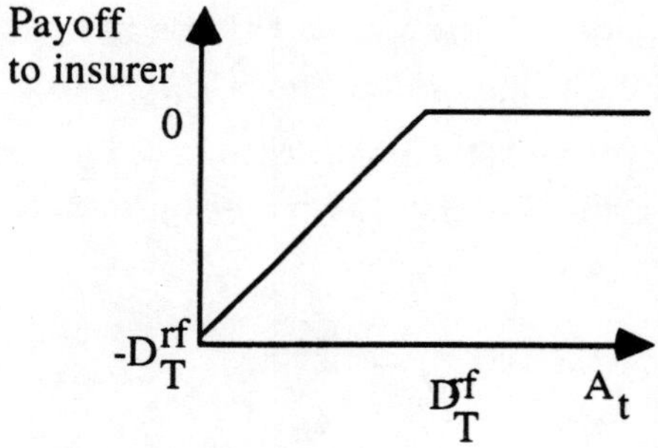

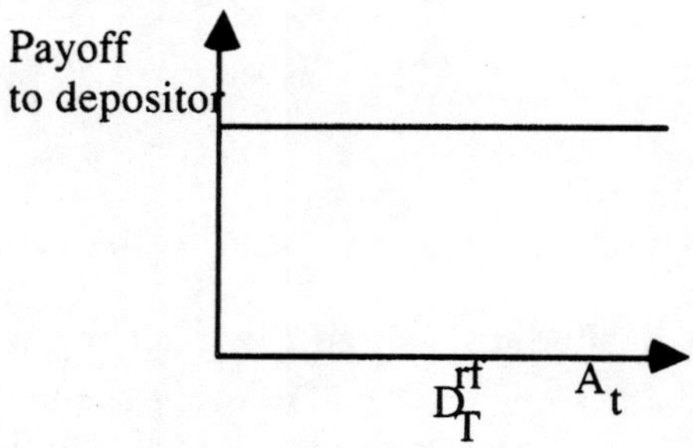

- if $A_T > D_T^{rf}$ the bank's capital value is equal to $A_T - D_T^{rf}$ the put option is not exercised and thus the payoff to the insurer is nil.
- if $A_T < D_T^{rf}$ the bank fails and exercises the put option (sells its assets to the insurer for an amount equal to D_T^{rf}). Depositors receive D_T^{rf} from the insurer and the value of capital to shareholders is nil.

The payoff to the bank in the presence of an option contract is thus the following. In case of losses on the bank's asset portfolio the losses to shareholders are limited to the capital intially invested plus the value of the premium paid to the insurer. In case of gains the return to shareholders can be unlimited. However it is not this specificity that should be stressed upon here. Indeed the payoff would have had the same profile if the bank were not insured losses to shareholders being limited to the initial amount of capital. In fact the insurance system can lead to a mispricing of the rate demanded by depositers (since deposits are considered risk free) that induces banks to take on more risk on their asset portfolio.

To summarize, at maturity T the bank receives from the insurer:

$$G(T) = \mathrm{Max}\,[\,0, D_T^{rf} - A_T]$$

Since the value of the put option on maturity depends on the value of assets its value G(t) on time t (with $0 \leq t \leq T$) will depend on the probability distribution of assets at time T. With the Black and Scholes valuation model the current value of the option that is at time 0 can be determined:

$$G(0) = D_T^{rf}\, e^{-r\,T}\, N(x_2) - A_0\, N(x_1)$$

where
$$x_1 = \frac{\log\frac{D_T^{rf}}{A_0} - (r + \frac{\sigma_A^2}{2})T}{\sigma_A \sqrt{T}}$$

$$x_2 = x_1 + \sigma_A \sqrt{T}$$

σ_A^2 measures risk (standard deviation of the rate of return on assets)
r is the risk free interest rate
N(.) is the normal cumulative probability function
Let $g = \frac{G_0}{D_0^{rf}}$ that is the current premium value per unit of deposit
$d = \frac{D_0^{rf}}{A_0}$ the leverage ratio
$\tau = \sigma_A^2\, T$ is the variance (volatility) of the return on assets during the term of the deposits

Rewritting the above expression it can be shown that:

$$g = g(d, \tau)$$

with
$$\frac{\partial g}{\partial d} > 0 \text{ and } \frac{\partial g}{\partial \tau} > 0$$

Thus the insurance premium increases with leverage and asset risk and the length of time separating the date of the next audit from today.

The value of the premium so obtained corresponds to that which should be charged in order to avoid a negative expected net worth for the insurer. If the actual premium per unit of deposit p (p = $\frac{P}{D_0^{rf}}$) is fixed and lower than the risk adjusted premium g then the difference g -p constitutes a subsidy supplied by the insurer. It can be easily shown that g -p is nothing but the spread between the interest rate required on uninsured deposits by perfectly informed depositors and the risk free interest rate. Now if p is fixed the extent of the subsidy will increase with g that is with leverage and asset risk. In other words if the insurer charges a fixed-rate premium the bank is encouraged to take on more risk to increase the subsidy. Thus a fixed-rate insurance premium creates a traditionnal moral hazard effect that can increase the default risk of the bank as well as that of the insurer. As a result since the insurance system either under an explicit or implicit form appears indispensable to avoid bank runs which can in turn threaten the whole banking sector (domino effects) the losses endured by the insurer agent have to be government financed incurring higher costs to taxpayers. A proposed way to solve this moral hazard incentive is to limit bank leverage by raising capital requirements i.e. imposing higher minimum capital to asset ratios.

Thus neither insurance system being perfectly fitted to avoid moral hazard incentives it appears necessary to turn to solutions in which regulation of banks are introduced.

Deposit Insurance with Bank Capital Regulation

The amount of capital issued by a bank is of great importance for several reasons. In fact capital can be considered to ensure essentially four functions (Harrington (1987)). The major function is that capital (equity) allows to absorb losses and thus prevents the bank from failing (buffer function). But it also increases the confidence of depositors, it makes the financing of the longer term projects possible and specifically for the banking industry it reduces the maturity or duration differential between assets and liabilities and thus decreases the exposure to interest rate risk. Thus, for all the reasons mentionned, for banks to be safe and sound higher capital positions are generally believed to be better than lower positions.

However because of market imperfections the desired level of capital banks are willing to issue can be different of that imposed by regulation. Since capital standards have rather significantly increased over the past decade in the U.S. in order to reduce the exposure of the FDIC but also in all other OECD major countries the issue of the effectiveness of capital regulation has widely been opened.

The effect of capital regulation on bank failure risk has been examined under alternative and competing assumptions. More precisely to admit that capital regulation can be of any use one must first recognize that capital markets are imperfect. Indeed if that were not the case the Modigliani-Miller capital structure indeterminacy principle would apply and therefore the question of an optimal leverage ratio and eventually of regulating the latter would not matter. First dropping the assumption of perfect markets the second step is to detect the nature of the assumed imperfection[3]. For instance should the stress be rather put on information asymmetries between bank shareholders and depositors or on incomplete markets or on both type of imperfections simultaneously ?

However among the various conclusions obtained by a great number of economists, most of the time, the extent to which the results are related to the capital regulation itself or to the institutionnal financial environment is not explicit. That is the presence of an explicit or implicit guarantee to depositors by the government is only implicitly taken into account in most models and the extent to which the results depend on a specific kind of guarantee remains unclear.

If in the U.S. it appears clear that more stringent capital standards can be considered as a response to moral hazard behaviour related to the subsidy provided by the current fixed-rate deposit insurance system the case of european countries is more ambiguous. In other words, if the *raison d'être* and the only purpose assigned to capital regulation in the U.S. is the limitation of the losses of the insurance fund (FDIC) its justification is, at least theoretically, less clear for other countries.

Within this framework deposit insurance is assumed to take place either explicitly or implicitly on a fixed-rate basis. If not one has to assume that bank depositors are insensitive to bank risk in the sense that they do not require an increase in the interest rate paid on their deposit to offset the increase in the risk of failure of the bank. Alternatively to explain that bank borrowing rates are unaffected by bank risk, fixed-rate deposit regulation can be invoked which for instance is still the case for France. However under this condition alone, banks would be unable to attract the

[3] Other than the straightforward reasons related to tax or bankruptcy costs considerations.

volume of deposits they wish in the first place. Eventually banks can be considered as benefitting from a rescue programme implemented by the authorities (lender of last resort) which avoids bank creditors the task of disciplinating the banking industry. At last bank depositors can be assumed to ignore the actual degree of riskiness of the projects financed by bank managers.

The issue of capital regulation has been addressed essentially under two competing sets of assumptions. First, banks can be considered as aiming to maximise the value of their expected profits or equity. They are then considered as risk neutral agents acting in an imperfect but complete market set-up (Kareken and Wallace (1978), Furlong and Keeley (1987), Artus (1990), Genotte and Pyle (1991), Rochet (1992)). Second, banks can be viewed as risk averse portfolio managers (mean-variance framework). Their objective is then to maximise the utility of their expected profits or equity in an imperfect because mainly incomplete market set-up (Kahane (1977), Koehn and Santomero (1980), Kim and Santomero (1988), Tarazi (1992), Rochet (1992)). Also, some developments attempt to combine the mean-variance framework with option's theory to price the subsidy provided by deposit insurance (Keeley and Furlong (1990)).

Banks as Value Maximisers

The major reason why banks can be considered as value maximisers is that bank shareholders or managers are able to diversify their personal portfolios (to attain their desired level of risk) by holding other assets in complete capital markets. However this implies that bank shareholders invest only a small fraction of their wealth in the bank. In other words in this framework not only capital markets have to be considered complete but the bank has to be owned by a large number of shareholders. In other words the banks involved are large publicly or widely owned institutions. Formal treatment of agency cost or bankruptcy costs considerations is thus here ignored.

Within this framework a number of papers show that under subsidized deposit insurance (fixed-rate insurance) it is necessary to restrict leverage in banking. This result is obtained applying option pricing theory to the banking firm following Merton (1977). In that case it is shown that the value of the subsidy provided by the insurer increases with leverage. The same result is obtained using state preference theory (Sharpe (1978), Kareken and Wallace (1978), Dothan and Williams (1980)). With both approaches it can be shown that for a given level of asset risk the relationship between the risk-adjusted insurance deposit premium g and the inverse of leverage ratio d is of the following form:

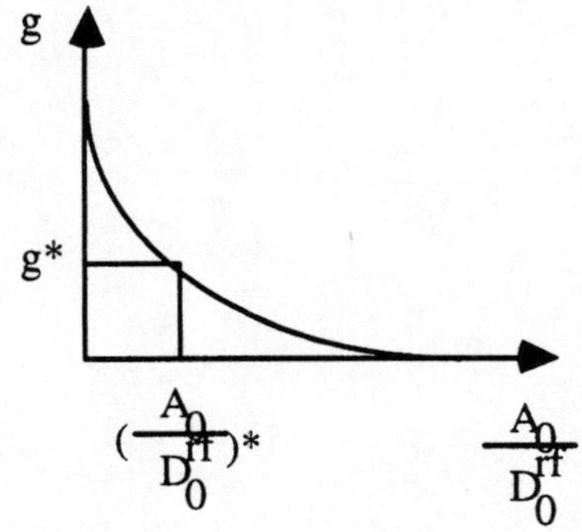

Given a level of asset risk an increase in the ratio of assets to the risk free value of deposits will reduce the per unit value of the insurer's liability. Therefore in the case where the insurer can also regulate the level of capital (state managed insurance agency) the value of the premium and the leverage ratio can be used as complementary tools. However as the allowed level of leverage increases the value of the premium to be charged increases at a higher rate suggesting that the risk-adjusted deposit premium could be too prohibitive in the absence of capital regulation or with low capital requirement.

However the question that arises is relative to the investment strategy and behaviour of banks with respect to regulation. In other words once the regulation has been implemented how are banks' investment sets altered and specifically how do banks react to the change ? Indeed nothing guarantees that once more stringent leverage is imposed by regulators banks will not restructure their asset portfolio. In fact when banks are supposed value maximisers the effect of capital regulation can be illustrated using option's theory. The value of capital to be maximised can be considered as a call option written by depositors to shareholders to buy the asset portfolio at maturity. The strike price is the value of deposits and the bank will exercise the call option only if the value of assets is higher than that of deposits. Since deposits are insured on a fixed-rate basis (or equivalently since depositors ignore the bank's default probability) the interest rate required by depositors is independant of risk (risk free rate) and moreover the option is written for free. Formally using the Black and

Scholes formula (Ronn et Verma (1986)) the value of capital C_0 can be expressed as:

$$C_0 = A_0\,N(z_1) - D_0^{rf}\,N(z_2)$$

where
$$z_1 = \frac{\log \frac{A_0}{D_0^{rf}} + \frac{\sigma_A^{\ 2}}{2} T}{\sigma_A \sqrt{T}}$$

$$z_2 = z_1 - \sigma_A \sqrt{T}$$

Since depositors do not require a rate greater than the risk free rate, to maximize its capital value the bank is encouraged to increase the risk (volatility) of its asset portfolio. At maturity the payoff to the bank is:

$$\text{Max}\,[\,0, A_T - D_T^{rf}\,]$$

that is while the payoff to the bank is at worse equal to zero it is potentially infinite. Since the value of the option (capital) is positively related to the volatility of asset return the bank is encouraged to increase the risk of its asset portfolio. In this framework the optimal risk taking of the bank results from bankruptcy cost considerations (reputation loss, liquidation costs...).

Therefore if regulators impose more stringent capital requirements on banks the direct initial effect is a decrease in failure risk. But to restore the pre-regulatory capital requirement optimum the bank reacts by increasing its asset portfolio risk and thus its failure risk. Furthermore according to some authors (Artus (1990)) the imposition of risk based capital requirement (Cooke ratio) would lead to the same result which rests basically on the limited liabiliy of the bank.

An opposite result is obtained by Furlong et Keeley (1987) using state preference theory. They insist that regulatory increases in capital requirements will not necessarily increase bank incentives to turn to riskier assets. That is while they recognize that banks will react by increasing asset risk the net effect is not necessarily a higher failure probability because the incentive to increase asset risk is lower when capital standards are higher.

Thus, globally, for value maximising banks the consequences of regulatory leverage restrictions on bank failure are difficult to assert.

Empirical studies on the net effect of capital regulation on the risk of failure (Furlong (1988), Tarazi (1992), Shrieves and Dahl (1992)) of banks provide unsatisfactory results because the increase in the risk of failure of banks in the 80's could be observed for banks indifferently. Therefore the extent to which the increase in failure risk was due to more stringent regulation cannot be clearly identified. Note that even when those studies tend to suggest that the effect of capital regulation on risk is positive (Shrieves and Dahl (1992)) the extent to which the result is related to capital regulation itself or to deposit insurance is unclear. Moral hazard phenomena related to deposit insurance cannot be precisely traced in empirical findings (Duan, Moreau and Sealey (1992)) although Grossman (1992) finds evidence of such behaviour in the 1930's in the U.S.[4]

BANKS AS UTILITY MAXIMISERS

If market are recognized to be incomplete to allow for perfect diversification, banks have to be considered as utility maximisers that is as risk averse portfolio managers. Risk aversion can also be put forward if it is assumed that most of the owners' wealth or portfolio is invested in the bank. In that case utility maximisation applies rather more on small owner-managed banks than large banks. Moreover if the presence of agency costs or bankruptcy costs due to conflicts of interest between managers and shareholders is taken into account again banks will maximise utility.

Following Kahane (1977), Koehn and Santomero (1980) and Kim and Santomero (1988) a bank can be considered as a price taker agent that can invest his wealth choosing among various combinations of a given number of risky assets say n while issuing a specific asset (that is deposits) at a fixed rate (Kahane (1977), Koehn and Santomero (1980) or random rate (Kim and Santomero (1988)) in all cases however independant of failure risk. Also the bank faces a leverage constraint that can either take the form of a simple capital to asset ratio or a risk weighted capital to asset ratio (Kim and Santomero (1988)). Formally the bank's problem is first to determine the efficient frontier that is the set of the combinations of assets that provide the lowest level of risk (variance of return on portfolio) for

[4] Note that according to Keeley (1990) this moral hazard incentive depends on the market structure of the banking industry. In deregulated and more competitive banking markets moral hazard incentives appear to be stronger. Indeed in regulated markets the fear of losing charters provides a discipline that is inexistant in deregulated markets with asymmetric information.

each level of expected return. Secondly, once the opportunity set defined the problem to solve is that of choosing the particular point that is the particular combination on the frontier that satisfies its preferences.

When capital regulation takes the form of a simple capital to asset ratio it is shown that higher capital requirements can lead to a result opposite to that expected increasing the risk of failure of banks. If banks do not react to the regulatory decrease in authorized leverage then more capital lowers the probability of failure of banks. However if banks react by reshuffling their asset portfolio in order to maintain their expected profitability (expected return on equity) then nothing guarantees a probabilty of failure lower than before. In extreme cases the risk of failure may be enhanced. To illustrate the possible reaction of a constrained bank consider the following situation:

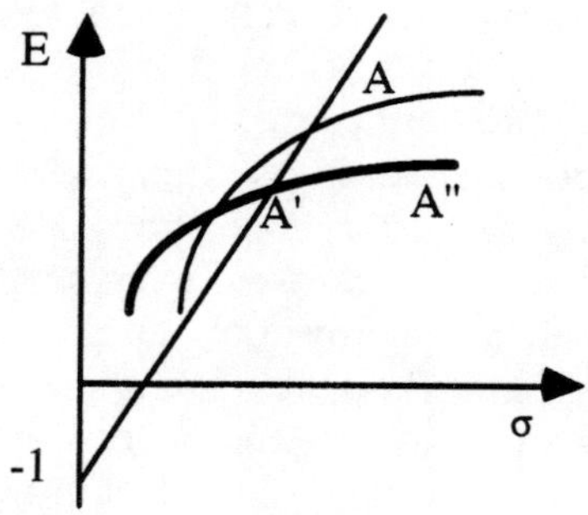

Initially the bank chooses a combination of expected return on capital E and risk σ on the efficient frontier that is represented by point A. If regulators consider that the probability of failure of the bank should not exceed a given level (combinations on the right hand side of the straight line are perceived as too risky) they will impose a higher capital to asset ratio. The result is first a shift of the efficient frontier downwards and to the left [5] and thus initially regulation achieves its goal the bank's combination of expected return and risk being now represented by point A' which is on the straight line that is at a tolerable probability of failure. However if the bank can react by reallocating its portfolio a case can be

[5] For formal proof see (Koehn and Santomero (1980), Kim and Santomero (1988), Tarazi (1992)). For an intuitive explanation however consider the traditional leverage effect $r_C = r_A + \lambda (r_A - r)$ where r_C: return on capital, r_A: return on assets, $\lambda = D/C$: leverage ratio, and r: risk free rate on deposits then: $E(r_C) = (1+ \lambda) E(r_A) - r$ and $\sigma(r_C) = (1+ \lambda) \sigma(r_A)$ thus more capital requirement (decrease in λ) leads to a decrease in both expected return and risk.

where to offset part of the reduction in expected return it could choose a combination that increases its probability of failure compared to the pre-hardenning of regulation for instance the combination A".

The recognition of such limits of capital regulation has indirectly lead to the imposition of constraints on the portfolio composition of banks. As noted by Kahane (1977) in order to avoid undesired effects the capital regulation of banks has to be coupled with the regulation of their asset portfolio. A way to achieve this goal is to introduce a risk weighted capital to asset ratio constraint that is impose a proper capitalisation rate for each asset component the rate being positively related to risk (Cooke ratio). In fact it can be shown (Kim and Santomero (1988)) that the theoretically correct weights should be defined in such a way that the bank's expected return on capital be bounded by E_b the expected return corresponding to combination A'. In other words as illustrated below the weights and the ratio fixed by regulators should make the efficient frontier become horizontal from A' so that any increase in risk becomes inefficient for the bank in the sense that it does not allow for higher return anymore.

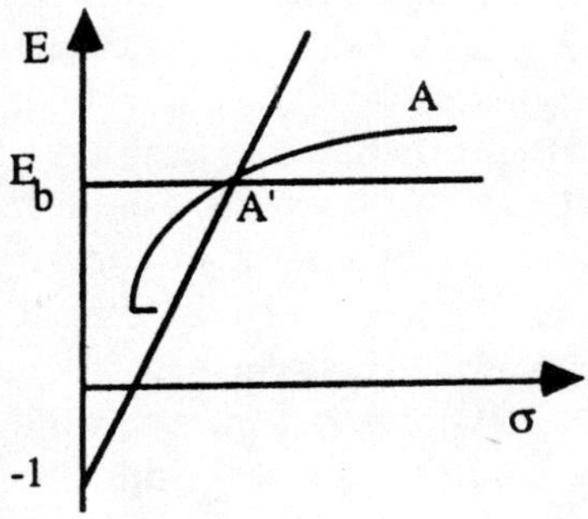

Formally the correct weights are shown to be dependant on the return on assets and deposits, on their variance-covariance structure and on the maximum level of failure probability fixed by regulators. In fact as shown by Rochet (1992) in the same framework a way to compute these weights is to make them proportional to the systematic risks (betas) of the assets.

Note that it could be argued that while most returns and risks can be considered as given to the bank (price taker) at least for some assets (loans in particular) the bank should be assumed to have a market power (price maker). The question is then: do the above results still hold ? Since the properties of the efficient frontier appear to be the same when the bank affects the return of a typical asset and when it takes returns as given for all assets (James (1976)) the answer seems to be yes.

While the above mean-variance framework is widely used it has severely been criticized by Furlong and Keeley (1987) and Keeley and Furlong (1990) on the grounds that it is inadequate to analyze bank failure risk and that the obtained results are thus derived from internally inconsistent assumptions. They argue that in the models used bank failure is not possible (bank failure is not taken into account since borrowing rates are independent of bank risk) and thus that the effect of regulation on bank failure risk cannot be studied in that context. While, intuitively, deposit insurance may seem to be a sufficient factor to explain why borrowing rates should and can be considered independent that is not the case. In fact Furlong and Keeley argue that with underpriced deposit insurance the effective borrowing rates would be lower as risk or leverage increases because the subsidy from the insurer (the value of the put option) is also higher. Moreover when bankruptcy occurs at worse shareholders only loose the initial amount of capital invested while their gains are potentially infinite. Thus it seems necessary to introduce limited liability into the model that is to recognize that the probability distribution of returns is truncated. Overall Furlong and Keeley conclude that in that case risk aversion alone is not sufficient to limit leverage and asset risk. And thus they point out that studying the effect of more capital on risk in a framework where it is not recognized that asset risk must also be limited by regulation is of no concern. In other words, implementing more stringent capital regulation without limiting the bank's asset risk with for instance bank examination should not be considered anyhow.

Moreover as shown by Rochet (1992) inserting limited liability in the portfolio model leads to a result where even correctly computed risk weighted capital requirements may fail in controlling the bank's behaviour when failure is very likely to occur. In other words when a bank's capital reaches a level so low that it is almost sure it will fail it may exhibit risk loving behavior that is choose riskier and riskier assets. This result suggests that continuous bank monitoring by supervisors may be necessary and notably that the regulator should close a bank before it effectively fails that is before its capital to asset ratio falls under a positive rate say 1%.

As a whole if banks are considered utility maximisers capital regulation appears insufficient to control bank risk behavior because the risk weights are difficult to assess for regulators and because in extreme cases even correctly computed risk weights can lead to the worsening of bank failure risk.

Conclusion

As a whole, for value maximising as well as utility maximising banks only a correct pricing (of deposit insurance premium or risk weights in the capital constraint) of risk can avoid a moral hazard situation where banks take too much risk. This result assumes that regulators or insurers are able to observe bank asset risk precisely. In that case the task of regulators and insurers is to solve information asymmetry problems among bank shareholders and depositors. However since information is difficult to collect two cases can be distinguished. If bank risk is underpriced moral hazard behavior still prevails and thus bank failure risk is not contained. On the other hand if risk is overpriced the structure of bank assets can be distorted the proportion of high risk assets being reduced (credit crunch). So this type of regulation is either inefficient or counterproductive. This explains why some economists reject it and specially when it comes to deposit insurance. The main argument is that it makes depositors completely insensitive to bank risk taking. Therefore alternative forms of deposit insurance are proposed in which depositors endure a part of bank risk playing at least a partial role in disciplinating the banking industry.

Alternative Deposit Insurance Systems

In order to limit moral hazard incentives of banks and the exposure of the insurer and the taxpayer different reforms have been suggested in the literature. The first set of reforms is designed to reduce bank risk incentives while eliminating the possibility of bank runs. The second set of propositions aims to increase market discipline in the banking industry in order to reduce moral hazard incentives while reducing but not eliminating the occurrence of bank runs completely. In fact in this second set market discipline is presumed to be enhanced because depositors have to monitor banks to some extent, constraining banks' risk taking.

Bank Run Protected Systems

Subordinated Debt

One type of arrangement consists in compelling banks to issue a certain amount of subordinated debt while maintaining the deposit insurance system. On the one hand a minimum subordinated debt to asset ratio would increase market discipline and reduce bank risk taking because of the marked to market feature of this type of junior debt. This however does not eliminate the incentive for depositors to run on banks. Thus on the other hand deposit insurance still remains necessary and even in a fixed-rate premium system moral hazard incentives are to some extent eliminated. Indeed as long as subordinated debt amounts to a sufficient level the rate paid on liabilities will be constraining and will serve as a signal to the market. However on the theoretical level applying a cash flow version of the CAPM (Capital Asset Pricing Model) Osterberg and Thomson (1992) show that the effectiveness of such a rule depends on the extent of forbearance by the insurer. Indeed forbearance by the insurer reduces the rate of return required on subordinated debt.

"Ex Post" Penalty

Another type of arrangement suggested by Baltensperger and Dermine (1987(b)) rests on a completely different mechanism. In this case there is no deposit insurance and depositors are considered responsible of bank losses even if they withdraw their deposits on time before bankruptcy. Thus the incentive for bank runs is eliminated because in any case depositors bear losses entirely. In practice however it is difficult to decide what date to choose to declare depositors responsible and specially how to compel them to repay other depositors in order to share losses with them. The fact that depositors are fully responsible should lead them to require a return in adequacy with bank risk therefore monitoring banks and thereby reducing bank failure risk. However the efficacy here, beyond practical implementation considerations, is directly related to the ability of depositors to observe bank risk. Indeed if risk is unperfectly observed a moral hazard incentive can lead to higher bank failure risk.

Marked To Market Deposits

Another proposition (McCulloch (1986)) is to price the value of deposits with respect to the value of assets financed. In this case the bank can be considered as a mutual fund the value of liabilities being continuously adjusted. However the success of such a system relies on the marketable feature of all assets. Although further securitization could effectively lead to the emergence of such institutions it appears difficult to implement in practice. Notably as long as market value accounting rules are not introduced in the banking sector this type of proposal cannot be considered.

Corporate Separateness

This proposal considers that basically banks can on the one hand issue only risk free deposits invested in marketable first order assets marked to market continuously and on the other hand create a risk taking corporation that is allowed to finance risky projects (Kareken (1986)). Depositors who hold risk free deposits have no reason to run even if the bank becomes insolvent. However as noted by Baltensperger and Dermine (1987(b) and Rochet (1991)) this would reduce the efficacy of the banking system in financing economic activity. Indeed the recognized functions of banks (transformation, liquidity service, economies of scope, information) may be altered if there is no cooperation between the two separated institutions.

The common goal of the above proposals is to increase market discipline in the banking industry while first preserving the system from the occurrence of bank runs. Other proposals still aim to increase market discipline while only partially preserving banks from runs.

BANK RUN NON-PROTECTED SYSTEM

A way to limit the moral hazard incentives of banks is to adopt alternative forms of deposit insurance that do not wholly cover depositors. A set of propositions consists of imposing a ceiling on insurance coverage per account or per individual at all depositary institutions. In each case the ceiling can be fixed or variable that is equal to some fraction of each account. An interesting feature of this system is that it protects small depositors who are presumed to be less informed. Thus this arrangement is designed to induce depositors with large accounts to monitor banks. It is precisely this ceiling on coverage that limits the prevention of bank runs because depositors will be willing to run for the repayment of the uninsured fraction of their deposits.

Through another type of proposal deductibles are introduced. The main feature in this case compared to the previous proposal is that all depositors (large and small) are induced to monitor banks.

Essentially these two sets of propositions can be analyzed through the two following forms. In the first version the guarantee provided by the insurer is limited. The second form is a deductible (that is the first say n monetary units are not insured in all cases (see Flood (1990) for detailed presentation).

Insurance With Coverage Ceiling

Under this deposit insurance arrangement depositors bear a part of the risk and this implies two main consequences. First the deposit insurance premium charged to the bank is lower than the premium under full insurance. Second the deposit interest rate required by depositors is positively related to bank risk taking. In this case it can be shown that the problem of the determination of the insurance premium and the interest rate on deposits can once again be formalized in terms of option's theory. In fact the insurer still writes a put option on bank assets at a strike price DT^{rf} to the bank as above. But now to hedge part of his risk he compells the depositors to write to him a put option on bank assets but with a strike price DT^{rf} - M (that is the amount of uninsured deposits, M representing the coverage ceiling).

The interesting implication of this deposit insurance arrangement is that the interest rate required on deposits can be computed from the put option written by depositors. And the rate can serve as a signal of the change in bank risk taking.

Such a system currently exists in many countries. For instance in the U.S. only the first $100 000 per depositor per institution are guaranteed (FF400 000 for France) (see table in introduction). However the effect of the insurance ceiling is widely reduced by the possibility of openning accounts in several institutions and also the fact that in practice the guarantee also applies for uninsured deposits. The reason is that full coverage is considered necessary to prevent bank runs.

Insurance With Deductible

In this case depositors bear the first losses endured by banks. In fact this arrangement is of special interest because it is similar to subordinated debt (junior debt) one of the propositions currently debated for increasing market discipline in the banking industry which was presented above. Indeed the rate paid on subordinated debt theoretically reflects a bank riskiness on the secondary bond market. In both cases option theory can be used to compute the rate of interest on such liabilities. More precisely depositors write a put option on the bank's assets A_T at a striking price D_T^{rf} to the bank and buy a put on A_T at a striking price D_T^{rf} - F (where F represents the deductible amount) to the insurer to partially hedge the risk on their deposits. The deductible provides a guarantee to the insurer because the strike price of the put option that he writes is only D_T^{rf} - F instead of D_T^{rf} as previously. In other words if the bank fails but losses are low enough the insurer is not sollicitated losses being completely beared by depositors.

Option valuation models allow to determine the interest rate required by depositors. However the meaning of this rate in terms of the bank risk taking is ambiguous. Indeed depositors simultaneously have long and short positions with two different striking prices. So the net effect of an increase in the volatility of bank asset return will depend on the current value of bank assets relatively to the two striking prices. More precisely, for low values of the current value of assets, depositors prefer a riskier bank asset portfolio because the rate of interest on their deposits is higher while it is the insurer that bears the risk of the potentially higher losses. Thus any decrease in the required interest rate by depositors does not necessarily imply that bank assets are less risky. Therefore the interest rate can no more constitute a signal of bank risk taking.

Globally all the proposals cited above (those totally as well as those partially protecting the banking system from bank runs) would be more efficient if bank accounting rules were based on market values instead of historical nominal values. Without such information insurers and depositors are not able to determine the actual (true) net worth and so the actual risk undertaken by the bank.

Also all the propositions presented above can be considered either with a government provided deposit insurance or with a private insurance. In theory private or public systems should be equivalent. However in practice government provided insurance has the advantage of being perceived as more credible to prevent bank runs. Indeed only public enforcement and government taxation power is likely to guarantee a protection perceived as perfectly reliable by depositors. In this case the aim of deposit insurance can be reached. In fact in practice government has actually played the role of the insurer's re-insurer. On the other hand private deposit insurance as long as it is based on competition will lead to a fairer pricing of deposit insurance premia. It would also reduce moral hazard incentives by enducing banks to take on less risk. However since less credible it would have to be protected by a public or private system of re-insurance. Moreover as suggested by Benston and alii (1986) it would be preferable to close banks before they actually fail (negative net worth). Indeed as mentionned above, when capital reaches a sufficiantly low level banks have more incentives to take risk increasing the extent of potential failure. This early closure possibility relies on a an enhanced discretionnary power of the insurer in enforcing the closure. Such a power is less likely to be given to private institutions.

EMPIRICAL EVIDENCE

On the empirical level a numerous amount of studies in the case of the US have analyzed the extent to which market discipline in the banking industry was effectively able to constrain the exposure to risk of banks (see Gilbert (1990) for a review of the empirical literature and for recent developments see). The problem here is to see whether discipline was corrupted because of unable investors and/or unwilling depositors to assess the relative degrees of risk assumed by banks at the individual level. If fact two questions are of interest here. First, are investors able of assessing individual bank risk? And second, if they are able to do so, do they effectively take risk into account when they require a given rate on their insured deposits?

In fact the answer to these questions appears to be clear. It seems that shareholders are able to assess bank risk since the required rate of return on shares in the banking sector is found to be positively correlated with risk. Thus information on bank risk seems to be at least partially reflected by share prices on the market. However when analyzing uninsured bank liabilities such as CDs (certificates of deposits) or subordinated debt (junior debt) more than half of the studies indicate that rates observed on the market are independant of bank risk. The only way to reconcile both results is to recognize that non insured debtholders are convinced that they will be repaid in full in case of bank failure. Since in practice in most cases a failed bank is merged with another bank which assumes all liabilities insured or uninsured debtholders effectively will not monitor banks even if they are able to do so. Particularly for banks considered as "too big to fail" the incentive for monitoring is presumably inexistent.

Thus unless subordinated debt is credibly perceived as such (that is risky) imposing a minimum subordinated debt to asset ratio will not increase market discipline and the rates of interest on such debt will not serve as a signal of the extent of the riskiness of individual banks.

Conclusion

The first solution found to financial instability related to potential bank runs is deposit insurance. However a simple fixed-rate deposit insurance is likely to lead to moral hazard incentives that increase risk of failure in the banking industry and generate social costs. Several solutions have been proposed to solve this problem: risk-adjusted insurance premia, prudential regulation, alternative deposit insurance systems, or removal of deposit insurance. All of these proposals rely on the assumption that an increase in market discipline is able to alter bank risk taking. In other words market discipline would replace or at least complement government supervision. Three questions are essential at this level.

First, do moral hazard incentives really exist? Empirical findings do not provide indisputable evidence.

Second, are banks able to reshuffle their asset portfolio easily? In fact even if the optimal reaction of banks, for instance to more stringent capital requirements, would be to increase the riskiness of their activity asset reallocation might be difficult to achieve for institutionnal reasons and cannot be instantaneous anyway.

Third, are liability and deposit holders able to assess bank asset risk to limit the risk assumed by banks? Again, empirical results provide contradictory conclusions. In fact as long as in practice even uninsured liabilty holders are sure to be repaid they have no incentives to analyze the market particularly when it is costly. An important step forward would be to introduce market value accounting in the banking industry which would guide not only deposit and liability holders but also supervisors and insurers.

Since market discipline is rather more difficult to rely upon specially in the case of transition economies with narrow financial markets and since market value accounting cannot be implemented, protective and prudential regulation based on market mechanisms cannot be considered. Only an individualized supervision of banks, that is close monitoring, is likely to ensure the soundness and the stability of the banking system. Techniques close for instance to the *CAMEL rating* system[6] existing in the USA can be applied to control bank risk at the individual level. However,

[6] Concerning bank supervision information collected by the authorities for individual banks are distributed according to 5 criteria: C (capital adequacy), A (asset quality), M (management competence), E (earnings) and L (liquidity). Once assessed the five criteria are weighted to obtain an index or score between 1 and 5. A bank scoring a 4 or a 5 is considered as experiencing severe deficiencies.

at present, this type of supervision appears difficult to apply. It seems crucial that bank balance sheets are first reorganized to exit the bad debts inherited from the past. Moreover inter firm high risk lending may have to be constrained.

REFERENCES

Artus P. (1990): "Le ratio Cooke et le comportement des banques", *Revue française d'Economie,* 5, Hiver.

Artus P., Pollin J.P. (1989): "les effets de la réglementation et le comportement des banques", article présenté au colloque de la *S.U.E.R.F.,* Sept.

Avery R.B. (1991): "Risk-based capital and deposit insurance reform", *Journal of Banking and Finance,* 15, Sept..

Baltensperger E., Dermine J. (1987(a)): "The role of public policy in insuring financial stability: a cross-country comparative perspective", in Portes-Swoboda Ed., *Threats to international financial stability,* London Cambridge University Press.

Baltensperger E., Dermine J. (1987(b)): "Banking deregulation in Europe", *Economic Policy,* 4, Avr..

Bank of International Settlements (1987): "*Proposal for the international convergence of capital measurements and capital standards_*", Dec.

Bank of International Settlements, (1986): *Recent innovations in international banking,* Basle, (the Cross report) April.

Benston G.J., Eisenbis R.A., Horvitz P.M., Kane E.J., Kaufman G.G. (1986): "*Perspectives on safe and sound banking, past, present, and future*", MIT Press.

Bernanke B.S. (1983): "Nonmonetary effects of the financial crisis in the propagation of the great depression", *The American Economic Review,* June.

Black F., Scholes M. (1973): "The pricing of options and corporate liabilities", *Journal of Political Economy,* May /June.

Blair R.D., Heggestad A.A. (1978): "Bank portfolio regulation and the probability of bank failure", *Journal of Money, Credit, and Banking,* 10, Feb..

Dermine J. (1988): "Assurance-dépôt et réglementation bancaire", *Revue d'Economie Financière* 5/6, Juin-sept..

Diamond D.W. (1984): "Financial intermediation and delegated monitoring" *Review of Economic Studies,* July.

Diamond D.W., Dybvig P.H. (1983): "Bank runs, deposit insurance, and liquidity", *Journal of Political Economy*, June.

Duan J.C., Moreau A.F., Sealey C.W. (1992): "Fixed-rate deposit insurance and risk-shifting behavior at commercial banks" *Journal of Banking and Finance*, 16, Aug.

Flood M.D. (1990): "On the use of option pricing models to analyze deposit insurance", Federal reserve bank of San Louis, *Review*, Jan./Feb..

Furlong, F.T. (1988): "Changes in bank risk taking", Federal reserve bank of San Fransisco *Economic Review*, Spring.

Furlong F.T., Keeley M. (1987): "Bank capital regulation and asset risk", Federal reserve bank of San Fransisco, *Economic Review*, Spring.

Furlong F.T., Keeley M.C. (1989): "Capital regulation and bank risk-taking: a note", *Journal of Banking and Finance*, 13.

Genotte G., Pyle D. (1991): "Capital controls and bank risk", *Journal of Banking and Finance*, 15, Sept..

Gilbert R.A. (1990): "Market discipline of bank risk: theory and evidence", Federal reserve bank of San Louis, *Review*, Jan./Feb..

Goyeau D., Tarazi A. (1992): "Evaluation du risque de défaillance bancaire en Europe", *Revue d'Economie Politique*, Mars-Avril.

Grossman R.S. (1992): "Deposit insurance, regulation, and moral hazard in thrift industry: evidence from the 1930's", *The American Economic Review*, Sept..

Harrington R. (1987): "La gestion par les banques de leurs actifs et de leurs passifs", *OCDE*.

James J.A. (1976): "Portfolio selection with an imperfectly competitive asset market", *Journal of Financial and Quantitative Analysis*, Dec..

Kahane Y. (1977): "Capital adequacy and the regulation of financial intermediaries", *Journal of Banking and Finance*, Oct..

Kane, E.J. (1989), *"The S. and L. insurance mess: how did it happen?"* Cambridge; MA:MIT Press.

Kareken J.H., Wallace N. (1978): "Deposit insurance and bank regulation: a partial equilibrium exposition" *Journal of Business*, 51(3).

Keeley M.C. (1990): "Deposit insurance, risk, and market power in banking", *The American Economic Review*, Dec..

Keeley M.C., Furlong F.T. (1990): "A reexamination of Mean-Variance analysis of bank capital regulation", *Journal of Banking and Finance*, 14.

Kim D., Santomero A.M. (1988): "Risk in banking and capital regulation", *The Journal of Finance*, Dec.

Koehn M., Santomero A.M. (1980): "Regulation of bank capital and portfolio risk", *Journal of Finance*, 35 Dec..

Lacoue-Labarthe D. (1993): "L'organisation de systèmes bancaires sûrs et efficaces en Europe centrale et orientale", *Cahiers économiques et monétaires*, Banque de France, 41.

Leland H., Pyle D. (1977): "Informational asymmetries, financial structure, and financial intermediation" *The Journal of Finance*, 32, may.

McCulloch J.H. (1986): "Bank regulation and deposit insurance", *The Journal of Business*, 59, Janv..

Merton R.C. (1977): "An analytic derivation of the the cost of deposit insurance and loan guarantees: an application of modern option pricing theory", *Journal of Banking and Finance*, Vol 1, June.

Modigliani F., Miller M.H. (1958): "The cost of capital, corporation finance and the theory of investment", *American Economic Review*, 48.

Osterberg W.P., Thomson J.B. (1992): "Forbearance, subordinated debt, and the cost of capital for insured depositary institutions" *Economic Review*, Federal Reserve Bank of Cleveland, quarter 3..

Paroush J. (1988): "The Domino effect and the supervision of the banking system", *Journal of Finance*, 63.

Raczko A. (1993): "Analysis of changes in the banking sector in 1992", paper presented at the workshop on financial reform in central european countries, *LARE* (25-28 march) University of Bordeaux I.

Peccioli R. (1987): "Prudential supervision in banking" Paris, *OECD*.

Rochet J.C. (1991): "Déréglementation et risque du secteur bancaire" Revue d'Economie Financière, 19, Hiver.

Rochet J.C. (1992): "Capital requirements and the behaviour of commercial banks" *European Economic Review*, June, 36.

Ronn E.I., Verma A.K. (1986): "Pricing risk-adjusted deposit insurance: an option-based model", *The Journal of Finance*, 41, Sept..

Sharpe W.F. (1978): "Bank capital adequacy, deposit insurance, and security values", *Journal of financial and quantitative analysis*, 13, Nov..

Shrieves R.E., Dahl D. (1992): "The relationship between risk and capital in commercial banks", *Journal of Banking and Finance*, 16, April.

Tarazi A. (1992): *"Risque bancaire, déréglementation financière et réglementation prudentielle"* Thèse de Doctorat, Université de Limoges, février.

Reputational Effects in the Lending Process and the Development of Banking Systems in Central and Eastern Europe*

David G. Dickinson
Department of Economics
University of Birmingham
Edgbaston, Birmingham B15 2TT
U.K.

Introduction

This paper is concerned with analysing how the process of bank lending is affected by a borrower's reputation, developed through long-term relationships between bank and customer, and hence on the development of the banking system. The issue is dealt with at a theoretical level, as well as being applied to an analysis of the banking systems in the emerging market economies of Central and Eastern Europe. In this respect, certain

* Prepared for a conference "Financial Reform in Eastern Europe", September 3-4, Prague, Czech Republic. Financial support from the EC under the ACE programme of the PHARE initiative, is gratefully acknowledged.

features of the model are designed to accommodate key institutional aspects of these economies.

The specific idea of reputation and its effect, both upon the behaviour of the bank and of the borrower, is a product of recent work which looks at banks as information processors and delegated monitors (Diamond (1989,1991) and Haubrich (1989)). Reputation here relates to the information, about past performance, which a lender uses to assess the borrower's probability of default. The particular subject of interest to Diamond (1989) and Haubrich (1989) is how the presence of these reputational effects can remove the moral hazard problem present in a debt contract, that a borrower has an incentive to invest in a riskier project once a loan has been granted, given that the choice of project cannot be monitored by the lender. Diamond (1991) extends this analysis to consider how reputational forces change the borrower's relative costs of borrowing through banks and capital markets, and argues that borrowers with a "high" reputation (earned by non-default over time) will find it cheaper to borrow through the capital markets rather than from the bank. An implication of this analysis is that banks will tend to provide finance for investment in the early stages of development of financial markets. It should be noted that banks forming long-term relationships with their customers is a well-established idea (e.g. Hodgman (1963), Wood (1975), and Blackwell and Santomero (1982), who argue that long-term relationships will lead to lower borrowing costs because of information advantages to banks of lending to existing customers although note the counterexample presented in Greenbaum, Kanatas and Venezia (1988)). Chan, Greenbaum and Thakor (1986) are interested in how repeated lending to customers is affected by the regulatory and financial environment. They argue that, since long-term relationships imply screening on the part of the bank, the costs of which are offset by surpluses earned from using the information to make fewer loans to customers likely to default, increasing competition, brought about by deregulation in the banking market, will reduce these surpluses and hence the value of the screening implied by long-term relationships. Lang and Nakamura (1990) introduce heterogeneity of borrowers, in the context of differential bankruptcy costs, and are interested in how learning about borrowers' quality, in the presence of both micro and macro risk, influences the dynamic behaviour of the credit market. In particular they show that unexpected shocks to the returns on loans have persistent effects, since the reduction in loans in the current period reduces the amount of information about lenders in the next period. Their analysis is the closest to the spirit of what is offered in this paper.

We are interested in incorporating the concept of reputation into a specific model of a bank, maximising long run discounted expected utility of profits through optimal asset selection and loan policy. The basic thrust of the model is that, in determining a bank's loan policy, the analysis must be conducted within a multi-period framework to capture reputational considerations a la Diamond, that borrowers are heterogenous in the sense that the probability of default varies across borrowers, and that the probability of default is subject to both macro (aggregate) and micro (borrower-specific) sources of risk. The model developed incorporates each of these features.

The remainder of the paper is divided into three sections. In the next section, we outline the model of a bank which we will use to analyse how reputation and lending interact, in the presence of both aggregate and borrower-specific sources of risk. The third section considers how this model can be applied to understanding the development of the banking sector in the emerging market economies of Central and Eastern Europe. The final section contains discussion of the policy implications of the analysis as a way of summarising the results of the model.

2. A Model of a Bank with Reputational Forces in the Lending Process

The simplest model which can be used to illustrate the arguments about borrower reputation and bank behaviour is one represented by the balance sheet below:

ASSETS	LIABILITIES
Loans to existing customers Loans to new customers Other Assets Required Reserves	Deposits Capital

A structure of this type has generally been the starting point for the analysis of the banking firm (see Baltensperger (1980), Santomero (1984) for surveys of the literature). The choice of endogenous and exogenous items of the balance sheet lead us into specific models of bank behaviour. The particular assumptions made here are that endogenous items are advances (to existing and new customers) and other assets, with reserves being set by regulation and deposits and capital being determined exogenously, the latter meeting regulatory requirements. Hence it is the asset side of the bank's portfolio which is the subject of specific analysis, while there is no role given to liability management (although we consider some aspects in the conclusion).

This highly stylised view of a bank can provide the necessary structure for us to examine how the bank's loan policy develops over time. It is sufficiently general for us also to consider the interaction between the bank's profit maximising activities and the regulatory regime under which it operates, and on how the starting point for the bank, in terms of its initial loan portfolio, influences the strategy which the bank follows over time.

Following O'Hara (1983) we will assume that the bank is run by managers who have the objective of maximising their discounted joint utility from consumption, financed by profits (this assumes that the share out between managers is settled so that it is in the interests of all to maximise the aggregate). We will also assume that the managers are (de facto, perhaps) owners and consequently we do not have to worry about dividend policy. This simplifying assumption does not detract from the main point of our analysis. The key decision which the managers of the bank face is to determine the intertemporal allocation of the bank's net worth, since this is the item which finances their consumption. We can formalise this decision in the following model.

The objective function can be written as:

$$\text{Max} Z_t = E_t \{ \sum_{s=0}^{\infty} U(C_{t+s})(1+p)^{-s} \} \tag{1}$$

where

$U(.)$ is a utility function obeying the Von Neuman / Morgenstern axioms
E_t is the expectation operator conditioned on information available at time t
$P_{t+s} = L^o_{t+s} r^o_{t+s}(L^o_{t+s}) + L^n_{t+s} r^n_{t+s} + B_{t+s} r^B_{t+s} - D_{t+s} r^D_{t+s}$
$- \gamma^o_{t+s}(L^o_{t+s}) L^o_{t+s} - \gamma^n_{t+s}(r^n_{t+s}) L^n_{t+s}$
$C_{t+s} = K_{t+s} + P_{t+s} - K_{t+s+1}$
C_{t+s} is manager/owners' consumption in time period t+s
K_{t+s} is the bank's net worth at time t+s
W_{t+s} is the total asset holding of the bank
L^o_{t+s} is advances to existing customers in time period t+s, with rate of interest $r^o_{t+s}(L^o_{t+s})$;
L^n_{t+s} is advances to new customers in time period t+s with rate of interest r^n_{t+s} ;
B_{t+s} is holdings of other assets at time t+s, with rate of interest rate r^B_{t+s}
$\gamma^o_{t+s}(.)$ is the default rate on loans to existing customers ;
$\gamma^n_{t+s}(.)$ is the default rate on loans to new customers ;

If the required reserves are a proportion k of total deposits, which are assumed exogenous, we can write the wealth constraint as:

$$W_{t+s} = (1-k)\, D_{t+s} + K_{t+s} \qquad (2)$$

and hence

$$B_{t+s} = W_{t+s} - L^{o}_{t+s} - L^{n}_{t+s} \qquad (3)$$

The assumption of exogenous deposits is for convenience and does not alter the nature of the problem that we are investigating. Note that it has been argued that the long-term customer relationship is important to the bank because it generates additional business for the bank (see Wood, 1975). This could be incorporated here by making deposits a function of the existing loan customer base, but this would not significantly affect the results presented, although it would add an extra facet to the benefits of an existing customer base. Additionally we shall assume that the solution to the bank's problem does not infringe the legally required minimum for bank capital (K*). Note that bank capital is the state variable of the system. In other words, the maximisation of discounted utility is consistent with the regulator's objectives. The rationale for this assumption is that failing to meet the legal capital requirement results in dismissal of the bank managers.

The above description of a banking firm will provide the framework in which we analyse the impact of reputation on the lending process and hence on the overall strategy which the bank adopts, with regard to asset selection. It is not a complete model of the banking firm given the assumptions made about choice and non-choice variables, but does allow us to bring out some of the key aspects of long-term relationships between banks and customers, and reputational effects in the lending process.

Note that banks are assumed to have some degree of monopoly power in setting interest rates for their existing customers, but not for new customers. The rationale for this is search costs (e.g. see Greenbaum, Kanatas and Venezia(1989)), where existing customers will look to their current bank to provide them with loans, rather than engage in costly search. These customers will be heterogenous in terms of their default probability, and γ^{o}_{t+s} represents the population default rate for them (the law of large numbers applies). New customers are, of course, of two types. There will be new entrants to the banking market, on which no information is available. There will also be those who have been turned down by their current bank as a result of an unsatisfactory loan performance. Given that this market is competitive and that information costs are sufficiently high that it is not profitable to try and distinguish between the two type of 'new' customer, a bank can expect a heterogenous set of both types of individual to apply for loans, with a population default rate

γ^n_{t+s}, in time period t+s. A key factor is that the γ^o_{t+s} £ γ^n_{t+s}, which is the reputation effect. Note also that both the default rates are functions of the level of loans granted. It is assumed that loans last for one period only. Hence, each period, the bank is faced with a new loan granting problem, with no existing loans being carried forward. This is equivalent to a situation where the bank can call in a loan at any time; hence continuation of an existing loan is the same as granting a new loan.

The bank makes decisions within an uncertain environment, and it is the form of uncertainty faced which has led to a number of different models of the banking firm. We shall assume that uncertainty relates only to the default rate - this allows us to concentrate on the impact of reputation on bank's decision-making. The default rate for new customers is assumed to vary from period to period with a time independent distribution. We can represent this as:

$$\gamma^n_{t+s+1} = \gamma^n(r^n_t) + \eta_{s+t}\gamma^{n\,\prime} > 0; \gamma^{n\,\prime\prime} < 0 \quad (4)$$

The first term $\gamma^n(r^n_t)$ is intended to represent the probability of default resulting from normal business failure; the dependency of the default rate on the interest rate is consistent with credit rationing models (e.g. Greenwald and Stiglitz (1981)). The latter term η_{s+t} is the disturbance which results from current aggregate level shocks and is assumed to be of a white noise stochastic structure.

The default rate for existing customers evolves in a fashion which represents two conflicting forces. There is a proportion of existing customers, each period, who default and hence lose that status. This has the effect of decreasing the size of the existing customer base and increasing the size of the new borrower set. In addition, the extension of the lending relationship with the other existing customers, has a reputational effect on the default rate. Consequently, the default rates depends upon the volume of loans granted to existing customers, and to the default rate inherited from the previous period. In order to capture these effects we will write the default rate for the existing customer base in the following form:

$$\gamma^o_{s+t+1} = a(L^o_{s+t+1}, \gamma^o_{s+t})\,\gamma^n_{s+t+1} (5)$$

and

$$\alpha^* \leq \alpha \leq 1; \alpha_1(.), \alpha_2(.) < 0; \alpha_{11}(.), \alpha_{22}(.) > 0; \alpha_3(.) > 0, \alpha_{33}(.) < 0$$

Note that the lower bound on a is a* (where a* > 0), to represent the fact that the minimum default rate is not zero (i.e. even known customers will default). When all customers are new α=1 and $\gamma^o_{s+t} = \gamma^n_{s+t}$. As the bank builds up a customer base we find that the default rate for repeated borrowing declines relative to that for new customers. If all customers were known to the bank, the default rate would be $a^{*}\gamma^{n}_{t+s}$. Macro risk affects new and existing borrowers in the same way. Although this is an arbitrary set-up, it is a simple analytical device to investigate the effect of reputation on bank behaviour.

3. The Model Solution and Implications

Given the setup of the model we can apply standard *dynamic programming* techniques to solve. This entails using a *value function* V(.) to represent the maximisation problem. This *value function* can then be used to find the optimising solutions for the choice variables.

The bank's decision can be written in the form:

$$\text{Maximise} V(K_t) = U(C_t) + E_t\left((1+r)^{-1} V(K_{t+1})\right) \tag{6}$$

and given, that the value function V(.) exists, the problem can be solved using the first order conditions for the problem represented by (6). These are:

$$\delta V/\delta C_t = U'(.) - E_t\left((1+\rho)^{-1} V'(K_{t+1})\right) = 0 \tag{7}$$

$$\delta V/\delta L^{o}_{t} = E_t\left((1+\rho)^{-1} V'(.)\, \delta K_{t+1} / \delta L^{o}_{t}\right) = 0 \tag{8}$$

$$\delta V/\delta L^{n}_{t} = E_t\left((1+\rho)^{-1} V'(.)\, \delta K_{t+1} / \delta L^{n}_{t}\right) = 0 \tag{9}$$

where

$$\delta K_{t+1} / \delta L^{o}_{t} = (r^{o}_{t} - \gamma^{o}_{t}) + r^{o}_{t}(.)'\, L^{o}_{t} - r^{B}_{t} - \alpha_1(.)\, \gamma^{n}_{t} L^{o}_{t} \tag{10}$$

$$\delta K_{t+1} / \delta L^{n}_{t} = (r^{n}_{t} - \gamma^{n}_{t}) - r^{B}_{t} \tag{11}$$

Note that it is assumed that other assets (B) are not a choice item, but evolve from the balance sheet identity.

The solution equations (7) - (11) can be easily interpreted. Choice of payment to managers from profits (C_t) is dependent on ensuring the marginal value from current consumption is equal to the expected marginal benefits from increasing the bank's net worth and enjoying higher profits (and consumption) in the future (equation (7)). The choice of loans to existing and new customers depends upon the relative benefits of placing those funds in the two loan categories, as shown in (8) and (9). These benefits are the present value of expected utility of the future consumption obtained from the marginal additional loans (set equal to zero for an optimum). The value, in terms of net worth (note that deposits and initial capital are assumed fixed), of additional loans are given in equations (10) and (11). Hence from equation (10) the first two terms are the additional return while the third term is the cost of using the funds to make the loan (note that we have assumed imperfect loan markets to existing customers). The final term is the change in the default rate from making an additional loan to an existing customer. For equation (11) the argument is very similar except that we assume that the new loan market is competitive, and that the default rate is not a function of the level of loans for an individual bank.

The solution equations are a set of non-linear partial differential equations which are not amenable to analytical solution. We could make some assumptions about the form of the utility function and the default function which would allow us to generate a tractable problem, or, alternatively, we could solve the system using numerical approximation, as has become popular in recent years. However we wish to employ this model only to gain some initial insight into the working of the reputational effects in the lending process, and to analyse the application of these results to the developing banking system in the transitioning economies of Central and Eastern Europe. Hence we shall use the basic framework outlined above to infer some simple comparative static results and to draw from these a number of implications for the development of the banking system. The full analysis of these results is contained in a separate paper, Dickinson (1994).

There are a number of effects which are interesting to consider when applying the model to the case of banking systems in Central and Eastern Europe. These are, in no particular order of importance:

(i) Effect of a change in the global default rate (γ^{g})

This impacts upon the default rate for both new and existing customers. It can be interpreted as the macroeconomic component of the default rate and could be the result of a change in the conduct of fiscal policy, or a shift in the toughness of monetary policy, for example. The effect of this change is to reduce K_{t+1} at existing optimum choice. Under certain condition (see Dickinson, 1994) this implies that consumption will fall as will the level of new and existing loans. The level of bonds will increase. Hence the acquisition of reputation is delayed for some borrowers and, consequently, the future level of banks loans is reduced. In this sense, current macroeconomic policy has long-lasting effects.

(ii) Effect of a change in the existing borrower default rate (α)

Suppose that there is a change in the financial security of existing customers. This could arise, for example, through significant changes in traditional industries, or through tougher loan policy at the bank (perhaps related to the relative poor performance of existing customers). The effect is similar to the case dealt with in (i) except that now only the loans to existing customers are affected. At the previous optimum there is a decline in K_{t+1} which impacts on all choice variables. However, under conditions identified in Dickinson (1994), there is a shift from existing customers to new customers in loan allocations. The long-term effect of this depends on whether the change in a is temporary or not. If the change results from a new loan policy then this may be long-lasting and consequently there will tend to be a smaller proportion of existing customers who receive loan extensions. The reputation process operates more slowly. If however the change is only temporary (decline of old customers to be replaced by new healthy ones) then the reputation effect will be re-inforced since the change in a can be seen as strengthening the loan portfolio and increasing lending to sound customers in the future.

(iii) Impact of a change in the discount rate (ρ)

A change in the discount rate has clear effects on consumption, a rise leading to an increase in consumption, for example. This change impacts on loan selection through the effect on K_{t+1} (in the case described this would fall causing a fall in loans to existing and new customers). Hence there is a reduction in the reputation effect and as a result the average default rate which the bank faces declines more slowly. The interpretation of an increase in the discount rate is that bank manager's are becoming more short-term in their outlook - perhaps because of increasing uncertainty about their likely future status in the bank.

(iv) Impact of a change in bond rate (r^B)/deposit rate (r^D)

We can consider the effect of a change in the exogenous interest rates, on bonds and on deposits. As the bond rate increases, for example through a desire of the government to move away from money-financed deficits, there is a substitution away from loans into bond (see Dickinson(1994) for the conditions), while if the deposit rate increases (for example as a result of more competition for savings among financial institutions) there is a redution in K_{t+1} which has the effect of causing a fall in loans both to existing and new customers (for details see Dickinson (1994)). Hence the reputation effect is less powerful and the overall default rate for banks will decline more slowly over time. For the case of a change in the bond interest rate we can note that this implies a long-lasting 'crowding-out effect', while for the deposit rate example we may observe that this implies competition may not be wholly beneficial to the allocation of finance although, of course, it may bring more savings into the financial sector and hence increase the amount of funds available for investment (this is the 'financial repression' argument for increasing real interest rates in developing economies).

(v) Impact of a change in required reserves (k)/ required capital (K)

The two potential policy variables in our model are the required reserves (kD) and the equity of the bank (K). We have assumed that these are exogenous to the bank. Suppose that there is a change in the required reserves of the bank. There will be a direct effect of this change on the wealth available for allocation into other assets which will impact on bank loans in the opposite direction to the change in reserves. Similarly there is an inverse relationship between the capital requirement and loans made by the bank (detailed analysis in Dickinson, 1994). An interesting implication of this analysis is that tightening the regulatory regime now will cause a decline in reputational forces in the lending process hence creating the need for greater regulatory tightening. This is a conflict which central banks need to face in determining the appropriate regulatory stance and to recognise the perverse results which may evolve when the lending process does contain reputational effects.

SUMMARY

The brief description of the comparative static properties of the model illustrate the impact of the reputational forces in the loan market, namely that any change, even if it only lasts for a single period will have persistent effects. Of course, even in the absence of reputational effects, the multi-period setting of the bank's decision problem would ensure that such changes would have longer lasting effects, but only in the context of the bank's net worth. The particular feature of the model here is that the loan market is directly affected.

4. Reputational Forces in the Banking Systems of the Transitional Economies of Central and Eastern Europe

In this section we will consider some of the key insights which may be gained from the model above. In particular, we shall be concerned with analysing how reputational forces will operate during the transition to a market economy, being undertaken by many of the former Socialist economies in Central and Eastern Europe.

The model has highlighted how long term bank - customer relationship can be advantageous to both parties. The well-managed bank will look to develop partnerships with their customers and, as a result, create a loan portfolio which is sounder (lower default rate) than would be the case if all customers were new. As a result, banks will offer existing customers preferential loan rates ensuring that there is an incentive for them to stay with the bank. The banking system will become characterised by these long term relationships.

However there are disturbances to this virtuous pattern. A tighter monetary policy (higher interest rates on government stock) will take funds away from the loan market, increasing loan rates as a result. There will be a detrimental effect on the default rate for new borrowers (the Greenwald - Stiglitz effect) and the failure to continue loans to some existing customers will reduce the soundness of the loan portfolio into the future. A deterioration in the macroeconomy will increase the default rate for all borrowers and result in a regression in the process of building long term lending relationships. Not only will banks tend to reduce lending in favour of fixed interest securities but also the increased default rate will put previously sound borrowers out of business and reduce the stock of existing borrowers to which the bank can lend.

The development of the banking system in the economies in transition has been affected by the sort of reputational forces we have introduced. The monobanking system has been broken up to create a commercial banking system. However this has been done by using the existing institutional structure and by artificially creating a number of commercial bank groups by amalgamating branches of the old state-owned monobank. In so doing the old lending relationships have been preserved.

During the early macro-stabilisation phase with a (relatively) stringent monetary policy operating, these relationships formed the basis of bank lending to the exclusion of new borrowers (private enterprises). This can be interpreted as a rational response to the environment which the banks faced. However, a further and very important incentive for this behaviour was that the banks inherited existing loans to the large, former state-owned enterprises which, if foreclosed would create financial problems for the banks themselves, particularly in the light of an inadequate capital base. The existence of 'passive lending' to these enterprises has been identified as a major problem during the early stages of the transition (see Begg and Portes (1992), who also identify the major problem of inter-enterprise credit replacing bank credit in a situation of tight monetary policy) and quite clearly prevents the operation of the reputational forces identified in the model of this paper. In the context of that model, the banks can ascribe a low default rate to existing loans, on the expectation that they will be continued. Hence there is an almost symbiotic relationship between the banks and the large, former state-owned enterprises. The problem has been exacerbated by the concentration of the inherited loan portfolio in certain industries and/or a region of the country. In order for a proper banking system to develop it is important to create the appropriate incentives for lending based on sound commercial judgment. There is a need for the banks' loan portfolio to be cleaned of *inherited* bad debts.

The exclusion of small and medium sized enterprises from the lending process, which can be ascribed to the type of bank behaviour described above, is also an important problem which needs tackling. The reputational model of the lending process highlights that these new enterprises, with no past credit performance, will find it difficult to obtain finance. As indicated this will be particularly true for banks with a large inherited customer base. The private banks which have been set-up could be a solution but they are necessarily wary of undertaking too risky a loan given that they must satisfy the normal regulatory requirements. The application of different regulatory standards, at least in the short term could ease this problem. Whilst this creates the potential for bank failure, as the loan portfolio grows, the reputational effects will bring the default rate and the capital requirement into closer conformity. The relaxation of regulatory requirements for this category of bank would also reduce the implicit tax on banks resulting from regulations and allow greater returns to be paid to depositors and dividends to owners of the bank, to compensate for the higher risks involved. Note that there is a conflict between the short-term costs (higher probability of bank default) and long-term benefits (quicker development of reputation among new borrowers) of relaxing the regulatory regime, which has been highlighted in the discussion of the model and its results.

In a similar vein, the regulators could also tailor their regulatory structure to reward the bank for prudent management. One way to achieve this would be to differentiate between loans which reflect the banks' development of long term relationships, and those which are more speculative and reflect risk-taking with new and unknown customers. This would create a reward for the type of activity which represents good bank management.

Methods of reducing the perceived default rate for new customers would clearly increase the attractiveness of loans and hasten the reputational process. The provision of accurate information on the credit-worthiness of new borrowers is an essential component of the creation of an efficient banking system. The results of the model suggest that a reduction in the default rate will assist in the development of a sound loan portfolio and this creates an incentive for the banks to engage in information gathering activities (we have not formally modelled this but it is clear from the model). However, there is clear free rider problem here, in that a bank which did not engage in information gathering activities could benefit from it by offering preferential rates of interest rates to borrowers who were existing customers of other banks and hence had a credit history. We assumed in our formal model that this process was halted by the existence of search costs for borrowers. These are likely to be higher during the early stages of bank development and consequently the free rider problem may be less significant. However, it is important for sharing of information on credit ratings to be a normal part of the operation of the banking market and should be encouraged by the central bank. The development of proper accounting systems and suitably trained staff to assess credit risks are also of importance to the process of reputation-building, in the sense that whatever information is available is available is used efficiently.

The objective function of the model also requires comment in the context of the developing banking systems of the former socialist economies of Central and Eastern Europe. The managers are assumed to maximise the present value of their consumption over an infinite time horizon. For the managers of the newly created commercial banks, the prospects for a long-lived tenure may be somewhat unlikely. Then it is straightforward to see that they will tend to consume more in the early stages of development (their discount rate is higher). Hence the reputational effects operate more slowly. In order to ensure that they use a longer time horizon, it is important to introduce the right sort of incentives. For example, building a managerial equity stake in the bank can make the managers value the longer term objectives implied by the reputational model.

5. Conclusions

We have considered a rather specific model of a bank which has highlighted some of the effects of reputation in the loan market and demonstrated that monetary and financial policy changes and the more general macroeconomic policy stance will influence the loan decisions of banks and that these current decisions have long-lasting impact on the loan market as a result of the breakdown in bank-customer relationships.

We have used the insights of this model to consider the development of the banking system in the economies in transition in Central and Eastern Europe and have argued that due account should be taken of the impact of reputational forces in the loan market in assessing not only how successfully the banking system is performing but also when determining the appropriate regulatory policy towards the banking system, particularly given the significance that the bank loan market will play in the provision of funds for investment.

This model is partial and incomplete and the results should be interpreted in that context. The concentration of the analysis on asset management ignores the fact that banks rely more and more on liability management. However, given the lack of competition between banks in the transitioning economies in Central and Eastern Europe, the rudimentary nature of banking and other finacial markets, and the lack of management expertise the emphasis placed on the asset side of the balance sheet may be a reasonable first approximation. Certainly the basic message of the model about the qualitative significance of reputational effects is unchanged. A further developemnt of the model would be to build the ideas presented here into an analysis of the credit market equilibrium. This would allow simulation of how the process of reputation can dynamically influence the rates of interest and the quantity of loans made to the three categories of borrowers (including the government).

BIBLIOGRAPHY

Baltensperger, E. (1980), "Alternative Approaches to the Theory of the Banking Firm", *Journal of Monetary Economics,* 6, 1-37.

Begg, D and **R. Portes** (1992), "Enterprise Debt and Economic Transformation: Financial Restructuring of the State Sector in Central and Eastern Europe", *Centre for Economic Policy Research,* Discussion Paper No. 965.

Blackwell, N.R. and **A.M. Santomero** (1982), "Bank Credit rationing and the Customer Relation", *Journal of Monetary Economics,* 9, 121-29.

Chan, Y-S, Greenbaum, S.I. and **A.V. Thakor** (1986), "Information Reusability, Competition and Bank Asset Quality", *Journal of Banking and Finance,* 10, 243-53.

Diamond, D. (1984), "Financial Intermediation and Delegated Monitoring", *Review of Economic Studies,* 51, 393-414.

Diamond, D. (1989), "Reputation Acquisition in Debt Markets", *Journal of Political Economy*, 97, 828-62

Diamond, D. (1991), "Monitoring and Reputation: The Choice Between Bank Loans and Directly Placed Debt", *Journal of Political Economy*, 99, 680-721.

Dickinson, D.G. (1994), "A Model of a Bank with Reputational Forces in the Lending Process", *University of Birmingham Discussion Paper.*

Greenbaum, S.I., Kanatas, G. and **I. Venezia** (1989), "Equilibrium Loan Pricing Under the Bank-Client Relationship", *Journal of Banking and Finance*, 13, 221-35.

Haubrich, J.G. (1989), "Financial Intermediation: Delegated Monitoring and Long term Relationships", *Journal of Banking and Finance*, 13, 9-20.

Hodgman, D. (1963), *Commercial Bank Loan and Investment Policy*, Bureau of Business and Economic Research, University of Illinois, Chicago, Illinois.

Lang, W.W. and **L.I. Nakamura** (1990), "The Dynamics of Credit Markets in a Model with Learning", *Journal of Monetary Economics*, 26, 305-18.

O'Hara, M. (1983), "A Dynamic Theory of the Banking Firm", *Journal of Finance*, 37, 127-40.

Santomero, A.M. (1984), "Modelling the Banking Firm", *Journal of Money, Credit and Banking*, 16, 576-602.

Stiglitz J.E. and **A. Weiss** (1981), "Credit Rationing in Markets with Imperfect Information", *American Economic Review*, 71, 393-410.

Wood, J. (1975), *Commercial Bank Loan and Investment Behaviour*, John Wiley and Sons, London.

THE SECOND BANKING REFORM IN TRANSITIONAL CENTRAL EUROPEAN ECONOMIES: AN ASSESSMENT*

Dominique Lacoue-Labarthe
Laboratoire d'analyse et de recherche économiques
Université Bordeaux I, France
Avenue Léon Duguit, 33604 Pessac

INTRODUCTION

Banking reform is closely linked to transition towards market economies in Central European countries. It was precisely the case in Hungary (1987), Poland (1989) and in the former CSFR (1990), among other countries. This reform essentially aimed at remodeling banking systems. Two groups of banking agents hived off from the former national monobank: a Central Bank, on the one hand, a number of administrative bodies called "banks", on the other hand. Some of these entities were previously created specialized agencies in foreign trade financing, mortgage loans etc. ; others stemmed from regional branches of the monobank structure. Later on, these bodies became genuine commercial banks when they were endowed with an advisory board and their capital was divided into

---

* Conference on Financial Reform in Eastern Europe Prague, September 3-4, 1993

shares sold to state-owned enterprises (SOEs), other public institutions, and in some cases, to foreign interests.

This two-tier public banking sector was completed by a third component consisting of a greater or lesser number of private banks in each country, depending on how liberal was the Central Bank in granting new licenses.

As far as macroeconomic adjustment is concerned, recession still goes on, except in Poland where signs of industrial growth are giving strong encouragement and hope to its watching Eastern neighbours. Inflation rates, indeed, already started to abate. The real sector may now look more sensitive to changes in command variables, particularly real interest rates which, recently, turned out to be positive. Budgets deficits, on the contrary, are deteriorating, and no significant inflows of foreign capital have yet been recorded as the IMF is still putting governments under strain, so that they hold on restrictive fiscal and monetary policies.

The financial situation may look even gloomier. Banking reform did not really succeed in solving the throbbing problem of bad debts. Surely, bad debts endanger creditors as well as debtors, pushing the former towards bankruptcy and worsening the budget deficit. Moreover, links between the state, SOEs and state-owned banks are still as ambiguous as they were under the command economy prevailing prior to political opening. Confusion of property rights, cross ownership between SOEs and state-owned banks and conflicts of interest hamper any attempt to build up consistent risk sharing and enterprise governance.

Banking reform neither prevented some banks, whether public or private, from becoming insolvent. A few bankruptcies were even officially declared in Poland last year. A credit crunch is also frequently reported. Besides, as a sign of further flaws in the banking sector, one can mention segmentation of deposit and credit markets, excessive sectoral or geographical concentration, insufficient capital adequacy, over-stated book value of loans, outdated systems of payments and inefficient supervision and control procedures by monetary authorities (Sheng, 1991.a ; Thorne, 1992). A rising risk of a major bank crisis and financial collapse is more and more hinted at.

In order to cope with this situation, a second banking reform was conceived in 1991-92 by the governments of these countries. This time, the reform aimed at prudential control and supervision of commercial banks. It is not, however, without consequences on the banking structure as it unveils banks' hidden insolvency. The latter cannot escape the following alternative anymore: either they go bust or they become a target for a merger. Besides, it certainly should not be taken for granted that simply defining, and perhaps even implementing, prudential control might prevent banks from a financial collapse.

At the center of most discussions and proposals for setting up a safe and sound banking system in transitional economies, we can clearly identify two crucial problems:

First, the issue of bank's profitability is essential insofar as it governs their medium and long-term perspectives as well as an efficient financial intermediation for the whole economy. Hence, one can argue that the first banking reform undermined the survival of the banks it had created, and that the second banking reform is just trying to give the banks a thrust forward, while it offers no guarantee at all as long as they are still saddled with bad debts strapping their profits.

The second problem deals with the attitude of banks towards risk, especially default risk. It is mainly a matter of capital adequacy and leverage, on the liability side of the balance sheet, related to the degree of risk included in the asset portfolio. The first banking reform actually generated a tremendous moral hazard problem in the whole banking structure, to the extent that it made banks completely unaffected by the risks they were supposed to bear. The new reform may well be, in this respect, demanding too much, too soon, in the guise of an extra amount of capital in accordance with the Cooke ratio standard prevailing among international banks. There is a possibility that this new requirement worsen former flaws affecting the banking sector as it might create a risk-loving behaviour with banks and increase financial instability.

Risk has multiple facets ; another one is systemic risk affecting payments and interbank transactions. Following the first set of reforms, this kind of risk appeared very acutely and monetary authorities proved totally unable, in certain circumstances, to cope with swindling and other failures of clearing procedures, if not simply causing more damages by their actions. Unfortunately, not much has really been done to allow for efficient monitoring and control on banks' behaviour in their mutual settlements.

In short, the new phase of banking reform only partially corrects the difficulties that arose in the wake of remodeling bank structures. Inherited problems linked to these changes are still hanging on and may hinder, from the start, the chances of the new reform to succeed. However, one may wonder whether things are in a fair way to improve, as they create a more comprehensive and consistent set of incentives and mechanisms, at least in the credit market.

1. Banks' Profitability

The former banking system was tailored to the requirements of a planned economy. The purpose of creating a single-tier banking sector was to ensure the allocation of financial resources necessary for the targets of the plans. Bank credit was not fundamentally distinct from budgetary subsidies. Banks did not have to select among credit applications according to their expected risk and return. Debt servicing was hardly a matter of concern because of roll-over credits or even perpetual loans procedures. Banks indeed were not used to monitor the creditworthiness of their debtors.

Following the first phase of reforms, the increase in the number of banks and the decrease in direct state control over banks provided, in principle, a greater scope for decisions based on profit maximisation behaviour. However, the constant large demand for credit by SOEs together with the reduced real resources of banks (due to tight monetary conditions and high persisting inflation), was not conducive to strengthening businesslike banking abilities and skills. In addition, the largest banks which are playing a decisive role in financing the economy, inherited a loan portfolio from the preceding period in which the proportion of doubtful and bad debts given to large SOEs in crisis was too high.

Unfortunately, neither the former nor the latter banking reform had succeeded in solving once-and-for-all the burden of this excessive indebtedness which definitely has kept preventing banks from achieving a sufficient level of profitability.

1.1. The Burden of Bad Loans on Banks' Profits

The different types of banks are not equally affected by the bad debts problem. The whole financial system is leaning under the burden of this inherited poison anyway.

1.1.1. State Owned Banks

Their balance sheets are particularly vulnerable. The bulk of non performing loans extended by the former national monobank was not equally distributed among the new state-owned banks when the two tier banking structure was created. Geographical proximity was used as the principal criterion for distributing bad loans among branches of the ex-monobank.

For instance, Katowice-based Bank Slaski received most of Poland's distressed steel and coal sectors on its books, while the Krakow-based Bank Przemyslowo Handlowy is still entangled in the recession of arms factories concentrated in the South-East.

An even greater concern stems from the fact that dynamic enterprises, who invested heavily in modern equipments and improved their productivity, are accumulating bad debts. They simply find it difficult to service their contractual debt to the banks as real interest rates turn out to be positive or, possibly, rising.

A drastic deterioration in general economic conditions took place the first two or three years following shock therapy in Poland or more gradual policies in Hungary and CSFR. The insolvency of the (ex) soviet markets causes serious liquidity problems for the large SOE's, which have sofar been unable to find new markets. Moreover, Western demand for agricultural production exported by central Europe has recently vanished, thus increasing the current recession. As a result, payment discipline deteriorated which entailed the dramatic increase in the creditors' losses.

1.1.2. Private Banks

Even if they have to cope with different situations, private banks have difficulties in obtaining a substantial share in the credit market. Mostly, these banks are of small or medium size, undercapitalized and they operate in restricted sectors and geographical areas. They do not collect many deposits either, and they keep complaining about unfair competition with large state-owned banks or specialized banks.

These banks' profitability is not really hindered by the burden of bad debts. They rather endure a lack of lending opportunities, because they are crowded out as their resources and reputation are not yet firmly established. Moreover, they cannot benefit from refinancing loans granted by the Central Bank. As the money market is all the more restricted and the international market is completely inaccessible, small private banks ultimately suffer from a liquidity squeeze.

1.2. Distortions in Banking Behaviour

Banks have been left deeply deprived, having to deal with their bad debts. The first reforms had not cancelled a fiscal procedure leading to hide accrued arrears in fictional bank's profit. Creditor passivity became a widespread behaviour among banks. Credit rationing is the usual reaction of banks confronted with a failure of interest rates to act as an equilibrium mechanism in the allocation process of financial resources.

1.2.1. Fictional Banks' Profits

Bank profits are a major source of fiscal revenues for the budget of the nation. The government would not encourage banks to make loan loss provisions since this would decrease profits, a large part of which is collected through taxation by the state itself. In fact, because of the strain on the budget, most governments are unwilling to concede pre-tax provisioning against bad debts. Consequently, banks have generally none or negligible loan loss provisions.

In addition, unpaid interests on outstanding credits are still capitalized in the banks' balance sheet as they are recorded under "accrued interests on future revenues" denomination. Since these foregone interests are treated as a current income for the banks, exemption from income tax is simply discarded.

Bank profits being artificially maintained in this manner create conflicting interests for the state. First, as the owner of banks, it has an interest in maximizing the value of its shares. The banks' stable profitability, high returns from the asset portfolios, low risks in extended loans, contribute to the capacity of banks to pay dividends. Second, as a tax collector, the state has an oppositive interest. It prefers to let banks produce high fictional profits from non performing and dubious loans expecting high return from taxes. In order to partially offset this fiscal levy, the state, as a stakeholder, votes against high dividends, contrary to the SOEs holding bank shares, enabling the banks to overstate their profits. Actually, this complex process leads largely to the deterioration of the banks' market value (Varhegyi, 1993).

For similar reasons, SOEs have the incentive to overstate profits and output and to hide such overstatement in their inventories, accepting to pay high taxes to the state. As a compensating device, they would rather stop paying their debt charges to the banks, arguing that banks achieved "excess" profits anyway. The effect of SOEs losses in the balance sheet of a state-owned bank simply implies that such losses are quasi-fiscal deficits that the state is ultimately responsible for (Sheng, 1991.b).

Moreover, banks are unwilling to cut new loans to ailing enterprises, refusing a responsibility for increasing unemployment in deciding which firms would survive and which would go bust. Political and union strains would not allow the banks to make such decisions which imply deep intrusion in firms'governance. The state itself is not prone to encourage direct conflicts between SOEs and state-owned banks.

1.2.2. Creditor Passivity

Even in countries where bankruptcy laws have been designed for many years, such as Hungary since 1986, banks are utterly reluctant to initiate procedures against insolvent debtors. As Mitchell (1993) puts it, it is not a matter of technical flaws in the legislation, but rather an implementation problem.

A primary explanation of creditor passivity appears when the expected value of creditors' claim is nil or negative. Over accumulation of obsolete equipments by firms, the absence of potential buyers of existing plants or the lack of any takeover project, combined with the existence of unavoidable costs to liquidate the ailing firm, lead the banks not to initiate the bankruptcy procedure.

The creditor bank may also take advantage in concealing the plight of its asset portfolio to its stockholders, particularly when the state itself holds a majority of shares. Disclosing its real illiquid or even insolvent net situation would prevent the bank from being an applicant for further privatisation. In case its name would be added to the list of problem banks by external auditors or rating agencies, the bank would deteriorate its own reputation, and reduce its own crediworthiness.

When the bank is unfolding its losses to the public, it also risks to arouse suspicion among depositors who may rather transfer their funds towards other banks. Aside from the risk of a bank run, private banks may durably lose market shares in collecting resources that will be gained by state-owned banks as long as it is well established in the depositors' mentality that the state offers unlimited guarantee to public banks' liabilities. Such latent runs can easily degenerate into general banking panics.

At last, if a bank is convinced that it may obtain any refinancing it needs from the Central Bank, when the value of its assets is shrinking, then neither itself nor its depositors have an interest in triggering off bankruptcies procedures against bad debtors. It is easier to roll over credits in favor of the ailing firm, in case it can restore its profits in the next future, or in case another creditor may initiate proceedings against the defaulting borrowers.

Creditor passivity is now widespread enough to be considered responsible for unjustified survival of a number of insolvent firms throughout Central European economies. Creditor passivity is never a debtor's right anyway. That is a reason why, in order to cope with their financing needs, firms will rather frequently turn towards informal loan procedures. Interenterprise credit, in the form of delayed settlements and arrears, is systematically resorted to, as requiring any company with debt payments more than ninety days overdue to file for bankruptcy, under threat of criminal proceedings against its managers, is never enforced.

Finally, there is much evidence that all the economic agents are equally sharing the plague of creditor passivity: firms, banks and, ultimately, the state itself through the inability of courts to enforce the law.

1.2.3. Credit Rationing

In the credit market, a number of firms cannot borrow the funds they need to finance their projects. Banks, under certain circumstances, simply refuse to satisfy the excess demand for loans by raising the interest rate above a certain level. According to Stiglitz and Weiss (1981), whereas moderate increases in the lending rate would normally elicit a higher volume of loans, further rate increases beyond that critical level would prompt a lower volume of supply of credit by changing adversely the quality of the pool of borrowers in favor of those in the high-risk category. Banks prefer to charge the lending rate which maximizes their expected profit and to ration the amount of credit supplied at that rate. At a higher rate of interest, expected profit would be lower for two reasons.

First, safe borrowers, who apply for financing a low risk-low return project, would be discouraged by an excessive cost of funds and would be likely to drop out of the market. This is the so-called adverse selection effect.

Second, other borrowers would be induced to choose projects with a higher expected return and, presumably, a higher risk of default – the adverse incentive effect.

If losses induced by defaulting borrowers exceed marginal gains consisting of interest payments, then the profit expected by a bank which would only satisfy the most risky borrowers should be less than the expected profit of a bank which would not raise its lending rate.

The hypothesis of credit rationing may prove useful to explain banks' behaviour (particularly small and medium-size banks) in transitional economies. Banks have to pay high information costs in order to screen and select projects among potential borrowers. They must decide under limited and asymmetric information. However, they have an interest in developing long-term relationships with their customers and providing them with an incentive to signal their attitude towards risky projects. Frequent adjustments of lending rates is, by no means, the best way to establish this kind of steady relationships, based on reliable debt servicing on the one hand and on regular renewal of loans on the other hand, that banks and their clients call for.

The principal shortcoming of this model of equilibrium credit rationing, when applied to banks dealing with financing transition towards market economy, is that it analyses the optimal response of a properly regulated bank, with adequate provisions for loan losses. As earlier mentioned, it is not exactly the case at present in central Europe and maximizing expected profits net of default has not yet the same significance as in Western economies.

Perhaps the most satisfactory explanation to the reluctance that banks display when financing risky industrial or commercial projects, lays in the generally low expected return associated with obsolete technology and other technical difficulties. Another reason might be the recession causing a depreciation in the value of real assets that firms are willing to acquire and affecting banks' portfolios and profitability.

1.3. Supervision and Control of the Loan Market

The second set of banking reforms designed in the beginning of the nineties aims at creating structures and mechanisms which might give the banks the necessary incentives to meet three fundamental functions that make them "unique" financial intermediaries (Rochet, 1993):

- managing, for their customers, means of payment and providing depositors with liquidity services. In central Europe, banks can only meet these requirements if their access to the market of desposits is not hampered by a monopoly of state-owned banks and public savings institutions.
- extending credit, that is financing those projects that could not obtain direct funding though the capital market, because these markets either are too small or are still too costly. This implies that all informal financing procedures such as inter-enterprise credit, delayed settlements, arrears be channeled towards a genuine loan market within a legal framework defining and enforcing a comprehensive set of contractual credit arrangements.

- transforming the mean maturity of deposits and loans, with reasonable and adequate liquid reserves that banks should keep in case of defaulting borrowers or of sudden liquidity need by depositors, so that illiquid banks should not be endangered.

Banks have no substitutes for assuming these roles (Lewis, 1992). First, they provide liquidity insurance, which guarantees that depositors can withdraw their holdings at nominal value whenever they want it. Second, banks select and monitor projects more efficiently than the market because of asymmetries of information banks having access at lower cost to hidden knowledge and hidden actions of borrowers. Third, banks produce efficient financial intermediation through the whole structure of their balance sheet maintaining in all circumstances a positive net worth, that is a value of their assets greater than (or equal to) the value of their liabilities (sight deposits and other debt items).

In order to implement these objectives, the second phase of banking reform found its inspiration in standard regulations and techniques existing in market economies abroad. Whether they fit or not specific aspects of transitional economies is questionable ; anyway, questions dealt with are essentially: cleaning banks' balance sheets, loan loss provision policy, risk limitation, new banks licensing and competition.

1.3.1. Cleaning Banks Balance Sheets

There are, in principle, several alternative solutions (Caprio and Levine, 1991). A first solution is inflation which diminishes the real value of debts – although their nominal amount keeps recorded in the bank's books. It is similar to taxing deposits through inflation. But, of course, as soon as inflation rises again, the bad loan problem is likely to quickly reappear (as in Poland in 1991).

A second option consists of transforming a large fraction of deposits into equity claims, particularly government deposits in banks. In compensation, banks would write-off an equivalent proportion of their claims on insolvent SOEs. But a deposit-for-equity swap raises the question of how efficient it would be to recapitalize banks using their own liquid resources.

A variant of this is the debt-equity swap which replaces bad claims on enterprises with equities. This option would lead banks to be in a position of directly managing a substantial part of the real sector, which is an area where they have no experience. Besides, put succinctly, bad debts equal bad equities ; acquiring equity in non-viable firms neither saves the firm nor resolves bank insolvency.

Debt-bond swap is a most popular and common approach to solving the bad debt problem. Bonds may be long term zero coupon Treasury bonds. Short-term T-bills, automatically rollovered, offer better protection of banks against inflation tax. Government guaranteed claims on privatisation funds are also an alternative. Even though the debt-for-bond swap is likely to be an important component of the solution, one must still choose between a stock or a flow option (Sheng, 1991.b). If all enterprise debts are substituted for government bonds in a once-an-for-all attempt to break with the past, this stock solution implies that tax collection will rise significantly. Substituting debt for bonds more slowly, over a sufficiently long time span, – a flow solution, would certainly be less costly, except for the interest rate risk incorporated in the public debt servicing by the budget, (unless bonds pay zero coupon, but still, banks have to bear a wealth effect affecting the present value of bonds received in exchange for bad debts).

Another related approach is to create a Debt Recovery Agency, an independent body which collects resources by issuing long-term bonds (possibly state-guaranteed) and which buys back outstanding loans to the banks and then resells them at a discount in a secondary market. Athough such an agency might raise fairness questions in determining which enterprises will benefit from such a transfer of debts and which shall not, this solution has the advantage of quickly clearing the bank's balance sheets of (part of) the inherited stock of debts incurred under central planning.

How come none of the three countries referred to in this paper could or would be willing to solve this everlasting problem of bad debts once-and-for-all. Poland tried, in the beginning of the transitional period, taxation of deposits through inflation. Hungary has offered a state guarantee on a part of dubious claims of banks outstanding by the end of 1987. These guarantees run for five years and are callable only upon initiation of liquidation proceedings on the debtors. The former CSFR, in March 1991, established a new Consolidation Bank (KON), which only function consisted in collecting and holding non-productive loans. Then, the government decided to remove a portion of the so-called TOZ loans, that is perpetual loans yielding 6%, with no amortization schedule, supposed to finance enterprises' inventories. Lastly, since a law of December 1992, Polish banks have been engaged in a vast program designed to enhance governance on over-indebted enterprises ; the nine big state-owned banks will then participate in the restructuring and privatisation of enterprises by offering them a wide range of debt-relief schemes in order to reduce their financial costs, such as partial debt write-downs and debt-equity swaps.

Although there is a wide range of options, one must note that they offer only partial solutions to the bad debt problem. Actually, this complex problem is closely linked to other difficult tasks and necessary reforms such as privatisation, structure of ownership, sequencing of reforms etc. Whatever the option, it all boils down to a problem of public finance, more precisely, of tax collection, as it is assumed by all economic agents that the responsability of the state is unescapable and deeply engaged. One must recognize however that is quite legitime for the government not to try solving the problem of bad debts by a once stroke fiscal bailout that no economy could stand in a phase of recession and which might create expectations of future government involvement, should bad debt problems reappear in the future.

1.3.2. Loan Loss Provisions

A priority of bank supervisors is to harmonize accounting standards between banks and enterprises. New rules have very recently been adopted or are still in preparation. It is not an easy task that Central European enterprise accounting reaches GAAP or Western European standards as all prior procedures are based on the established Soviet classification of accounts designed to maintain control over plan fulfillment. Besides, the design of any new chart of accounts for banks will have to be harmonized with the accounting law for enterprise accounting, and a translation chart from the old accounts to the new accounts will have to be drawn up. Beyond this legal aspect, new accounting standards will probably not be reached until after there is is a large pool of accountants and auditors trained in GAAP, and the whole process will take a lot of time.

Elements of the new accountancy legislation introduced in Hungary, for example, in December 1991 and January 1992 include interesting measures dealing with monitoring credit risks. First, any company with debt payments more than three months in arrears must file for bankruptcy. Second, companies are requested to follow new accounting standards for asset depreciation and to make provisions against dubious accounts receivable from pre-tax profits. For commercial banks, the legislation also requires new procedures for making provisions against bad loans. Banks are required to classify their assets as:

- substandard if their involve "large branch risks" ;
- doubtful if the borrower made losses in the preceding two years or is more than 60 days in arrears ;
- bad if the defaulting borrower is in bankruptcy proceedings.

New rules further require that provisions be made against 20%, 50% and 100%, respectively, of the non-productive loans in these three categories.

In November 1992 Poland has adopted a comparable set of accounting bank and enterprises standards. Provisions are also required against non-performing loans extended by banks, as they must enter one of the five categories of the new classification. The design of a new legislation of this kind was in preparation in Spring 1993, in the Czech Republic, where difficulties in enforcing the bankruptcy law, in close connection to the bad debts problem, caused some delays.

If banks do not receive a fiscal incentive for making provisions against bad loans, in order to maintain their profitability, then banks are forced to charge high interest rate spreads which generate margins to cover these bad debts. As a result, good debtors, that is sound and profitable enterprises, have to pay high borrowing costs which might endanger their future growth ; as a matter of fact, the most progressive part of the economy pays for the burden of SOEs debt, resulting in a counter-productive transfer of real and financial resources.

Banks have also to plough their profits back into operations, thus curtailing their tax payments. Government tax collection from the banking sector in Hungary, for instance, are down by more than half, in 1992, compared with 1990 (when they accounted for nearly 8% of fiscal revenues). This too might increase strain on the private sector if it results in higher taxes. Anyway, provisions against new non-performing loans are the only means to prevent the old bad debts problem to reappear again and again. As usually, this sort of mutualization of individual problems has a social cost which has to be taken in charge by the state, since bad loans have created a negative externality diminishing social welfare.

1.3.3. Bank Risk Limitation

Adequate management of a bank requires a diversification of its asset portfolio as well as avoiding excessive concentration of loans on a single borrower or a single sector. According to the new rules designed in the second phase of banking reform, a risk limit, that is a limit to lending to a single customer, has been fixed up to 15% of assets in Poland, and up to 25% of capital in Hungary and in the Czech Republic.

Loans to a bank's single shareholder create a risk of discrimination against other borrowers and a risk of fraud if lending conditions offered to the stakeholder are too obviously off market lending rates, amortization schedule, etc. Limits are up to 5% of the bank's capital in Hungary, up to 15% in Poland and in the Czech Republic.

In the new prudential regulation, different banking models have been followed. On the one hand, Hungary has opted for the US-Japan model of separation between the commercial and investment banking functions. Commercial banks are thus restricted on the volume of investments they can make (up to 15% of capital), whereas investment banks, on the contrary, can hold up to 100% in long term investment (bonds or equity of any single company). On the other hand, in Poland and the Czech Republic, banks are universal and allowed to perform all functions. The regulation is thus very liberal and banks can invest in long-term investments such as real estate, securities or equities, up to 25% of their capital and reserves.

As for separation between banks and commerce, the American legislation has not been followed at all. A single individual or commercial company can hold a bank up to 100% of its capital in the Czech Republic, 50% in Poland and 25% in Hungary. There is no limitation on foreign holdings in any of these countries.

Another issue of ownership of banks is the traditional separation of ownership of banks from regulators or borrowers. Conflicts of interest arise when state-owned banks are also shareholders in private banks. It would generally be preferable to "freeze" ownership of such shares in a trust fund or a fiduciary institution, before eventual sale through privatisation.

1.3.4. Bank Licensing and Competition

In its enthusiasm to open markets, Poland adopted a very liberal licensing policy of new banks, creating easy conditions of entry in the financial industry. In the beginning of 1989, 18 new banks had been licensed, 86 by the end of 1991. Hungary had a more cautious policy since the number of banks reached 27 by the end of 1991 against 19 in 1987. In the CSFR, there were 7 new banks in 1990, 27 by the end of 1991 and 45 one year later.

Minimum capital for a new commercial bank has been fixed to the equivalent of USD 13.3 m. in Hungary, 6.6 m. for a specialized bank, and under the Financial Institutions Act, the Banking Supervision Committee is allowed ample scope for licensing of new institutions. In Poland, the threshold was initially particularly low (PLZ 20 bn, that is USD 2 m.) and minimum capital was suddenly, and rather unexpectedly (Raczko, 1992), raised up to PLZ 70 bn. In addition, some banking services, such as holding foreign exchange accounts, for instance, are now restricted to banks whose capital is not inferior to PLZ 105 bn.

These two opposite cases illustrate, on the one hand, a cautious policy of stable development of private banks and, on the other hand, a wildcat attitude in which too many small banks compete for a limited amount of business in a market dominated by large state-owned banks anyway, followed by a much more restrictive entry policy. The first Polish experiment was rather disappointing as the small private banks did not reach a critical size, did not succeed in capturing enough lending opportunities and in achieving a sufficient profitability. The more restrictive licensing policy is clearly intended to create a new structure in the banking industry where a small number (perhaps 10 to 15) medium-sized private banks would provide more competition than the present structure of large state-owned banks competing (inefficiently) against too numerous small banks. Moreover, it is clear that the Central Bank is willing to exercise a tighter control over the aggregate supply of credit and that an excessive dispersion of credit sources among too numerous institutions was thought to be a hindrance.

It is frequently argued that joint-ventures with foreign banks would be a satisfactory means to import bank skills, capital and technology. Twinning agreements between foreign and domestic banks have been largely used in Hungary and are more slowly introduced in Poland and in the Czech Republic. There is obviously a nationalist reluctance to widely open entry to fully-owned foreign banks but given the shortage of skills and experience in banking at present, a long time span may be likely before all needs can be met on a purely domestic basis.

High minimum capital requirements for licensing new banks may signal a deliberate policy from the supervisory and control authorities aiming at enforcing safe and sound banking industries. However, excessive capital requirement also brings in accusations of inefficiency, as private initiative is severely hampered, and of inequity because the private sector does not generally have the amount of cash necessary to meet such regulations. Lastly, it is not sure that so-to-speak infant (private new) banks can easily, from the start, reach a sufficient profitability to establish a basis for further growth. It is not only a matter of profits but also a question of risk-taking. From that viewpoint, neither the first, nor the second, banking reform was a real success.

2. Banking Risks

There are many dimensions to banking risks. A first type of risk is moral hazard created by the first banking reform in the transitional economies of central Europe. A number of born-insolvent banks, according to GAAP standards, are artificially maintained. A second kind of risk is systemic risk present in systems of payments outdated and obsolete.

Moral hazard and systemic risk are, in great part, the legacy of the ancient planned economy but we argue that the first banking reforms have worsened them. Far from addressing directly these issues, the second banking reforms added new constraints, such as the capital adequacy guidelines issued by the Basle Committee tending to the goal of 8% of risk assets. A question is how meaningful can a situation be, where no adequate loan loss provisions have yet been made. What use can a very demanding regulation as the Cooke ratio be, when simply booking newly required loan loss provisions would leave many of the banks with negative capital ? Isn't the capital adequacy requirement redundant with respect to the loan loss provisioning rule ?

2.1. Moral Hazard in the Banking Sector

Moral hazard may be defined as an asymmetric behaviour in which a bank will retain higher profits than expected results when the situation is favourable, whereas it will be unwilling to assume losses when an unsatisfactory outcome affects its results. Thus, a bank always has an incentive to supply loans on riskier projects at higher interest rates. It is typically a risk lover behaviour. In most circumstances, this attitude threatens the financial stability of a banking system when a sufficient number of uninsured banks make systematically risky choices.

2.1.1. Aversion to Closing Insolvent Banks

Insolvent banks usually do not go bankrupt in Central Europe. Three official failures have been reported in Poland for the last two years. In one case, at Lublin, a two-day bank run of depositors led to a prompt lifeboat operation to protect depositors in Pierwszy Komercyjny Bank. Of course, in most cases, banks closures were linked to an anecdotal affair – fraud or swindle. Of more concern is the fact that, last Spring, eight medium-size private banks, generally considered as very promising, were reported insolvent. In Hungary, two of the largest commercial banks, both state-owned, Magyar Hitel Bank and Kereskedelmi Bank, are technically insolvent and require massive injection of capital. In the Czech Republic, hints at potential insolvency of several banks, according to internationally accepted accounting standards, are circulating.

A handful of Western countries also provide examples of the aversion to closing and liquidating insolvent banks. Over the past several years, the regulators have much more often tried to allow the banking authority some time to formulate and implement a reorganization of a failing bank, and then to provide the resources to execute the planned rescue. The typical response to the impending insolvency of a bank is to merge the failing bank into a healthy bank (a purchase and assumption transaction, in the FDIC's terminology), or to recapitalize the bank to keep it in operation. The legal process by which a failure is supposed to be resolved – closing the bank, implementing bankruptcy procedure and liquidating the assets – is rarely followed for a bank of sizable proportions.

Indeed, the traditional "too big to fail" argument is often advocated by those people who contend that handling bank failures through assisted mergers is less expensive and less disruptive to the bank's depositors and loan customers, as well as to the local merchants and the general community, than a closure. The truth of this argument is hard to deny, provided there exists, in the banking sector, some program designed to improve the mechanisms for maintaining financial order and not to involve a state commitment to rescue every defaulting bank.

The point is that this kind of program, whether modeled on a form of insurance, which is in essence a loss sharing scheme, or mutual aid pact, has not yet been created in transitional economies of Central Europe. Up to that moment, only deposit protection or guarantee is offered by the state, on a restricted basis to the sole state-owned banks and for certain types of deposits only. There is a widespread belief that deposit guarantee is a collective good that must be offered by the state which, in the end, is the ultimate risk bearer in the economy. Implicitly, the cost of this protection is not supposed to be charged to the banks or their customers, but rather covered by the budget of the nation. This, obviously, generates a moral hazard problem in the banking sector.

As said earlier, despite various incidents, big state-owned banks are systematically sustained by the state, on behalf of the common good as interpreted by more or less populist political parties and unions. This raises, among others, the question of why private banks do not benefit from the same treatment as state-owned banks when confronted to solvency problems. They have no protection or guarantee of deposits mechanism to offer. When a private bank is failing, the monetary authority chooses a special commissionner and an assisted merger, or else recapitalisation is organized. The outright solution of initiating a bankruptcy procedure, leading eventually to a liquidation of the failed bank, is discarded on the ground that winding-up of a failed bank would threaten the very structure and existence of the whole private banking sector. It is argued that if the shareholders of a failed bank refuse a merger solution as organized by the banking authority, then a transfer of funds by depositors towards the protected or guaranteed public banks must be expected. This "spontaneous" reflux of deposits would be a substitute for a bank run ; let's call it a "crawling" bank run, or a "suggested" run, as it is used as an argument to justify a restructuration of the banking sector.

It is rather clear that the Polish monetary authorities want to reduce the number of banks operating in the private sector. The rise in the minimum capital requirement allowing to keep a bank in operation goes in the same direction. Thus a widespread program of assisted purchase and assumption transactions will presumably be implemented. What is not entirely clear though is whether state-owned banks are systematically going to be taking over private banks, before they are themselves privatised, or only private banks will be merged in order to reach a bigger size.

Although there is a scope to restructure the whole banking or the private banking sector, in countries where the licensing of new banks has been too liberally granted, it should be clearly understood that competition is also regulated by exit conditions. Industrial organization teaches that the normal way of regulating exit from an industry is bankruptcy and liquidation of failing competitors, not mergers or purchase and asumptions transactions assisted by a public authority.

Bankruptcy, indeed, is a consequence of insufficient profitability. Taking over a non profitable firm by a profitable one can curb the buyer's results and threaten its own survival. It is precisely what happened when the former national monobank was carved out in order to create the two-tier banking sector. Bad debts had been similarly hived off, leading to desastrous initial financial conditions of the newly created state-owned banks. Repeating a similar procedure today would be an error. Restructuring an industry by the only means of mergers and acquisitions and by refusing bankruptcies and liquidations will not be sufficient to restore competition and profitability. It would be in the best interest of the banking system that a strict bankruptcy law should be enforced, so that the credibility of banks kept in operation could improve.

2.1.2. New Capital Adequacy Requirements

The second phase of banking reform introduces a new norm which is similar to the EC ratio of solvency or to the Basle Committee on Banking Supervision Cooke ratio. The banks capital must be maintained at 8% of risk-weighted assets. It is yet a target which must be met by the end of a transitional period (1993 in Hungary, 1995 in the Czech Republic).

Adopting this norm is justified insofar as all banks are now commercial banks, including state-owned banks or former administrative bodies. As joint-stock companies, these banks engage a commercial responsability. This has different meanings anyway, according to each particular statute. A state-owned bank is virtually fully guaranteed by the state, either on the asset side of its operations (bad loans), or on the liability side (deposits, capital), which contradicts commercial responsibility of a joint-stock company. Private banks, on the contrary, benefit from no guarantee or protection, neither public or private, except for their own funds. In short, a state guarantee plays the same role for a state-owned bank as its capital for a private bank. In other words, its capital is almost redundant for a state-owned bank.

As their budget constraint is quite different, the two categories of banks react differently to the increase in their capital ratio, that is in the proportion of their own funds with respect to the amount of deposits and other debts they issue. For a given size of its balance sheet, a bank must decrease its leverage if it has to raise its capital ratio.

Portfolio theory asserts that low risk adverse banks prefer a relatively high leverage (low capital) and a relatively high risk in their assets portfolio. The level of risk and the capital ratio of a bank should thus be positively correlated. As a consequence, when prudential regulation requires an increase in a bank's capital ratio, it tries to restore the rate of return on this capital by raising the degree of risk on its asset portfolio.

It has frequently been reported that big banks in industrialized countries, notably the United States, adopted this type of behaviour, although it is still questionable whether it is due to the required increase in capital ratio or to specific factors such as the former flat rate insurance premium collected by the FDIC to insure deposits. Thus a moral hazard problem arises in the banks attitude.

The prospects completely differ in Central European economies. First, banks will find it very difficult to raise new own funds: the stock market is limited, all banks are not listed, cost issuance of equity shares is high etc. Subordinated debt securities, which are less costly to issue and which can enter tier two in the Cooke ratio, have not been legally created yet. As for state-owned banks, the state as a stakeholder cannot simply recapitalize the banks by bringing in cash, because of its budget deficit and because priory has been given to solving the bad debts problem.

Supposing that the shortage of external capital prevents banks from reaching their new capital adequacy requirement, the monetary authorities will have to request banks to plough their profits back into operation. Remember however that banks have to provision, from the same source, against their non-performing new loans and that the stock of bad debts outstanding has not been absorbed yet. It looks like there were too many objectives for only one instrument. Because of this deadlock, banks will be likely to increase the degree of risk in their loans in order to raise profits. In turn, this will lead them to increase provisions against riskier loans, causing lowered pre-tax profits, and so on. A way to get out of this dilemma implies reducing the volume of extended credit so that the quality of loans can be improved, but in that case, growth financing would be altered.

It results that the new capital adequacy required from banks might be either inefficient if banks cannot reach the norm, or even adverse if bank risks increase rather than diminish. Moreover, the probability of a credit crunch cannot be discarded. Lastly, the credibility and reputation of the banking authorities would probably not be strenghened in case these bad results would follow.

In industrial countries, it is frequently argued, particularly by bankers, that the increased capital ratio provoked at the same time a flight to quality (a substitution of non risky Treasury bonds to risky loans in banks portfolio), a credit crunch and an incresed risk in assets portfolios. Although this conjunction of effects is questionable, the role attributed to the capital ratio is supposed to be reinforceed by the existence and shortcomings of the insurance deposit scheme.

In transitional economies, the state guarantee of state-owned banks could play the same role as the insurance deposit program in industrialized countries, generating an even stronger moral hazard insofar as there is no bankruptcy at all neither in the public, nor in the private banking sector.

One might conclude that, confronted to conflicting goals, the banking authorities should clearly display what their preferred order of sequencing in banking reform is. It seems reasonable to recommend that provisioning against new bad loans be given a firm priority and be strictly enforced, checked and explicitly sanctioned in case of offence. Fiscal incentives should be granted for persuading the banks that provisions are in their best interest. The new capital adequacy regulation could be delayed further until privatisation of banks becomes more effective. Besides, it should never be forgotten that the Cooke ratio was conceived, by its authors themselves, as a regulation which should be restricted to those banks having an important volume of business in the international capital market (wholesale deposits and borrowings in the euro-markets, brokerage and issuance activity on foreign and international equities or bonds, financial engeneering etc.). Moreover, these internationally active banks must have a very stringent disclosure policy of their accounts ; they receive a rating from auditors and rating agencies. All these constraints seem beyond what could realistically be required from most transitional banks in Central Europe at present.

2.1.3. Banks Privatisation

When a state-owned bank is managed independently from the state or the banking authorities, it is sensible to require that it conforms to the capital ratio regulation. This might even serve as a proof of the bank autonomy, which implies that the state or the regulator signals the market that it will not necessarily rescue this bank in case of default. In France or in the UK where public banks have been in operation for years, (and still are), it was found that this signal was not as clear as it should be. In other words, because of moral hazard, a state-owned bank, even independently managed, might be a victim of its insufficient credibility in the market and, for instance, be forced to pay an extra risk premium when it is borrowing in the interbank market or issuing certificates of deposit. Privatisation is certainly the best clarification to offer to market participants, provided though, for the sake of the whole banking system, that a stringent regulation be organized by the banking authorities.

Privatisation of enterprises is more and more extended in Central European economies, whereas bank privatisation is much more delayed. This sequencing is deliberate in Hungary. In the Czech Republic and in Poland, privatisation of SOEs and state-owned banks is contemporaneously conducted. Both methods have benefits and costs which will not be discussed further in the present paper. Mullineux (1993) offers a spurring discussion of these issues.

The long-awaited privatisation program in the Polish banking sector started last Spring when two, out of the nine state-owned banks created in 1988, were offered to investors. It was first, in April 1993, the succesful privatisation of Wielkopolski Bank Kredytowy (WBK), in Poznan, with Henry Schroder Wagg, the City merchant bank as advisers ; the Bank Slaski (Gornoslaski Bank Gosdoparczy), in Katowice, then will follow with the French Paribas as counsellor. In the case of the WBK, for instance, selling state shares raised PZL 200 bn. for the Treasury through the public offer of 20% of the shares to small private investors. A further 7.2% was allocated to large investors, both domestic and foreign, while 14.3% of shares was reserved for employees, with the Treasury retaining 30%. The rest of the bank's capital, 28.5% in new shares, was subscribed by the European Bank for Reconstruction and Development for PZL 210 bn. (USD 12.7 m.), meaning an injection of new capital.

Other methods of privatisation can be planned, and probably will be in the near future, as several other banks are included in the privatisation pipeline. Assistance and participation of a bank of development, as the Polski Bank Rozwojo (PBR), created in 1990, or the Polish investment bank would allow to use the funds made available by the G-7 in favor of a program aimed at sustaining the convertibility of the zloty.

In any case, banks privatisation is closely related to the long-awaited, and so frequently announced, overhaul of balance sheets and recapitalization issue. One might argue that gradualism, in that matter too, may prove wiser than a hasty mass privatisation program in the banking sector. Privatisation is not a miracle solution as it makes banks vulnerable to mismanagement caused by those frequent conflicts of interests between shareholders and managers, and other failures in the market mechanisms (externalities, asymmetrical information, destructive competition) leading to financial instability. It should also be recalled that where a private banking sector exists, it is of the utmost importance that the public authorities learn to regulate it in the general interest rather than discriminate in favor of the state-owned banks sector alone. Privatisation cannot be self-justifying ; the state must provide financial stability and continuity in financial intermediation.

2.2. Systemic Risk

This type of risk appears as soon as a single bank refuses (voluntarily or not) to consider the impact of its actions on other participants in the banking system (Dietsch, 1993). In every lending operation, a bank, through the risk that it takes, transfers an extra risk to any bank which holds a claim on it in the interbank market. It follows that the social cost of risk is superior to the sum of the individual costs incurred by participants in the system. The financial system is thus permanently exposed to risk, a situation potentially generating financial instability.

Potential failures are particularly hampering in the interbank system of settlements and clearing of payments. Weaknesses of banking supervision in that area are frequently revealed. Security must then receive great attention from the regulators.

2.2.1. Failures in the System of Payments

Restructuring systems of payments was largely overlooked in the first phase of banking reform. The risks involved in running a banking system without speedy telecommunications to help clearing and other interbank transactions were dramatically underlined by the ART-B scandal, in 1991. There are at least two important features in that affair. First, a swindle based on large loan operations collateralized by fraudulent guarantees is discovered with considerable delay by the banking authorities, revealing serious negligence and leading to subsequent removal of the then Central Bank president. The second feature is related to the issue of obsolescence in interbank settlements processing. The private BHK bank, recently closed down by the Central Bank, helped ART-B conduct a big cheque-kiting operation where billions of zlotys were simultaneously deposited in different banks around the country, taking advantage of slow communications. This type of operation involved drawing cheques on an account which did not have sufficient funds and banking them on a second account. The account holder then made use of the "non-existent" funds in that account before the cheques could be processed, cleared and, finally, dishonoured.

Recent theoretical work outline how the very technical features of payments system may be destabilizing in case of failure of a debtor. In some cases, net payments are settled after clearing of reciprocal debts and claims between participants. If a debtor is defaulting, then the market authority has no other choice than to cancel ex post all subsequent payments made by those banks which used their received claims to make their own settlements. A solvent bank may become illiquid after its claims have been cancelled and then, in turn, it threatens all the banks which hold claims on it.

Modernizing the technology of payments is thus a (costly) priority. To bring Poland, as an example, to international standards, a company set up by the Central Bank (Narodowi Bank Polski), the Polish banking union and several individual banks will link 17 cities and handle interbank transactions. It will operate along NBP'own wire to expedite settlements in a new clearing system, KIR (Krajowa Izba Rozrachunkowa) playing the role of central authority and coordinator of payments. Fears remain (Raczko, 1993) that access to this modern, less costly and safer system might be restricted to the state-owned banks, thus altering competition among banks and discriminating the private sector.

Most importantly, the new projects must be designed in such a manner that risks are minimized. Removing moral hazard is a necesity, which implies that the authority must have a capacity to repeal individual gross payments made by defaulting banks without being forced to validate all net payments ex post. In other words, irrevocable gross settlements are best suited to limitate contagion of defaults. Reforming clearing systems in a fragile financial environment should take this issue of gross v. net payments as a basis for bringing about more safety in the banking sector.

2.2.2. *Safety Net for Depository Institutions*

The state is the guarantor of last resort of financial stability since it is the sole authority which might stop a bank panic and mitigate the resulting impact on real transactions and financial activity. It is thus very difficult for the state to disengage from running altogether the supply of credit and subsidies, the demand for loans, the ownership of enterprises and banks, the lender of last resort and the function of ultimate guarantor of depository institutions.

The Central Bank, which is a state-owned bank, must indeed be the lender of last resort, providing liquidity assistance for supporting a troubled bank when there is a risk of liquidity squeeze of significant scale developing throughout the banking sector. In economies with well-developed money markets and the common practice of liability management, a bank does not usually develop problems unless its solvency is to some degree questionable. When a liquidity problem is unfolding, as Goodhart (1988) puts it, it is often impossible to gauge how serious the threat of insolvency is in the time available to prevent the troubled bank from affecting other institutions and possibly disrupting the entire financial system. Thus, at the critical moment, the Central Bank may not be able to serve as the lender of last resort.

It also happens that failing banks are not closed soon after they have turned insolvent (or are not closed at all, as said earlier). The principal reason is that the supervisory authorities are unable to value with certainty a bank's loan portfolio which represents the bulk of its assets. If insolvency could be declared immediately upon its occurrence, the moment the bank's net worth fell below zero, which might be feasible if all its assets were marketable, the losses to the bank's creditors would be sufficiently small that the Central Bank could absorb these losses without seriously impinging on its budget.

Despite the regulation and supervision of banks and a mechanism for providing liquidity assistance, which are the traditional functions assumed by the Central Bank, deposit guarantee is thus thought to be necessary. It should be recognized that supervision, regulation and deposit guarantees all work towards the prevention of bank failures, although deposit protection also encourages risk-taking by bank management and thus creates a greater need for regulation and supervision of individual banks.

Bank supervision as a necessary condition for safe and sound banking has been accepted. There is a wide scope for supervising and regulating banks although the banking authorities must be aware that there in a cost to regulation and that excessive rules and regulations can stifle innovation and competition. The regulatory role of supervisors must be tempered by their institution-building function (Sheng, 1991.a). Attention has therefore to be paid, in on-site supervision, to the operations of the payments system, the chart of accounts, reporting system, internal controls etc., which represent the basic functioning of commercial banks.

In any case, a full range of penalties and sanctions must be specified and enforced when banks are breaking the rules. Withdrawal of a license is an efficient substitute for stockholders' forbearance. Removal of faulty managers by the regulators may bring some relief to weak or neglectful stakeholders. The ART-B bank affair led to an urgent strenghening of bank supervisory procedures in Poland.

Whether the Central Bank itself or an independent state agency should be in charge of bank supervision is questionable. The US Comptroller of the Currency is an independent Treasury agency which is sharing supervision with the FDIC and the Fed. In Germany, the Bundesaufsichtsamt für das Kreditwesen is independent from the Bundesbank. Hungary had a preference for the German model in this matter. As a matter of fact, several issues are at stake and the question of an independent regulatory authority cannot be solved separately from the issue of the Central Bank's independence with respect to the government. Whatever solution is considered appropriate, a key issue is avoiding conflicting interests and promoting coordination between the various agencies constituting the safety net of depository institutions.

Conclusion

This paper has attempted to show the interdependence of issues in bank reform. Banks cannot be made healthier if enterprises are not cleaned-up from their bad debts. Banks cannot be privatised separately because of cross-ownership by SOEs, and vice versa. Restructuring the public bank sector alone, without defining clearly the share and roles of the private sector at the same time, necessarily leads to an incomplete reform.

Although it seems hardly impossible to design a one-stroke and comprehensive plan of reform, the method of small steps and partial changes may prove harmful. The first banking reform has created a moral hazard problem that the second reform leaves largely unresolved. Loan loss provisions and new capital adequacy rules may interfere and lead to inhibiting banks. A reasonable time schedule should be introduced considering that a capital adequacy rule makes little sense when applied to unregulated loss making banks.

As for individual banks behaviour, the most difficult task of regulators seems to give them the necessary incentives to get over the difficulty of assessing asset quality and the required level of loan loss provisions. Borrowers, too, must be educated and should systematically engage more own funds in their projects, collateralize their borrowings and maintain long-term relationships with their bankers, so as to improve the information that banks use in their lending decisions. Self-protection which can be reached through internalization of costs, is a close substitute to external regulation which is costly too.

Bankruptcy costs will play an essential role as this procedure becomes more and more familiar. An important part of conflicts stemming from agency relationships between bank managers and stockholders depends on the value attributed to this element. Unwary banks are transformed into risk adverse financial intermediaries, provided that the bank authorities do not systematically rescue all failed banks. A complete safety net, including a deposit guarantee scheme, must be organized which does not commit the Central Bank – or even worse, the state itself or the Treasury – to be the ordinary guarantor of deposits. Otherwise, moral hazard in the banking sector will never be eliminated.

As can easily be seen, the second phase of banking reform in transitional economies is far from being the final step in this time cousuming, hard process of building new institutions and consistent regulations.

References

Begg D. and **R. Portes** (1993), "Enterprise Debt and Financial Restructuring in Central and Eastern Europe", *European Economic Review,* vol. 37, 396-407.

Begg D. and **R. Portes** (1993), "Enterprise Debt and Economic Transformation: Financial Restructuring in Central and Eastern Europe", in C. Mayer and X. Vives, eds, *Capital Markets and Financial Intermediation,* Center for Economic Policy Research, Cambridge, Cambridge University Press.

Belka M. and **A. Mullineux** (1993), "Hardening the Micro Budget Constraint: Bank Behaviour and Corporate Governance in Poland and the (Ex-) CSFR", University of Birmingham, International Finance Group.

Calvo G.A. and **J.A. Frenkel** (1991), "Credit Markets, Credibility, and Economic Transformation", *Journal of Economic Perspectives,* vol. 5, n° 4, Fall, 139-148.

Caprio G. and **R. Levine** (1991), "Reforming Socialist Economics: Issues for the Financial Sector", World Bank, Financial Policy and Systems Division.

Carter P. (1992), "Financial Sector Reform in Central and Eastern Europe", European Investment Bank *Papers,* n° 18.

Coricelli F. and **A. Thorne** (1992), "Creating Financial Markets in Economies in Transition", World Bank, ECA-MENA Technical Department.

Dietsch M. (1992), "La protection contre le risque systémique et la fonction de prêteur en dernier ressort", Commission bancaire (France), *Le risque systémique,* Rapport 25 mai ; annexes, vol. 1.

Goodhart C.A.E. (1988), "Bank Insolvency and Deposit Insurance: A Proposal", in P. Arestis, ed., *Contemporary Issues in Money and Banking,*London, Macmillan, 49-68.

Hrncír M. and **R. Matousek** (1993), "Financial Intermediation in the Former Czechoslovakia – Lessons and Progress Evaluation", Czech National Bank, Institute of Economics.

Lacoue-Labarthe D. (1992), "Setting-Up a Safe and Sound Banking System in Central and Eastern European Economies", Paper presented at the Workshop on Financial Reform in Poland and the Evolution of a Single EC Banking Market, University of Birmingham.

Levine R. and **D. Scott** (1992), "Old Debts and New Beginnings: A Policy Choice with Dynamic Implications for Transitional Socialist Economies", World Bank, Financial Policy and Systems Division.

Lewis M.K. (1991), "Theory and Practice of the Banking Firm", in C.J. Green and D.T. Llewellyn, eds, *Surveys in Monetary Economics,* vol. 2, *Financial Markets and Institutions,* Oxford, Basil Blackwell for the Money Study Group, 116-165.

McKinnon R.I. (1991), *The Order of Economic Liberalization ; Financial Control in the Transition to a Market Economy,* Baltimore, Johns Hopkins University Press.

Mitchell J. (1993), "Creditor Passivity and Bankruptcy: Implications for Economic Reform", in C. Mayer and X. Vives, eds, *Capital Markets and Financial Intermediation,* Center for Economic Policy Research, Cambridge, Cambridge University Press.

Mullineux A. (1993), "Privatisation and Banking Sector Reform: Lessons from Poland", Paper presented at the Xth Annual Conference on Monetary Economics and Banking, Bordeaux, France, june, 10-11.

Raczko A. (1993), "Analysis of Changes in the Banking Sector in 1992", University of Lodz, Institute of Economics.

Rochet J.C. (1992), "Towards a Theory of Optimal Banking Regulation", Banque de France, *Cahiers économiques et monétaires,* n° 40, 275-284.

Sheng A. (1991.a), "Bank Supervision in Central and Eastern Europe", World Bank, Financial Policy and Systems Division.

Sheng A. (1991.b), "Bad Debts in Transitional Socialist Economies", World Bank, Financial Policy and Systems Division.

Stiglitz J. and **A. Weiss** (1981), "Credit Rationing in Markets with Imperfect Competition", *American Economic Review,* 71, june, 393-410.

Thorne A. (1992), "The Role of Banks in the Transition: Lessons from Eastern European Countries' Experience", World Bank, ECA-MENA Technical Department.

Várhegyi E. (1993), "The Modernisation of the Hungarian Banking Sector", in I.P. Székely and D.M.G. Newbery, eds, *Hungary: An Economy in Transition,* Centre for Economic Policy Research, Cambridge, Cambridge University Press, 149-162.

Financial Reform and Growth

Some Lessons of the Chinese Experience for Central and Eastern Europe*

Christian Bordes
University of Bordeaux (I), LARE

Introduction

The Chinese economic system started to change in 1978 when the Chinese authorities embarked on a path of economic reforms introducing gradually market-oriented economic policies. The challenge of these reforms was to create an economic system that generates self-sustaining econonomic growth under conditions of stable prices. More precisely, China's reformers have managed to implant versions of all the elements of the East Asian approach for getting out of poverty: 1) land reform that sharply raises incomes in the countryside; 2) a transfer of profits and labour from farming to industry; 3) high savings rate which finance industrial investment; 4) low taxes; 5) vigorous domestic competition; 6) an openness to foreign influence. The reform gave farmers and enterprises greater autonomy in production and investment decisions in response to market forces.

---

* Prepared for the Conference on "Financial reform in Central and Eastern Europe", Prague, Czech National Bank, 3 - 4 September 1993.

The growth performance experienced since the implementation of the reforms has been truly outstanding and has sustained itself for a decade and a half in the face of two recessions [see Table 1]. China doubled per capita income in one decade. There is a large and growing literature on the reasons for this success [see, *inter alia,* Hussain and Stern (1991); Mao and Rivera-Batiz (1992); McMillan and Naughton (1992); Gelb et al (1993)]. Faster growth has been associated with: 1) the agricultural reforms; 2) opening to international trade; 3) the development of collective relative to State-owned enterprises; 4) the shift ot the regional allocation of central government spending and taxation [Mao and Rivera-Batiz (1992)].[1]

Table 1: Annual average growth rate

1952 - 1970 *	4.8
1952 - 1957 *	6.4
1957 - 1970 *	4.2
1965 - 1970 *	6.3
1971 - 1977 **	4.6
1978 - 1983 **	8.1
1984 - 1988 **	11.3
1985 - 1989 ***	9.2

Note: *: GNP [Source: Rawski (1975) p. 41]; **: Net National Income [Source: Hussain and Stern (1991) p. 145]; ***: GNP: Morgan Guaranty Trust Company [Source: Morgan Guaranty Trust Company (1993)]. The official data on national income differ from those used in market economies. National income is the sum of net output value of agriculture, industry, transportation, construction and commerce. These are the so-called "material" production sectors of the economy. The coverage of national income in Chinese statistics excludes the value added in "non-material sectors" such as banking and finance. Chinese national income figures approximate the United Nations concept of Net Material Product.

This impressive growth performance has been achieved without the benefit of a well developed financial system. China still has a "primitive" and highly regulated financial system. This absence is puzzling: normally,

[1] It is frequently argued the reforms have generated divergence across provinces and thus seem to contradict neoclassical convergence [See, for example, The Economist, June 26th, 1993, p. 65]. However, Mao and Rivera-Batiz (1992) show that the usual perceptions of the Communist period and of the regional impact of the reform are not valid. The pre-reform period was characterised by insignificant or even expanded regional divergence rather than the widely-toted egalitarianism. On the other hand, significant regional convergence in income levels is observed over the post-reform period.

high growth would be expected to require an efficient financial system to generate high saving and investment rates and an efficient allocation of resources. In a recent paper, Andersen (1993) examines the experience of four other rapidly growing Asian economies - Indonesia, South Korea, Taiwan and the Philippines - wich present mutatis mutandis the same characteristics: an impressive growth performance without the benefit of efficient financial markets. His main conclusion is that, "at early stage of economic development", "efficient financial markets are helpful but not essential to economic growth. At a later stage, however, the absence of financial market liberalization may retard growth" (p. 67). To examine the robustness of this conclusion, China is a case of particular interest and will add another dimension to the range of experiences already examined.

The study is organised in the following way. Section 1 provides a brief overview of the - theoretical and empirical - links between financial liberalization and growth. The high growth performance during the eighties despite the primitive character of the Chinese financial system is the subject of Section 2. Section 3 considers the main obstacles to further development and the necessity of a financial reform.

1. Financial Reform and Growth: An Overview

1.1. Financial Reform in Theories of Economic Growth

There are basically two categories of economic growth theories: those based on the traditional Solow (1956) growth model and those based on the concept of endogenous growth. The traditional economic growth models imply a positive relation between financial market development and the level of income per capita. In these models, financial reform[2] can be related to the level of the capital stock per worker or to the level of productivity, but not to their respective growth rates. Income rises following the increase in capital generated by financial reform, but the rise does not generate ever-increasing growth rates [Figure 1]. Financial reform increases the level of income by its positive effects on saving and invest

[2] Throughout the presentation, we identify the financial reform with the financial liberalization and we suppose that financial liberalization is decisive in achieving financial development. This last affirmation is not generally accepted. For a different point of view, see, for example, Arestis and Demetriades (1993).

Figure 1: Traditional growth model:
Increase in income due to financial reform

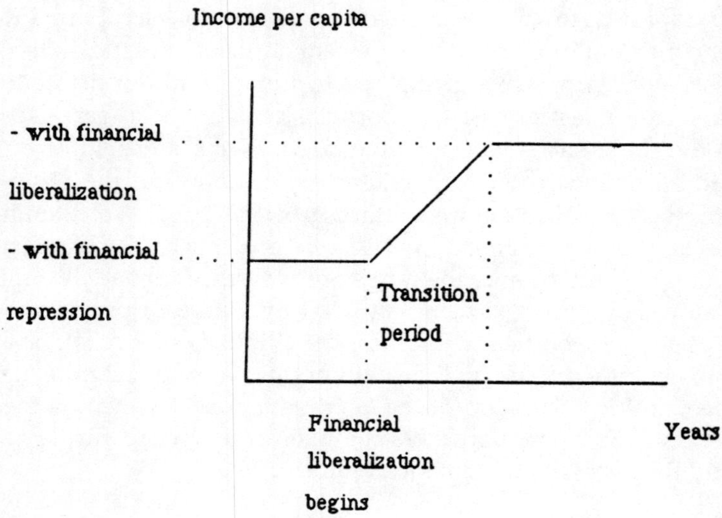

Figure 2: Endogenous growth model:
Increase in growth due to financial reform

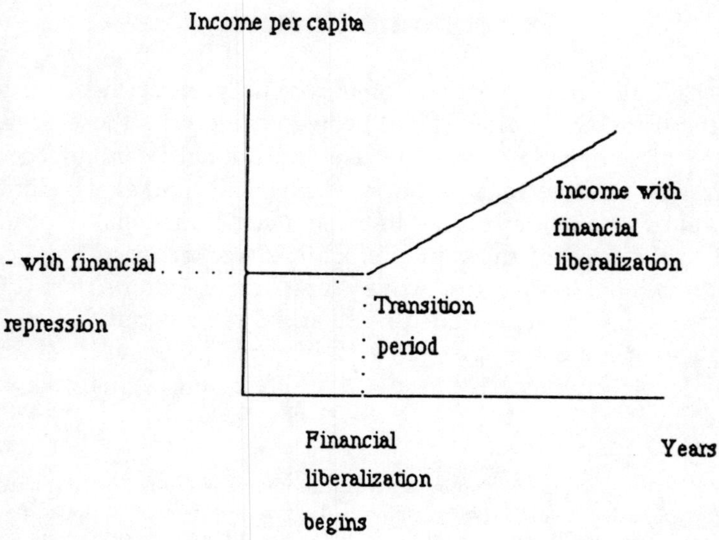

Box 1

Financial Reform in Endogenous Growth Theory

This box explains potential effects on growth resulting from financial reform found in the basic endogenous growth model [see Pagano (1993)]. Suppose that: 1) population is stationary; 2) the economy produces a single good that can be invested or consumed; 3) capital depreciates at the rate d per period; 3) a proportion 1 - f of the flow of saving is lost in the process of financial intermediation; 4) there are N identical firms, each producing output $y_t = B k_t^a$ with its capital stock k_t. The key assumption in the theory of endogenous growth is that there are spillovers. A simple way of capturing this idea is to suppose that B is considered as a parameter by the individual firm but actually responds to the average capital stock according to $B = A k_t^a$. On the basis of these assumptions, aggregate output (Y) and gross investment (I) are given respectively by the following two equations:

$$(1)\quad Y_t = A K_t$$

$$(2)\quad I_t = K_{t+1} - (1 - \delta) K_t$$

Capital market equilibrium requires:

$$(3)\quad \phi S_t = I_t$$

Combining (1), (2) and (3) - and writing s = S / Y- yields the following equation for the growth rate:

$$(4)\quad g = A \frac{I}{Y} - \delta = A \phi s - \delta$$

Financial reform affect growth by affecting: 1) s, the private saving rate; 2) A, the social marginal productivity of capital; 3) f, the proportion of saving funnelled to investment.

ment (more on this *infra*), but it does not increase growth in the long run because technological progress and the rate of growth in the labor force - which are the determinants of the rate of growth of the economy and are supposed to be exogenous - do not depend on the presence of a liberalized financial system.

In recent years, the "new" growth theories and the associated empirical work have greatly advanced our knowledge of the factors associated with long-run growth. Some recently developed endogenous growth models have tried to capture the process behind financial development. Most of these models imply a positive relation between financial market development and growth rates and assess financial reform as an element of the growth process [De Gregorio and Guidotti (1992); Andersen (1993); Pagano (1993)]. In these models, financial reform can affect growth: 1) by raising the private saving rate; 2) by increasing the social marginal productivity of capital; 3) by raising the proportion of saving funnelled to investment [see Box 1]. As opposed to the traditional growth model, there are no diminishing returns to capital when other factors are held constant; so, raising the level of capital by financial liberalization can lead to ever-increasing growth rates [Figure 2]. Therefore income growth will tend to be faster among countries that have a liberalized and well-developed financial system that is favourable to the accumulation of capital.

1.1.1. Financial Reform And The Private Saving Rate

The influence of financial reform on the private saving rate was the principal mechanism in the financial repression models proposed by McKinnon (1973) and Shaw (1973). Financial repression can be illustrated by the following figure [Figure 3] proposed by Fry (1982). The flow of saving - which is increasing in the real interest rate (r) - is viewed as the supply of investible funds while the demand of investment is a decreasing function of r. Given the initial schedules of savings and investment, the (equilibrium) interest rate should be r^* but has been set by the government or central bank at r_1, limiting investment to I_s. At r_1 the excess demand for savings is I_d - I_s. With no discrimination and savings limited to I_s, the interest rate would tend to r_2 and the rectangle [I_s - O] ¥ [r_2 - r_1] would be either the profits of the monopolized banking system or a sum spent by competing banks in building branches to attract deposits. If the quasi-rents earned by financial intermediaries and the tax revenue extracted from them are entirely spent on private and public consumption, the detrimental effect on growth can be very high; of course, this effect is tempered if they are partly spent on investment. High interest rates (real and nominal) are associated with an easing of financial repression. These rates reflect a high demand for capital, in turn indicating the high productivity of additional investment. Therefore, higher interest rates are associated with higher growth rates.

1.1.2. Financial Reform and the Productivity of Capital

Another avenue by which financial reform may affect growth is by altering the efficiency (or "the quality" as measured by the average productivity of investment), as opposed to the quantity of investment. Here, it can be supposed that in a "repressed financial system" some investment projects have a marginal productivity which is lower than the equilibrium rate of interest - r^* on Figure 3 - because bankers will ration credit arbitarily and not on the basis of the relative productivity of proposed investment projects [Arestis and Demetriades (1993)]. However that may be, most of endogenous economic growth models imply that financial repression, credit quotas and priority loans adversely affect resource allocation and economic growth. Therefore, financial liberalization is likely to draw capital away from relatively inefficient self-financed or informally financed projects toward projects having a high rate of real return. As an economy liberalizes domestically the set of investment opportunities available to the banking sector should be larger than the set available to the informally organized market [Cho (1990)]. Only under extreme circumstances would informal markets be able to match the allocative performance of an unfettered banking system. Informal markets are likely to find themselves constrained by a smaller information set, further enhancing the banking sector's relative advantage in terms of efficiency. Moreover, having access to attractive liquid financial assets inhibits bad physical investments with low or negative yields; at the same time, such access encourages intertemporal arbitrage for making good investments [McKinnon (1991), Ch. 2; Burkett and Vogel (1991)]. Thus, attractive financial assets and productive physical capital seem to be complementary and one can reasonably expect a positive link between financial depth and productivity growth.

Figure 3: Financial repression

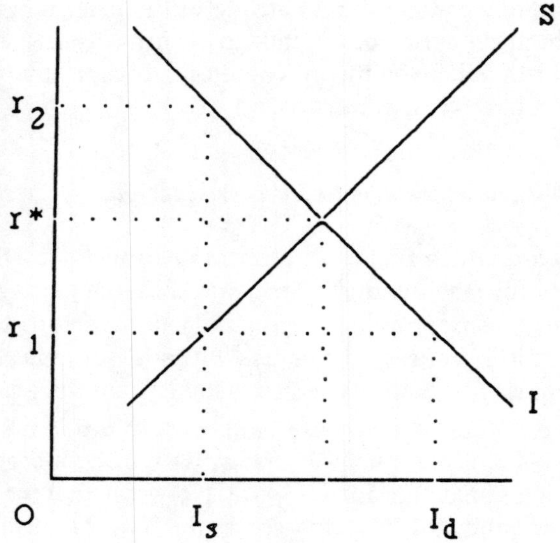

Source: M. Fry (1993) p. 733

A number of observers express concern that financial liberalization does not produce such healthy results. These positive effects presuppose the setting up of efficient screening and monitoring procedure by banks as well as a strenghtening of supervision in step with deregulation [Andersen (1993)]. There is also the risk that a rise in asset price volatility causes misallocation of resources. For example, Malkiel (1992) has provided evidence that U.S. stock prices reflect short term growth prospects far more now than in the 1960s, giving managers of firms an incentive to focus on the short run. The increased financial market volatility, sustained deviations of capital market prices from fundamentals, and misallocation of savings that occurred in the 1980s in most market economies are taken by several authors as unavoidable, natural consequences of financial liberalization. Moreover, when real lending rates are raised beyond a certain limit they create problems for highly averaged enterprises and may lead to adverse selection and incentive effects.

1.1.3. Financial Reform and the Proportion of Saving Channeled to Investment

Typically financial liberalization and positive real deposit rates provide incentives for households to increase their financial saving. This raises the lending possibilities of the banking sector for financing investment. However, the "neostructuralists" object to that conclusion arguing that, in the process, deposits move from the informal - the so-called "curb markets" - to the formal sector [Taylor (1983)]. Therefore, funds available for investment do not necessarily rise and will actually decline if reserve requirements in the latter are high. According to the "neostructuralists", the easing of financial repression may not lead to higher saving and growth rates. They argue that informal, loosely organized intermediation will occur in economies whose primary financial intermediary is a repressed banking sector. An easing of interest rate ceilings would allow banks to compete more aggressively for capital, thereby shifting it from the informal markets to banks. However that adjustment would not necessarily lead to more saving and more growth because banks are faced with reserve requirements that would tie up a significant quantity of the newly attracted funds. The neostructuralists contend that for financial liberalization to work - i.e., raise saving and investment and therefore the growth rate - higher interest rates must not only attract funds to the banking sector but, on net, increase the total pool of savings (in both the banking and informal sectors) by enough to offset the loss to required reserves imposed on the banking system [see, for example, Burkett (1987)]. In addition, it cannot be assumed that an increased intermediation role for the formal sector leads to a more efficient allocation of capital as the informal sector usually has well developed screening procedures though at high costs for the borrowers [Taylor (1983)].

In fact, the question is wether the informal sector or the formal sector is more efficient. Even informal intermediaries - if they are pooloing savings - must hold some reserves against "withdrawals". Moreover, because the formal banking system often has access to sources of temporary funding and insurance not available informally, the banking sector may actually be able to get by with a lower overall ratio of reserves to deposits. Further, as the absolute size of the banking sector expands, a simple appeal to the law of large numbers provides some predictability of the demand for withdrawals - that is, as the number of depositors increase deposit flows will become increasingly predictable. Bencivenga and Smith (1991) have presented a model where savings can be held in liquid forms or in fixed capital and where financial intermediaries face reserve-requirement restrictions. Their main conclusion is that, under reasonable assumptions (relative in particular to savers' risk aversion), an economy with formal financial intermediaries is likely to invest more of its savings in capital than an economy relying on informal finance and thus will enjoy a higher growth rate.

1.2. Empirical Evidence on Financial Reform and Growth Across Countries

The evidence on the effects of financial liberalization on growth comprises econometric works and "case" studies. The conclusions of the econometric studies of the relationship between growth and financial development are somewhat mixed. They typically focus exclusively on development of the banking sector. The standard measure of financial development is the ratio of M2 to GNP. If financial repression is lifted and the banking sector allowed to function effectively, the result will be growth in banks' balance sheets and thus a rising ratio of M2 to GNP. McKinnon (1989) examines several Pacific Basin economies, for the period from 1971 to 1980, in search of evidence that an easing of financial repression coincides with higher real rates of economic growth. Countries are grouped into three categories: countries with positive real interest rates, moderately negative real interest rates, and severely negative real interest rates. Countries belonging to the first group have high financial asset growth and real growth whereas countries belonging to the last group have low and often negative rates of financial growth and real growth. In the early 1990s, important new empirical research for the World Bank over a huge sample pooled in cross section [80 countries] and time series [30 years:1960 - 1989] provides further strong empirical support for the link between financial depth and high productivity growth [Levine (1992); King and Levine (1993)]. However, some other econometric results are inconsistent with the existence of favourable effects of financial liberalization on growth [Arestis and Demetriades (1993)].

Recently, the experience of rapidly growing Asian economies has been a matter of great interest to observers. Generally, these countries have adopted a very cautious approach and the pace of their financial reforms has been very slow. They managed to maintain a tight grip on their banking system and on their interest rates which are still not determined by the free market [Fry and Nuti (1992)]. On the basis of this experience, the main conclusion of a recent study by Andersen (1993) - focused on Indonesia, South Korea, Taiwan and the Philippines - is that, in early stages of development, dynamic growth can occur even if financial markets are rigid and tightly controlled. In three of the four economies - Indonesia, South Korea and Taiwan - "impressive growth and inflation performance has been achieved without the benefit of competitive and well developed financial markets... Regarding the growth performance of the Asian countries, it seems that it can mainly be ascribed to stable and export-oriented policies, supported by savings and investment rates, ... and political leaders with foresight." In some cases, financial liberalization has had negative effects. Andersen notes that in some economies, saving fell after credit ceilings were abolished because households responded to the relaxation of constraints by taking on more debt. In some cases, the pace of deregulation has clearly been too fast and did not allow sufficient time for creating the necessary supervisory bodies. This problem led to a severe financial crisis in the Philippines and instability in Indonesia. In otner cases, the pace has been too slow. This hampered real growth in South Korea and created unsustainable speculation in real estate and equities on Taiwan. Andersen sees the following lessons from his study: 1) In the early stage of development, efficient financial markets are helpful but not crucial for economic growth because a large portion of income growth comes from small family-owned firms that finance themselves; 2) Authorities in the four countries studied appear to have been foresighted and able to pick winners, somewhat offsetting inefficiencies resulting from suppression of market forces; 3) Credit selection and suppression of market forces have limitations, particularly when it comes to meeting the needs of small, high-tech firms; excess demand in such markets also tends to result in speculative bubbles which eventually affect real growth; 4) But as expansion continues, failure to liberalize financial activities can create economic distortions and retard growth. The case of China will add another dimension to the range of the experience of other Asian countries.

2. The Early Stage of Chinese Development: Growth Despite a Primitive Financial System

2.1. The Mono-Bank System and Macro-Control in Pre-Reform China

In 1978, the People's Republic of China operated as a planned economy based on a series of five-year plans stipulating medium term national economic goals. Eighty percent of population worked in the farming sector where the collective form predominated. The State-ownership form was dominant in industry and commerce. Like all socialist governments, pre-reform China's government depended for its revenue on the retained earnings of the industrial firms it owned. All economic activities were conducted according to the State-designed plans, under close State supervision.

The Chinese financial system worked according to the cardinal principles of Socialist finance: State monopoly of banking which meant that the right to provide banking transactions, establish new banks and abolish or reorganise existing banks belonged to the State; development of banking institutions'network; "democratic centralism" in the organisation of banking transactions and in bank management in order to fulfil the single credit-monetary policy of the State; concentration of all monetary transactions in banks; and the State monopoly in carrying out transactions in foreign currency [Panova (1988)].

Projects were financed with budgetary grants. China's banking system was little more than a means of directing credits to State enterprises according to the the central credit plan [see *infra*]. China had one bank. The People's Bank of China [PBC] (founded in 1949) acted not only as a central bank but also as the country's one commercial bank. The PBC monitored the financial aspects and financed the investments of the central government's annual economic plan. It also monitored the payments of enterprises, received their deposits, and extended credits in the domestic currency. The central bank functioned as a department of the finance ministry, which in turn had his role determined by the central plan. The PBC, as well as the central planning bodies, sought to plan, in detail, credits for each enterprise and association. The management of these credits was fully centralized. The PBC was only responsible for providing working capital to enterprises. The PBC followed cash plans and credit plans from the State Planning Commission and its branches passively provided financial resources to the enterprises according to the plan. The term "central bank" was misleading as it should have been more appropriately called "central accounting office" [Poenisch (1991)]. In reality, the PBC was little more than the government's cashier, mechanically executing the plan's orders for investment and credit.

In China, as in all centrally planned economies, there were two distinct and separate financial circuits. The first circuit - the so-called "transfer balance circuit" - corresponded broadly to the production sector (i.e., the government and the State enterprises as well as State farms). Within that sphere, all entities had to keep "transfer balances" at designated banks and made payments to one another only through credits and debits to those balances. These transfer balances were not checkable in the normal sense.[3] In order to convert transfer balances in currency the approval of the relevant bank was necessary. Enterprises were on a "soft money circuit" [McKinnon (1993)]. They received credit from banks and made payments to other enterprises and budget entities via current bank accounts, while paying wages and salaries in cash. They were enjoined from holding household cash balances and had to hold noninterest deposits with the State bank in several categories of quasi-blocked accounts. These accounts have been subject to arbitrary seizure and confiscation by the government as an informal method of tax collection.

The second circuit - the so-called "cash circuit" - served the household sector which received personal incomes in cash and paid for consumption goods in cash. This circuit consisted of payment flows between households on the one hand and government agencies and enterprises on the other. Unlike transfer balances, currency was freely transferable and could be used to purchase anything on the market - subject to the availability of goods and services. Cash was used by households and non-gouvernments units socialist enterprises used cash only to pay wages and in return received cash, only for goods sold to consumers - cash which was deposited with the central bank.

The Chinese authorities attempted to regulate currency issues through deliberate financial planning. The financial plan was the counterpart of the physical economic plan. It was composed of the Government budget, the Credit plan - which set out the expected sources and uses of banking funds - and the Cash plan - which specified the planned change in currency in circulation as a net result of cash transactions between the government sector (including enterprises) and households (including the farm sector). All three plans were simultaneously constrained by a national flow-of-funds identity. China's bank-credit policy was guided by the "real bills doctrine" - which contends banks must finance only working capital needs [see, Humphrey (1982)].[4] As cash was used only for wage payments and payments to rural households through procurement of ag-

---

[3] Depositors could not draw upon them for making payments to third parties and each transfer was subject to explicit approval by the bank holding the balance, to ensure that the payment had received prior authorisation by the proper authorities and that all papers relating to the transaction were in order.

[4] At the beginning of the eighties, Cheng (1981) wrote: "Chinese economists like to stress that the real-bills doctrine is a specialist feature of socialist finance, in contrast to the bank financing of non-productive, speculative activities common in capitalist economies. In their view, adherence to the doctrine accounts for the Communist success in stabilizing prices, while departures from it are a basic cause of inflation" (p. 28).

riculture products, it was the cash plan that determined households' demand. Because there was only one bank and no other financial intermediaries and no financial instruments other than credit, control of cash and credit were effective [Qian (1993)].

Originally, China's banking system was little more than a means of directing credits to State enterprises according to the central credit plan. Three banks either performed special functions or served specific sectors: the Agricultural Bank of China (ABC) served the agricultural sector; the People's Construction Bank (PCBC) financed plant- equipment and infrastructure projects for enterprises and government units; the Bank of China (BOC) handled foreign-trade financing and foreign-exchange administration. Banks distributed fiscal funds to enterprises, with no interest and repayment obligations, for financing fixed-capital investments and regular working-capital needs. In contrast, they lended banking funds to enterprises for meeting transitory, revolving working capital needs, with definite interest and repayment obligations. Banks were responsible for watching over the two channels and guarding against the mixing of funds in a manner that would sabotage the separation principle.[5], [6]

2.2. The Profound Liberalization of the Real Sector

The years of economic reforms since 1979 can be divided into two periods - before the Third Plenum of the 12th Central Committee of the Chinese Communist Party in 1984, and after.

[5] The separation principle emphasized the distinction between permanent and transitory needs of capital. According to this principle, financial surplus arising from labor should be used for capital formation without interest and repayment obligation. The theory asserted that: 1) bank credit should be limited to temporary financial needs - such as fluctuations in inventories, agricultural credit between planting and harvest, goods in transit, gaps between receipts and payment, ... - and that banks must charge interests on the use of such funds so that they could pay the depositors; 2) funds needed for fixed capital formation and working capital should be provided through government budget appropriations and disburded through banks without interest and repayment obligations [Cheng (1981].

[6] At the time, according to some western observers the Chinese economic performance were good. For example, in 1973, Wassily Leontief wrote: "It works. This is the conclusion that I brought home after observing the animated life on the crowded streets in five large Chinese cities, visiting communal farms, factories, and schools, and watching the endless panorama of the Chinese countryside glide by during long railroad trips through the eastern provinces. The 800 000 000 people seem to enjoy a decent, purposeful, and organized life, an equitable distribution of income and, for the time being at least, social harmony and peace. The contrast with the sea of misery and utter destitution enveloping the small islands of conspicuous prosperity and opulence in the rest of the so-called underdeveloped world is so striking that it is almost unbelievable" [Atlantic Monthly, March 1973, p. 74 quoted by Maxcy (1975)].

In the first period, the Chinese government emphasized reform of the agricultural sector. The first wave of reforms: 1) concentrated on freeing farmers from the suffocations of the commune system; the "working-unit" system of commune was abolished and the reform carried out the family-based production system; the reform meant effectively distributing the land to the families, which are now responsible for the production and are allowed to lease their land, even if in principle it belongs to the State; 2) created a market-economy in food by freeing prices for most food except grain; 3) eliminated the central government's monopoly over foreign trade; China's policy made an about-turn from "self-reliance" to an "open-door to foreign countries": experimental "special economic zones"- that are completely exempt from import and export tariffs - were also set up on the coast to attract foreign direct investment.

The next two rounds of reforms - in 1984 and 1987 - dealt instead with industry. The driving force has been competition without setting the matter of ownership and the question of property rights. The Chinese reform proceeded by building up a market-orientated sector around the existing State sector. There has been no privatisation drive or even a resolute attempt to reform the State-owned sector. Hundreds of thousands of the new manufacturing enterprises - now simply called "township and village enterprises" (TVEs) - were owned largely by townships and villages. The TVEs were market-driven and outside the web of official price and output controls. The State-owned enterprises (SOEs) - much larger scale State enterprises - remained under the ownership and control of the central government. Step-by-step, the pricing and financial arrangements facing the old SOEs were also rationalized, but at a more deliberate pace lasting over a decade [McKinnon (1993)]. At the same time, economic policy objectives have dramatically changed from "adjustment" aimed at holding down economic growth to "advancement" aimed at promoting expansion. Simultaneously, the relation between the provinces and the central government has changed with the central government diminishing its importance in relation to provincial governments. A policy of transferring net resources toward the lower-income provinces began to take place. The government abstained from a detailed determination and targeting of provincial activities. They received more flexibility to act in the context of a broad incentives program, that covered agriculture, industry and trade [see Mao and Rivera-Batiz (1992)].

Because the nature of the reforms being undertaken in China differ from those occurring in Central and Eastern Europe [CEE], a comparison between the two experiences is interesting. First, contrary to the situation which prevailed in CEE, China's reform started in the countryside and continued without interruption for long enough to create an economy that can stand up to the State economy. Second, China's communist government was never organized or thorough enough to clamp on to the economy and society the sort of planning and other controls that the Soviet and Eastern European leaders managed to achieve. Third, China's - in contrast to the CEE's countries of the 1970s and 1980s - has an economy open to the outside world. Finally, one of the main differences is that the Chinese authorities decided to "cross the river by feeling the stones underfoot" while Central and Eastern European countries took the "headlong plunge" strategy.

2.3. The Emergence a Two - Tier Banking System

2.3.1. The Banking Reform

China was the first country to introduce a banking system superficially similar to the one used in market economies [see White and Bowles (1988); Poenisch (1991)]. In 1978, the PBC was separated from the Ministry of Finance and granted a ministerial rank. In 1981, the China Investment Bank was established to channel World Bank loans to China. In 1983, economic policy makers undertook a major overhaul of the financial system in an effort to provide a more flexible and dynamic financial sector. The People's Bank of China was established as a central bank. Subsequently, its commercial activities were transferred to a newly created bank, the Industrial and Commercial Bank of China [see Figure 4]. Meanwhile, the other three State banks were encouraged to expand outside their traditional areas - agriculture, construction and trade finance. They have been allowed to compete for deposits and loans in the other's previously monopolized markets, and enterprises have been allowed to open accounts with more than one bank. However, all four banks have remained highly specialized in their operations. In 1987, another step was taken to revive a competitive banking system when China's State banks monopoly was ended by the opening of the Shangai's Bank of Communications.[7] While new financial assets - shares and bonds - began to be

[7] This was the first non-state bank since 1949 that was allowed to compete for both local and foreign-currency business. It was also the first to issue its own shares, with 50 % taken by the central government, 25 % by the municipal government of Shangai and the remaining 25 % in the hands of other institutions and individuals. This made it, at least in principle, the first China bank since 1949 thas is accountable to shareholders. And it was to be given greater

traded and international financial flows took more importance, the domestic banking system has been changed: 1) a wider range of financial assets and services was introduced to promote saving and banks - in conjunction with new institutions such as credit cooperatives, postal savings schemes and other special savings banks - were charged with the responsability of collecting sufficient savings to maintain the investment rate; 2) the reform was aimed at replacing central planning as the sole mechanism for achieving macroeconomic balance and at developing the instruments of monetary policy (especially the control of the volume of credit) for achieving macroeconomic control of the "market socialist" economy; 3) the reforms gave more independence to the banks and established a branch banking system under the supervision of the PBC

Whereas the PBC was responsible for all commercial banking in China, this was then spun off to the four "specialized" banks, which today account for around 85 % of banks assets, and to "comprehensive" banks (of which there are now about eight) [see Figure 4]. The "specialized banks" are government departments. The largest is ICBC (Industrial and Commercial Bank of China). A great part of their loans are made up for reasons of policy. These policy loans [8] are made not just at the behest of the authorities in Beijung, but also on the initiative of local governments and even of the banks themselves which get special benefits from policy lending. "Comprehensive banks" are joint-stock companies whose shares are held by the central government, by provincial and local governments, and the rest by State-owned industrial firms. Their sole aim is to make profit and unlike the specialized banks, they cannot call on the central bank to make good their losses. They make no policy loans; all loans are decided strictly on commercial grounds. They don't face the quantitative credit controls imposed on the specialized banks.

The PBC is now responsible for the control of the total volume of credit in the economy and, together with the State planning bodies, assumes a measure of responsability for macroeconomic control. The levers at its disposal are the interest rate, the reserve ratio, directives and quantity rationing through the credit plan. The PBC has considerable power to affect the lending activities of the specialized banks and is charged with ensuring that the specialized banks' volume of lending is in accordance

flexibility to determine interest rates, within a narrow range set by the government [see The Economist "A yuan for change", April 18, 1987, pp. 73-4].

[8] Policy loans are subsidies (to agriculture products through procurement and subsidies to State-owned enterprises due to price distortions or inefficient operations - and loans for development purposes [Qian (1993)] pp. 32 - 3.

with planned targets. For this purpose, the PBC has a number of branches to supervise and lend to the specialized banks. In the current framework, the PBC combines the functions of a central bank, the government financial regulatory agency, and the supervising agency of the specialized banks exercising control rights on behalf of the State. The central bank's mission is at least two faceted: it is responsible for macroeconomic management as well as policy lending for structural adjustment. The PBC and its branches allocate tasks of policy lending to specialized banks and make policy loans directly in some cases as well.

Today, there are six commercial banks (with 120 000 branches among them), a few regional banks, and rural and urban credit co-operatives with a total of 60 000 branches. The big four National Specialized Banks still dominate the banking system.

2.3.3. *The Diversification of Financial Institutions*

Since the mid-1980s there has been an explosion in the number of non-bank financial institutions engaged in domestic currency lending, direct investment and trust business. They arose rapidly as a response to strict credit quotas imposed by the PBC to the banks. Now, there are seven types of Non-Bank Financial Intermediaries [see Figure 4]: 1) the Trust and Investment Corporations (ITICs) established by the central and regional governments; by the end of 1992, there were more than one thousand trust investment corporations run by bank branches and government at all level, CITIC - China International Trust and Investment Corporation - is the largest;[9] 2) securities companies; 3) leasing companies; 4) finance companies; 5) rural credit cooperatives; 6) urban credit cooperatives; 7) insurance companies.

2.3. 4. *The Development of a Capital Market*

Capital market development in China has been relatively fast compared to the reform of the banking institutions. During most of the 1980s, the government ran a budget deficit and tried to finance part of it by issuing

[9] CITIC is really a development bank. Its main role is to bring western technology and business methods to bear on the pressing need to modernise the Chinese economy (hence the dominant role played by its overseas operations). CITIC reports directly to the Chinese government's State Council, or Cabinet. It is closely linked with both government and the Communist party at the highest level [see Holberson (1993)].

Figure 4 : China's financial institutions

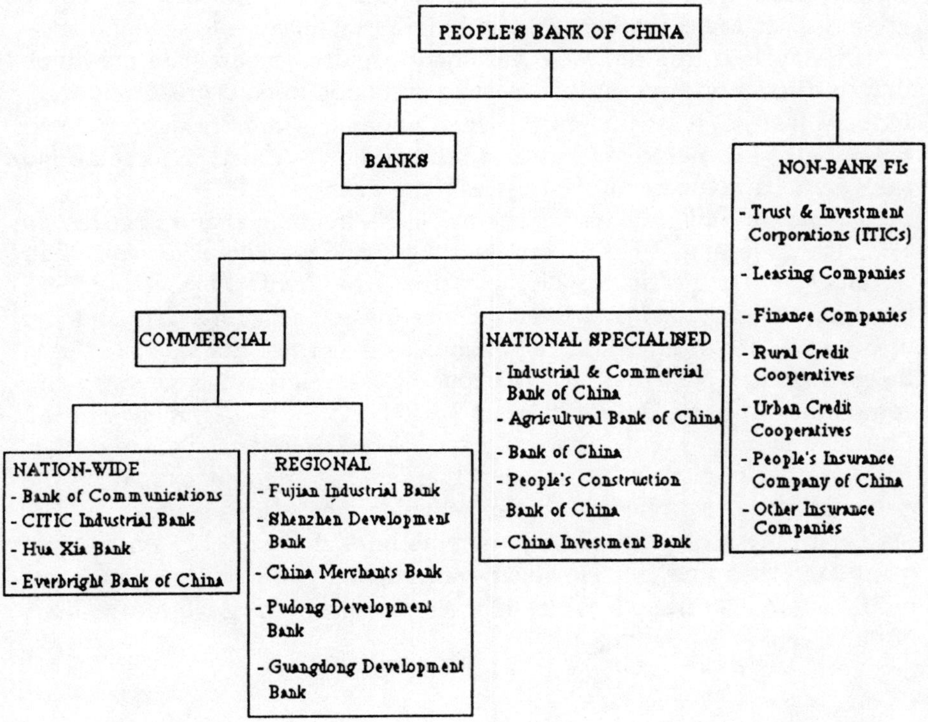

Source : Deutsche Bank.

bonds.[10] Until 1991, allocations of bonds was through mandatory planning with very low interest [Qian (1993)]. Chinese households did not have to weigh up the relative returns on a range of investments. State workers simply found their pay cheque slashed and a State bond in place of the missing cash. Many workers sold them for nominal sums to speculators.[11]

In May 1991, the central government decided to eliminate the involuntary distribution system of government bonds to enterprises and individuals. Instead, it set up a new system under which more than 5 000 retail outlets nationwide can buy and sell bonds.[12] But in 1993 forced bond sales were back and compulsory sales have taken place.[13]

Currently, China has two stock markets - in Shangai and Shenzen. In 1992, the government has encouraged these two markets to expand their trading and listing activities in other parts of the country. In October 1992, it set up two regulatory bodies to cover the securities markets and has drafted a series of laws and regulations on securities markets. Recently, the government has attempted to expand the foreign exchange swap and commodity markets. In addition, in May 1992, the government opened China's first futures and options market, the Shangai Metal Exchange.

The development of commodity markets has been supported by the government's price reform program - which means that it now controls prices of only a handful of "key" commodities that are sold on government-controlled markets. However, more than a half of these "key" commodities are also traded in free markets in which the government does not intervene.

---

[10] Under current Chinese laws local authorities are prohibited from issuing municipal bonds. However, they can raise funds through enterprises and local banks controlled by them. In recent years, local authorities have encouraged firms and local financial institutions to issue bonds.

[11] After the military crackdown on pro-democracy demonstrators in 1989 some speculators made a fortune buying state bonds dumped by workers who believed that the Communist Party would fall and the bonds would be worthless

[12] Institutional and individual brokers are paid by commissions from the central bank. The PBC - which licenses securities dealers - has opposed the rapid development of the securities industry seeing it as a threat to the banks.

[13] See "An offer they cannot refuse", *The Economist*, June 26th 1993 p. 66.

2.4. Growth Despite a Primitive Financial System

Following the first wave of reforms, agricultural output and productivity rose sharply.[14] Whereas farming output per head did not go up at all between the mid-1950s and 1978, in the first half of the 1980s, real value added in agriculture went up by 7 % a year while the number of people working the land went down. The growth of farmers' output quadrupled from 2 % a year in 1958 - 78 to 8 % a year in 1979 - 84. Real incomes in the countryside grew spectacularly: rural incomes doubled in six years.

Table 2: Level of per capita GDP

	- GDP per head, $ -		GDP, $ bn
	market exchange rates	purchasing power parity	purchasing power parity
China	370	2,460	2,870
India	275	1,255	1,105
Brazil	2,525	4,940	770
Mexico	3,700	6,590	590
Indonesia	650	2,770	510
South,Korea	6,790	8,635	380
Thailand	1,780	5,580	320
Pakistan	400	2,075	240
Argentina	6,870	5,930	190
Nigeria	275	1,560	190
Egypt	655	3,350	180
Philippines	820	2,400	155
Malaysia	2,980	7,110	130

Source: World Bank,OECD.

Following the second wave of reforms, economic growth has also accelerated owing to the development of the industrial sector while income per capita has also sharply increased. Since 1979, real GNP has grown by an average of almost 9 % a year [see Table 1]. In the 1980s the real growth of China's output and exports vastly outstripped that of the Soviet Union and India and even overtook Taiwan, South Korea, Singapore and Hong

[14] Grain output grew by a third in six years, cotton almost trebled, oil bearing crops more than doubled, fruit production went up by half.

Kong. China's GDP has been a cause of controversy for years. Converting China's GDP in 1992 into dollars at the official exchange rate yield $440 billion, or $370 per head, an income per head only slightly higher than India's [see Table 2]. However this figure is misleading. It is badly understated and China's social indicators - life expectancy, daily food consumption, not to mention household ownership of consumer durables [15] - are less like those of the 25 poorest countries on earth (of which China is officially one) than like those of middle-income countries with dollar GNPs five time as big [Guonan and Garnaut (1992); Gelb, Jefferson and Singh (1993)]. Using purchasing-power parity suggests a GDP of $2 870 billion in 1992 or 2460 per head. China appears more as a middle-income than a poor country and to have outstripped India in PPP terms. If China hits its targets - the Government recently announced a ten-year "development strategy" according to which over the next decade GDP growth is supposed to average 6 % - by 2002 the economy will be eight times bigger than it was in 1978.

3. The Further Stage of Chinese Development: The Necessity of a Financial Reform

3.1. Unsustainability of Growth: Inflation and the Stop-and-Go Cycle

Since the start of the economic reforms, China has registered recurrent phases of overheating and external disequilibrium. The process of reforms has been regularly threatened by the overheating of the economy: to fight inflation, Chinese authorities have used direct administrative controls, thus suspending the liberalization process. It became simultaneously more and more difficult for them to cope with these recurrent phases of acceleration in inflation and increasing external deficits.

In the first half of 1980s, the rapid increase of money supply did not lead to inflation and the price level was kept quite stable. Monetization of the rural sector played an important role in keeping price level low. In the second half of 1980s, there was a shift of monetization from the rural areas

[15] Nearly 70 % of Chinese urban households now have colour televisions and 81 % have washing- machines ["Chinese puzzles", *The Economist*, May 15th 1993, p. 75].

Table 3. Indicators of real developments

	80	81	82	83	84	85	86	87	88	89	90	91	92
GNP [1]	7.9	4.4	8.8	10.4	14.7	12.8	8.1	10.9	11.3	4.4	4.1	7.7	13.0
Industrial output [2]	9.3	4.3	7.8	11.2	16.3	21.4	11.7	17.7	20.8	8.5	7.8	14.5	22.0
Fixed investment [4]	2.9	-12.5	28.0	14.7	22.7	27.3	13.3	14.7	10.4	15.5	1.2	18.8	28.2
Retail prices :													
- Period average	6.0	2.4	1.9	1.5	2.8	8.8	6.0	7.3	18.6	17.8	2.1	2..9	5.3
- End of period	22.2	2.6	0.1	3.7	4.8	10.7	6.2	9.1	26.7	6.4	2.2	4.0	6.7
Current account [4]	0.3	0.9	2.1	1.5	0.8	- 4..0	- 2.6	0.1	- 1.0	- 1.0	3.2	3.6	1.5
Budget balance [4]	- 3.3	- 1.3	- 1.4	- 1.7	- 1.5	- 0.5	- 2.0	- 2.2	- 2.4	- 2.4	- 2.1	- 2.5	- 2.5

Source: Bell et al. (1993), Table 18, p. 66.

Remarks: [1] Real GNP : annual percent change ; [2] Real gross industrial output : annual percent change ;
[3] Real gross fixed investment : annual percent change ; [4] In percent of GNP

Table 3: (following) Indicators of real developments

	1960s Average	1970s Average	1980s Average
Growth rate of per capita GNP	1.21	5.53	7.62
Inflation	1.08	0.75	8.15
Investment ratio	0.21	0.30	0.35
Efficiency (IOCR)	0.16	0.25	0.26

Source: Gelb, Jefferson, Singh (1993), Table 2.

to the urban ones [McKinnon (1993) a, b]. However, the price level started to rise and inflation got out of control in 1988 and reached more than 50% at an annual rate for several months in that year. In the period of 1990 - 92, the government deficit continued to climb and monetary expansion grew even faster, the price level nevertheless remained stable

Since 1978, the Chinese economy has been characterised by a stop-and-go cycle [see Figure 5], alternating between loosening administrative controls and bold economic reforms in the "go" phase, and reimposition of controls and a cautious attitude towards further reforms in the "stop" phase [Komiya (1989); Hussain and Stern (1991)]. Here we concentrate on the last two episodes.

Figure 5: The stop and go cycle

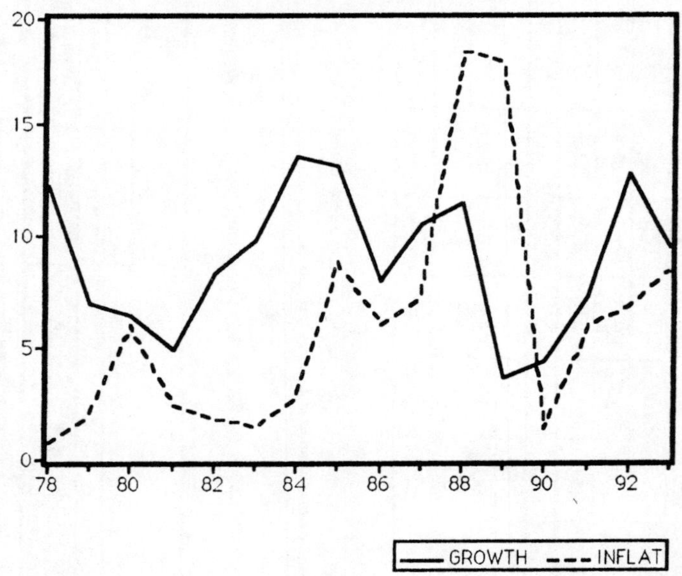

In September 1988, panic buying and bank runs persuaded the government that the inflation-prone reforms were jeopardising stability. An anti-inflationary policy package was implemented: 1) total investments for 1989 were targeted to be cut by 20 %; 2) in the financial area, the government intended to raise the savings rate by raising interest rates on deposits and by introducing deposit rates with interest rate linked to the price index, as well as severely restraining bank loans - credit was strangled

Table 4. Financial indicators

	80	81	82	83	84	85	86	87	88	89	90	91	92
Domestic Credit	22.3	13.1	11.2	12.8	31.4	31.3	34.1	22.3	18.9	17.1	23.7	20.2	22.8
Curency, % change	...	...	...	...	...	23.3	19.4	46.7	9.8	12.8	20.2	30.0	...
M1, % change	...	...	...	...	...	...	26.7	16.9	21.0	6.6	19.2	23.0	36.0
M2, % change	24.1	19.7	13.1	19.2	42.4	17.1	29.3	13.2	21.0	18.4	28.0	26.4	31.3
Net Domestic assets	...	...	...	...	...	...	33.9	21.5	20.7	18.3	24.1	25.0	32.7
Currency / GDP	...	...	...	...	...	11.5	12.6	12.9	15.2	14.7	14.9	16.0	...
M1 / GDP	...	...	...	...	...	39.0	43.6	43.8	42.5	39.9	43.0	47.5	...
M2 / GDP	...	...	...	...	...	60.8	69.3	73.7	71.8	74.7	86.4	97.0	...
M1 / M2, %	...	...	...	...	...	64.1	71.6	59.4	59.2	53.4	49.8	49.0	...
Real interest rates													
- Household 1 year	- 0.6	3.0	3.9	4.3	3.0	- 1.6	1.7	- 0.1	- 9.9	- 6.5	6.5	4.7	
time deposit													
- Household 3-year	0.1	3.7	4.9	5.3	4.0	- 0.5	2.3	- 1.0	- 8.9*	- 4.7*	8.0	5.4	...
time deposit													

Source : Bell et al. (1993) ; Qian (1993).

Remark : * Cost of living adjustment not included.

and the little that got through was directed to State-owned business - and money supply; 3) concrete measures to control prices have also been taken. These harsh administrative methods bankrupted millions of small firms ["township and village enterprises" (TVES)] in the private sector.[16] Inflation fell from over 18.6 % in 1988 to 2.1 % in 1990. The price was the collapse of economic growth from 11.3 % in 1988 to 4.1 % in 1990 [see Table 3]. Unemployment rose. So did the government's budget deficit. But in 1990 China had turned its trade deficit to a trade surplus.

In 1990, no longer able to bear the unemployment and budget strains of austerity, China's government released a vast amount of liquidity into the economy. Until the first quarter of 1991, prices did not rise, but output did. The continuing rapid increase in liquidity has underwritten a capital surge. In 1992, overall money supply increased 31.3 % and bank credit surged 22.8 % [see Table 4]. In 1992, real GDP growth was 13 %. The growth was unbalanced.[17] Since 1992 the economy is once more overheating. The overall rate of inflation edged up only to 5.3 % in 1992, but capital goods prices climbed 13.4 % and urban prices jumped 11.0 %. A speculative property boom has got out of hand. The overall trade surplus narrowed reflecting faster import growth driven by strong domestic demand. Bank credit and investment spending have continued to rise quickly during the first half of 1993. In the middle of July, the Government introduced an "economic readjustment" program - mainly based upon administrative measures - to tame runaway inflation, restore financial and fiscal order and improve the country's external balances. Four weeks later, a massive economic reform program to begin in 1994 was announced and a high speed growth strategy was - once again -endorsed by the authorities [see Box 2]!

3.2. The Need for Financial Reform

There is a growing feeling that substantial reform of the Chinese financial system is desirable. The stimulus for financial reform comes from many directions.

---

[16] During 1989, 3m TVES went under or were taken over (even though proportionally four or five times as many state enterprises as TVES were loss-makers.

[17] Amid a booming construction sector, the demand for capital goods surged 17.9 % in 1992, whereas the transportation sector grew just 3.4 % and overall energy production only 3.2 %.

3.2.1. The Deterioration of the Government's Fiscal Position

The implicit revenue system began to unravel naturally as liberalization began [see, for example, McKinnon (1993 b)]. First, the government-owned share of industrial assets began to fall. A huge amount of the economy has escaped from State's hands. In 1979, State-owned businesses accounted for nearly 80 % of China's industrial output. In 1990, the figure was 54 % and the split is now 50 - 50. (They still account for 60 % of industrial employment). In every category, State-owned businesses are declining and the non-State one rising. In 1990, the output of State-owned industries grew by only 3 %; the industrial output of collectives was up by 20 % and that of foreign joint ventures by more than 50 %. The State has lost a lot of its power to raise revenues. With economic liberalization and the competition it brings, government's revenue base shrinks: consolidated government revenues have fallen as a share of GNP from around 35 % in 1978 to little more than 15 % today.

Second, price decontrol and industrial competition from both domestic and foreign sources tended to shrink the profit margins in all industrial enterprises; many once (artificially) profitable SOEs became loss makers. The State-owned enterprises are still subject to strict planning and retain past inefficiencies. Around two-thirds of State companies lose money even in boom years. The government spend 14 % of its budget on subsidies to keep State-firms running, but that alone is not enough.

3.2.2. The Use of the Financial System to Cover the Deterioration

The lack of well-functionning money and capital markets is especially critical. Since 1978, China's government has been using the financial system to cover the deterioration of its own fiscal position. The reason is that the banks have become the government's main instrument for keeping unprofitable State-owned industrial companies in business. Chinese firms and households have vastly increased their holdings of financial assets - such as cash and savings deposits - encouraged by the fact that the government has, by and large, kept real interest rates positive.

Box 2

THE "NEW GROWTH STRATEGY"

(to begin in 1994)

In the middle of November 1993, the Communist Party announced a massive economic reform program to begin in 1994. The key components of the "new growth strategy" are the following:

1) *External sector*: The Government will abolish many import subsidies, cut import tariffs substantially, allow Chinese enterprises direct access to international markets, and terminate foreign exchange earning quotas. The dual exchange rates will be merged into a single unified exchange rate (to be a "managed" floating rate).

2) *Pricing policy*: The government will free coal prices and raise its own grain purchase prices to support farmers.

3) *Enterprises, ownership issues*: In addition to granting a great deal of autonomy to managers, the Government plans to sell and lease nonprofitable State-owned companies. It will allow the public to buy and hold about 80% of listed companies' total equities, although it will maintain its control over the number of State-owned companies that go public.

4) *Fiscal policy* : The Government will cut the corporate income tax rate to 33 % from the the current level of 55 %. It aims to collect 60 % of total taxes (of which 20 % will be redistributed to poor provinces), compared to the current 30 % level.

5) *Financial sector*: The Government plans to strengthen the central bank by modeling it on the U.S. Federal Reserve. To move away from traditional administrative control, it plans to introduce open market operations. The Government will form three policy banks to support exports, agricultural and infrastructure projects and will allow commercial banks a great deal of independence in making credit decisions. It also plans to expand and regulate several financial markets.

Source: "Emerging Markets Economic Outlook", 1993, quarter 4.

China's saving rate is 38 % of GNP (one of the world's highest) and most of it is accounted for by the holdings of households.[18] However, the Chinese financial system is unable to transmit China's huge pool of savings to the place it can usefully be invested. China's banking system cannot cope with the twin pressures of increased demand for finance for modernisation and the drop in State revenues that resulted from rural reforms. Despite limited but successful experiments in interbank trading, the flow of capital has remained mostly from the State down - rather than between banks and savers; and what money was available was often inefficiently channelled. Despite the reforms, China still operates a primitive financial system. The State banks hold more than 85 % of all financial assets. This causes problem because Chinese banks are prey to moral hazard. Limited deregulation on the liability side has caused banks to compete for deposits by offering relatively attractive (though often still negative, in real terms) rates of interest. On the asset side, however, banks not only know that the government's will rescue them from any bad loans they happen to make - they get told to make bad loans. They are used by the government principally to channel credit to State-owned industrialist firms (less than 20 % of bank lending goes to the non-State sector). The balance sheets of the "specialized banks" are in terrible shape. The "comprehensive banks" are not allowed to adjust rates for risk or to balance the term structure of deposit and loans, so they make hardly any long-term loans. Apart from their profitable foreign-exchange dealings, they seem to be little more than credit agency that provide some industrial firms with working capital.

3.2.3. Primitive Tools of Macroeconomic Controls

Chinese authorities are using a variety of instruments to try to bring credit under control and redirect it to more productive investments. However, only a couple of the tools at their disposal are of the indirect sort: changes in interest rate and in government spending. The authorities must, in fact, rely on quantitative credit controls. At the moment, the credit quotas plan is the central piece in the control mechanisms of the central bank. Each year PBC disaggregates credit quotas to each specialized banks, which in turn disaggregate to their branches. Credit quotas

[18] Household financial assets as a share of GNP are already 51 %, compared with 54 % in Japan in 1954. Household bank deposits increased by more than 16 times in real terms between 1978 and 1991; they are now around 1.2 trillion yuan ($ 210.5 billion) equivalent to more than 40 % of GNP.

are strictly enforced and are a binding constraint for specialized banks. The second most important tool of the central bank is its credit to specialized banks. Four main problems are generally associated with the use of these tools [Qian (1993)]: 1) a misallocation of resources; 2) fine tuning is hard; 3) the boundary between the cash and credit circuits [see *supra* 2.1.] is increasingly blurred; 4) using credit quotas becomes a less and less effective method to control money supply. In particular, the fact that the volume of credit soares regularly suggests that specialized banks do not abide by the rule according which credit ceilings are established for each of them. Of course, the PBC can move short-term interest rates and reserve requirements, but these tools of monetary control remain primitive and are in the nature of administrative fiat, they do not play very important roles so far. Administrative methods are inevitable so long as China's indirect economic levers remain primitive. When the fight against inflation is the priority, workers in State-owned firms are forced to buy government bonds; loans for "speculative" purposes - especially in property and construction - are called in; State-owned banks are ordered to demand repayment of the loans they have extended to "non-bank financial institutions".[19]

3.2.4. Some Recent Steps in the Direction of Financial Reform

The need for financial reform has led the Government to move the issue to the front of the agenda and to take significant steps in that direction [see Huan (1993)]. The PBC no longer fully controls and regulates the securities markets.The government has increased the number of banking licenses granted to foreign banks.[20] Recently the government has decided to permit foreign banks to conduct yuan business. [21] Until recently banks have had to hand over more than 90 % of their total profits to the central bank - which accounts for about one-fourth of total central government revenue. Once local taxes were paid, the banks were able to retain less

---

[19] From 1983 to the end of 1988, there has been a gradual shift toward using indirect instruments such as reserve requirements and the deposit-lending ratio to achieve financial control. Inflation in 1988 disrupted these experiments, and starting from the fourth quarter of 1988, strict credit quota controls were again imposed.

[20] By the end of January 1993 foreign banks and other financial institutions had opened 231 representative offices and 67 branches in China and have made a significant dent in the trade finance market.

[21] Although the tax rate on foreign banks that do so will be 55 % compared with 15 % on those foreign banks which only conduct business in foreign exchanges, so the effects may be small.

than 2 % of profits that they made. Nor were banks responsible for losses from bad loans [Huan (1993)]. Recently, the central government has allowed the establishment of several local banks and banks owned by some big companies. It has significantly reduced the number of "policy loans" that it ordered specialized banks to make in the State sector. Instead, it has urged them to base their lending decisions upon expected profits and risk calculations. In addition, it has set up new banks to finance major infrastructure projects that it endorses. The central government also decided to grant greater autonomy to most banks. Their fiscal burden has been reduced - with the tax rate on them only 55 %. Moreover, the government is intervening less in their business operations. As a result, commercial banks now have a much stronger incentive to reduce risks on their loan exposures. However, these measures are timid compared to the tasks that are still on the reform agenda.

3.3. Proposals for Restructuring the Chinese Financial System

China has reached the point at which it can no longer avoid a comprehensive financial reform. At this stage of the liberalization process, modernising China's financial system appears as a sine qua non condition for the success of the transition to a market economy. While there is an agreement on the need of a gradual reform, there are some disagreements over the "optimal" transition.

3.3.1. Gradualism With an Explicit Sequencing Rather Than a "Big Bang"

A first solution would be to try to do as much as possible with little concern for sequencing, i.e. the so-called "big-bang" approach. The main problem confronting designers of such a reform is similar to the one facing the planners of an economy: they need to know a lot [McMillan and Naughton (1992)]. Moreover, the experience seems to suggest that, in transitional economies, such a financial big bang can lead to a lose of monetary control and a worsening of moral hazard in bank lending. Therefore, the preferred financial reform should be gradual and must decide the order of the internal financial liberalization taking into account the three main problems of the transition: 1) excessive or unjustified trade credit; 2) overhang of enterprise bad debt; 3) weak capital base of the banking system. Two broad approaches are being discussed.

3.3.2. First Approach: The Adoption of a Version of Japan's "Main Bank" System

Because it takes years for fully operating financial markets to develop, an economy in the process of transition will lack, in any case, efficient financial markets [Tirole (1991)]. As far as China is concerned, it is generally admitted that it is unlikely that the stock market will play a major role in allocating financial resources in the near future. A solution would be for China to adopt a version of Japan's "main bank" system where banks with large stakes in the firm - both as creditors and as equity holders - monitor the managers' decisions and use their expertise, resources, and information to help corporations in restructuring and investment decisions. The establishment of such a system would result in the supply of funds through banks' credit screening. Banks would begin monitoring the performance of borrowers, thereby contributing to improving investment efficiency.

Three main arguments are put forward in favor of such a solution: 1) "Transforming the four specialized banks into commercial banks of the kind of city banks in Japan will be less costly and faster than destroying the existing system and building everything from the scratch"; 2) "Scarcity of expertise and human capital in the financial sector is one of the major constraints in China. The integrated monitoring by the main bank has the advantage of using scarce monitoring resource better"; 3) "A bank-orientated financial system is compatible with a variety of arrangements, this kind of flexibility is valuable in the transition" [Qian (1993)].

According to this approach, the following institutionnal changes must be quickly completed: 1) division of responsability of the fiscal sector and the financial sector; 2) establishment of a China's Development Bank on the basis of the People's Construction Bank of China [see supra 2.2.2.] - with explicit mission of development lending and not for profit maximization - and commercialization of the four specialized banks; 3) establishment of a "Second-Tier" Banking by the entry of regional banks - using current employees and facilities of branches of the PBC at the county and municipality levels - and the further expansion of urban and credit cooperatives; 4) development and regulation of non-bank intermediaries and informal financial institutions [Qian (1993)]. Many Chinese economists disagree because "they think bank lending is hopelessly entangled with government industrial policy" [22]

3.3.3. *Second Approach: The Adoption of a Dual Financial System*

The second approach to China's financial system restructuring proposes a financial reform with two successive stages [McKinnon (1993 a, b)]:

Stage One: A dual financial system is adopted. Unreformed State enterprises - the "within-the-plan-system" - continue to have access to bank credits which are tightly controlled. Bank lending to market-oriented non-State firms and reformed State firms - the "outside-the-plan system - is prohibited. Therefore, liberalized enterprises can only raise funds from retained earnings and from the nonbank capital market not involving traditional enterprises, and the two components of the financial system are insulated from each other. The primary objective is to encourage firms to use monetary assets, rather than physical assets, as a store of value. Simultaneously, the public finances are improved through expenditures reduction and the establishment of a proper tax system with the institution of an internal revenue service capable of directly taxing all enterprises as well as the agricultural sector.

Stage 2: The traditional sector is still credit-constrained. The base of bank lending is deliberately but very carefully broadened to include the liberalized enterprises. Commercial banks begin limited and fully collateralized short-term lending to liberalized enterprises according to the principles of the "real bills doctrine": they lend only to finance the build up of "productive" short-term assets, such as inventories or accounts receivables, that can be realized if assumed. The stage is set to allow liberalized enterprises to grow very rapidly compared to the "within-the-plan system" which is phased out. Households are brought systematically under a personal income tax.

The main difficulty, associated with Stage One of this program, is how the intended insulation between the two systems could be implemented. The "within-the-plan-system" could arrange transactions with the "without-the-plan system" to escape the reglementations. Moreover, McKinnon does not suggest when firms belonging to the "within-the-plan-system" are to be liberalized or closed, how the central planning of their inputs and outputs and fixing of their prices can be consistent with a free

---

[22] "China's financial system: Still in the Middle Kingdom", The Economist, December 12th 1992, p. 82.

market environment for firms belonging to the "without-the-plan system" that sell or buy from the traditional firms. Another difficulty, associated with Stage Two, is the use of the rule proposed by the "real bills doctrine", since that was the rule applied in the past (see *supra* 2.1.) and "bad habits will doubtless persist" [Portes (1993)].

3.3.4. The Monetary Control

The introduction of a control mechanism of global demand through interest rate is necessary [see, for example, Bank of Japan (1989)]. To allow the effective functioning of such a mechanism several reforms are necessary. A priority must be given to the creation of a short-term interbank market where interbank financing should take place through market mechanisms. Lending and deposit rates need to become more flexible. Hovever, "it might well be the case that imposing credit quotas is the only effective way to constrain the State-sector from expanding because many State-owned firms are not sensitive to interest rates if they face the soft budget constraint. Enforcing strict credit quotas for them is the only way to harden the budget constraint" [Qian (1993)]. Several other reforms would be desirable. First, a responsability system - like in the business sector - is required in the banking sector. Second, reforms in the enterprise sector are necessary to allow the functioning of the interest rate mechanism with respect to demand for funds.

REFERENCES

Andersen, P. S. (1993): "Economic growth and financial markets. The experience of four Asian countries", in "*Finance and the international economy: 7*", edited by R. O'Brien, The Amex Bank Review Prize Essays, *Oxford University Press.*

Arestis, P. and **Demetriades, P.** (1993): "Financial liberalisation and economic development", in "*Money and Banking": Issues for the twenty-first century*" (edited by P. Arestis), *St. Martin's Press*, pp. 287 - 303.

Bank of Japan (1989): "Recent developments in the Chinese economy: Economic reform, its success and problems", Special Paper, No. 176, April.

Bell, M. W., Khor, H. E., and **Kochhar, K.** (1993): "China at the threshold of a market economy", *International Monetary Fund,* Occasional Paper 107, September.

Bencivenga, V. R. and **Smith, B.** (1991): "Financial intermediation and endogenous growth", *Review of Economic Studies*, pp. 195 - 205.

Brainard, L. J. (1991): "Reform in Eastern Europe: creating a capital market", in "Finance and the International Economy: Volume 4", *Oxford University Press*, Reprinted in Economic Review, *Federal Reserve Bank of Kansas City*, January / February, 1991, pp. 49 58.

Burda, M. (1991): "Economic reform in China: Dicussion", *Economic Policy*, April, No. 12, pp. 178 - 80.

Burkett, P. (1987): "Financial "repression" and financial "liberalization" in the Third World: A contribution of the critique of neoclassical development theory", *Review of Radical Political Economy*, No. 1, pp. 1 - 21.

Burkett, P. and **Vogel, R.** (1991): "Financial assets, inflation hedges, and capital utilization in developing countries: An extension of McKinnon's complementary hypothesis", *Quarterly Journal of Economics*, August.

Cheng, Hang-Sheng (1981): "Money and credit in China", Economic Review, *Federal Reserve Bank of San Francisco*, Fall, pp. 19 -36.

Cho, Y. J. (1990): "McKinnon - Shaw versus neostructuralists on financial liberalization: A conceptual note", *World Development*, No. 3, pp. 477 - 80.

Cunningham, T. J. (1991): "A liberal discussion of financial liberalization", *Economic Review*, Federal Reserve Bank of Atlanta, November - December, Volume 76, No. 6, pp. 1 - 8.

De Gregorio, J. and **Guidotti, P.** (1992): "Financial development in economic growth", *IMF Working Paper*, No. 82.

Financial Times (1993): "China", Thursday November 18, Section III.

Fry, M. J. (1982): "Models of financially repressed developing countries", *World Development*, Volume 10, No. 9, September, pp. 731 3.

Fry, M. J. and **Nuti, D. M.** (1992): "Monetary and exchange rate policies during Eastern Europe's transition", *Oxford Review of Economic Policy*, No. 8, pp. 27 - 43.

Gelb, A., Jefferson, G., and **Singh, I.** (1993): "Can communist economies transform incrementally? The experience of China", in "*NBER: Macroeconomics Annual, 1993*", pp. 87 - 149.

Groves, T., Hong, Y., McMillan, J., and **Naughton, B.** (1992): "China's evolving managerial labor market", Working Paper, *University of California*, San Diego.

Groves, T., Hong, Y., McMillan, J., and **Naughton, B.** (1993): "Autonomy and incentives in Chinese State enterprises", Working Paper, *University of California*, San Diego.

Guonan, M. and **Garnaut, R.** (1992): "How rich is China?", *Australian National University,* Working paper.

Hoenig, T. M. (1993): " China's economic growth with price stability: What role for the central bank? ", Economic Review, *Federal Reserve Bank of Kansas City,* First Quarter, Volume 78, Number 1, pp. 5 - 10.

Holberton, S. (1993): "Profile: China International Trust and Investment Corporation", *Financial Times,* November 18 1993, Section III, p. XII.

Huan, G. (1993): China's financial reform", *Morgan Guaranty Trust Company,* Economic Research Note, February 19.

Humphrey, T. M. (1982): "The real bills doctrine", Economic Review, *Federal Reserve Bank of Richmond,* September / October.

Hussain, A. and **N. Stern** (1991): "Effective demand, enterprise reforms and public finance in China", *Economic Policy,* April, No. 12, pp. 141 - 186.

King, R. and **Levine, R.** (1993): "Finance, entrepreneurship, and growth", presented to the Conference "*How do national policies affect long-run growth?", World Bank.*

Levine, R. (1992): "Financial intermediary services and growth", *Journal of the Japanese and International Economies, December,* pp. 383 - 405.

Malkiel, B. F. (1992): "The cost of capital, institutional arrangements and business fixed investment: An international comparison", paper presented at the Osaka-Wharton Conference on "*Corporate financial policy and international competition*".

Mao, Z. and **L. A. Rivera-Batiz**: (1992): "Growth and regional convergence in transitional regimes: China", *University of California,* San Diego, Working paper.

Maxcy, G. (1975): "A bourgeois economist looks at China", *Lloyds Bank Review,* January, Number 115, pp. 27 - 41.

McKinnon, R. I. (1973): "Money and capital in economic development", *Brookings Institution,* Washington.

McKinnon, R. I. (1989): "Financial liberalisation and economic development: a reassessment of interest policy in Asia and Latin America", *Oxford Review of Economic Policy,* No. 4, pp. 29 - 54.

McKinnon, R. I. (1991): "The order of economic liberalization: Financial control in the transition to market economy", *John Hopkins University Press.*

McKinnon, R. I. (1993 a): "Macroeconomic control in liberalizing socialist economies: Asian and European parallels", in "*Finance and development: Issues and experience*", edited by A. Giovannini, *Cambridge University Press,* pp. 223 - 56.

McKinnon, R. I. (1993 b): "Financial growth and macroeconomic stability in China, 1978 - 92. Implications for Russia and other transitional economies", Working Paper, Department of Economics, *Stanford University*, to be published in the *Journal of Comparative Economics.*

McMillan, J. and **Naughton, B.** (1992): "How to reform a planned economy: Lessons from China", *Oxford Review of Economic Policy*, Vol. 8, NO. 1, pp. 130 - 43.

McMillan, J. and **Naughton, B.** (1993): "Evaluating the dual-track system", Working Paper, *University of California*, San Diego, January.

Morgan Guaranty Trust Company: "Emerging market economic weekly" and "Emerging markets economic outlook", various issues.

Newbery (1991): "Economic reform in China: Dicussion", *Economic Policy*, April, No. 12, pp. 181 - 6.

Pagano, M. (1993): "Financial markets and growth. An overview", *European Economic Review*, No. 37, pp. 613 - 22.

Panova, G. (1988): "Recent developments in Soviet banking", *National Westminster Bank Quarterly Review*, August, pp. 31 - 38.

Poenisch, H. (1991): "The new central banks of Eastern Europe", *Central Banking*, No. 4, reprinted in Deutsche Bundesbank / Auszüge aus Presseartikeln, Nr. 42, 7. Juni 1991, pp. 11 - 15.

Portes, R. (1993): "Discussion on "Macroeconomic control in liberalizing socialist economies" by R. McKinnon", in "*Finance and development: Issues and experience*", edited by A. Giovannini, *Cambridge University Press*, pp. 257 - 60.

Qian, Y. (1993): "Lessons of the Japanese main-bank system for financial system reform in China", Working Paper, *Stanford University*.

Shaw, E. S. (1973): "Financial deepening in economic development", *Oxford University Press.*

Taylor, L. (1983): "Structuralist macroeconomics: Applicable models for the Third World", *Basic Books*, New York.

Discussant's Comments on Chapter 11

Clas Wihlborg

Dickinson develops a very interesting model of the impact of borrowers' reputation on bank behaviour and specifically on banks' willingness to lend to old and new customers when shifts occur in the general level of default, the interest rate level in the economy, and the required deposit reserve ratio. Reputation is a very important economic resource in financial relations. The topic of the paper is therefore important and especially interesting for transition economies.

Old and new customers have different probabilities of default in the model. The latter build up reputation over time by surviving. Banks keep these customers because of monopoly power caused by search costs. It cold be added also that the bank has a partial monopoly on information about old customers.

A general increase in the default rate as well as an increase in the bond rate induce banks to substitute bonds for loans in their portfolio and to increase the share of old borrowers. All effects are long-lasting, because after a reduction in the customer base it takes time to build up the same number of borrowers with low probabilities of default.

Dickinson asks how reputational forces of the type analyzed in the model apply to transition economies. One aspect is that the incentive to provide new loans is low because of the inherited customer base with bad loans. Another aspect is that it will take time to develop a new "sound" customer base and to increase the willingness to finance new ventures. Dickinson suggests that governments could speed up the process by encouraging sharing of information by means of, for example, rating agencies.

The conclusion that sharing of information could speed up reputation creation depends on the bank's monopoly power being created by firms' search costs. If the monopoly power instead is created by an information advantage created by monitoring, then required sharing of information could reduce banks' investment in information gathering and reduce their willingness to take on new customers.

It is possible that Dickinson's conclusions are overly pessimistic. The basis for this belief is that borrowers are unable to "speed up" reputation creation. There exist signalling devices for the borrowers, for example in their choice of capital structure and offers of collateral. Furthermore, banks can offer a menu of loans with different conditions inducing a degree of self-revelation among borrower categories.

Linking the reputation analysis to the value of the option to renege on loans could throw additional light on reputation creation. The reputation of the borrower could be viewed as inversely related to the value of the option to renege. This way of looking at reputation makes it a forward looking concept. The value of the option to renege declines if the borrower faces high costs of reneging. Those costs would be high if, for example, the borrower has made substantial investments in project-specific assets and human capital.

These reputational considerations should not be seen as attempts to reduce the reputational effects of Dickinson's model. A model must focus on particular economic mechanisms and the backward looking concept of reputation used in the model certainly has great validity. The cost of making a model tractable is that the economic policy implications become more narrow. In this case, I believe that the application of the model on financial markets in transition economies leads to excessive pessimism about the ability of borrowers to become credible bank customers.

Finally, I would like to emphasize one important conclusion of the model. I refer to the long-term consequences of short-term macroeconomic policies that affect the banks' lending behaviour. Policy-makers (in all countries) should bear in mind that the use of seemingly short-term policy instruments can have serious long-term repercussion through their effect on stocks of informational and human capital.

Subject Index